A LEGACY OF HOPE

STORIES FROM ROYAL FAMILY KIDS™

COMPILED BY WAYNE TESCH

Royal
Family KIDS
CELEBRATING 25 YEARS

RFK Press
Royal Family KIDS, Inc.
3000 W. MacArthur Boulevard, Suite 412
Santa Ana, CA 92704

Published in partnership with

ISBN: 9781940269825
Library of Congress: 2015952900

Printed in the USA
Cover design by Robin Black, Inspirio Design

CONTENTS

INTRODUCTION

My involvement with Royal Family KIDS began at six o'clock on a random Monday morning, seated in a stale Las Vegas casino lobby. While listening to the jingling noises bouncing off nearby slot machines, I didn't know what burned worse—my eyes, from the desert allergies, or my throat, from the cigarette cloud wafting in from the casino. I was waiting impatiently for Brett, the vice president of a large shoe company, to show up for a meeting he had called before he boarded a plane to escape Las Vegas. I would be trapped all week at the World Shoe Association trade show, and, on this particular Monday morning, thanks to the rowdy shoe-industry party I had attended the night before, my mood was especially foul.

At the time, I was working for a charity that collected footwear from shoe companies and individuals to give away to people in need, almost always to distribution partners in Africa, Haiti, Southeast Asia, or other remote parts of the world. We shipped them overseas, so Americans wouldn't try to return them to Nordstrom's for cash or store credit. A big part of our job was schmoozing industry executives, who typically threw away millions of pairs of perfectly good shoes to protect their profit margins.

Brett came rushing up, his carry-on bags in tow, sweating and huffing. He flopped down in the leather lobby seat across from mine. I couldn't tell if he had actually gone to bed the night before or if he had just kept the party going until our meeting. Either way, I looked forward to wrapping up the meeting quickly so I could crawl back in bed for an extra hour of sleep.

"I've got some news for ya," Brett said, looking over the top of his expensive bifocals. "Corporate is letting me give you guys ten thousand pairs of brand-new athletics for kids, like you asked."

Suddenly, my day brightened. Our charity had always struggled to find good quality shoes for children, especially athletic pairs from one of the top brands in the world.

"Wow, Brett, this is wonderful. Thank you!" I blurted. "I'm assuming we have to distribute out of the US?"

"That's the thing," he said. "I told them what you guys told me last night and, just this once, you can give the shoes to needy kids here in America."

I was excited and thankful. He waved me off with a smile. "Just make sure you give them to the best organization you know of that works with kids," he said, shaking my hand before hopping into his taxi.

Immediately I thought of Royal Family KIDS and their larger-than-life CEO, Wayne Tesch. I hadn't spoken to Wayne in fifteen years, but what Brett had said about finding the best organization for American children suddenly jarred my memories loose. What I remembered most about Wayne was the way he made me feel. I felt valued, even though I was just a random college kid joining his family for dinner.

Back then, Wayne and his wife, Diane, had shared with me their vision to take foster kids to summer camps to help break the cycle of abuse and neglect through healthy relationships. I thought it was crazy enough to be successful; but I hadn't thought about it again until I was standing outside that Las Vegas lobby, wondering which organization would benefit most from a bunch of new shoes. There was no question in my mind it would be Royal Family KIDS.

This is how feeling valued can have a positive impact, even years later. Maya Angelou wrote, "I've learned that people will forget what you said, people will forget what you did, but people will never forget how you made them feel."

The kids we serve may not remember that we let them eat as much bacon as they wanted, or that we stood shivering in a light rain because they wanted to keep firing arrows at the archery target, or that we endured listening to the "rap remix" of the Royal Family KIDS theme song for the eight hundred and forty-fifth time because they wanted to sing it again. But years later, when reflecting on what went right in their turbulent lives, they will remember a group of people who made them feel loved, valued, and safe when they needed it most.

That's what Royal Family KIDS is all about: the power of making moments matter enough to a child that their future pivots away from despair and toward *hope*. This incredibly important moment starts with our choice—yours and mine—to participate in the messy adventure rather than watch it pass by.

Twenty-five years ago, two people stepped forward in faith and started a Christian organization that would focus on kids in the foster care system.

They made the intentional decision to live out their faith by seeking "the least of these"—the foster children living invisibly in their own communities. When Wayne and Diane Tesch founded Royal Family KIDS, they had no idea they were launching a movement that would serve over 100,000 children around the world. Nor could they have imagined that tens of thousands of adults would rise to give their time, talent, and treasure to build up shattered children. But that is exactly what happened.

Most of the time, we focus on telling stories from the foster child's perspective, and rightly so. But in this book, you'll read dozens of stories from the adults' point of view—counselors, camp directors, activity coordinators, mentors, RFK staff members, a songwriter, a youth pastor, a nurse, and more. And, yes, we've also included a few former campers who look back on their experiences with the eyes and hearts of adults and now understand first-hand the challenges and joys that come from serving children at camp and club.

The ongoing decision of new volunteer leaders to step forward in faith and make a difference for foster children in their own cities is what makes Royal Family KIDS possible. Although the statistics are overwhelming, most people don't respond to facts and figures. People are hardwired to freeze when presented with big numbers—it's a classic case of "analysis paralysis."

If I post government figures showing that four hundred thousand children are currently suffering in the alternate universe called Foster Care, many people feel vaguely sad and wish the government would do something more effective to address the issue. If I claim that recent studies prove that one hundred thousand of these kids are at risk of being exploited and sexually trafficked, most people would get angry and look around the room to see who might serve on a committee to tackle the problem. If I report that Los Angeles County has the highest number of kids in foster care, yet RFK has only *two* active programs there (when we need 424 more), almost everyone donates a little money so we can recruit new volunteers and improve the situation. But when I share a true story about a nine-year-old girl named Jessica living in a group home in Bellflower, California, who desperately needs to meet you in order to a have a terrible future altered, you might feel compelled to stand up.

Jessica needs you to mentor her in a Christian environment. To not run away on her twelfth birthday, she needs to hear that the God of the universe loves her. She needs committed prayer warriors to help her avoid turning to the streets, where human vultures will pick her apart until she dies of a drug overdose before age thirty.

The truth is, there are many little kids like Jessica who we never meet in time, and our only barrier is locating, inspiring, and training more volunteers to intervene in the life of a foster child. Even when we do get the children to camp, the best outcomes are never guaranteed—just ask any one of this book's authors. Each of them has seen both miraculous outcomes and gut-wrenching losses. We are waging an all-out war, and our only weapons are love, prayer, and time.

You *can* and *do* make an eternal difference. What a wonderful opportunity to worship God by living out your faith and changing the trajectory of children's lives. What an amazing gift to have your own life reshaped by His will. What eternal joy will come from the people who will be in Heaven because you stepped forward to minister to orphaned and abandoned American children when presented with the opportunity.

We can't be frustrated by the overwhelming numbers of children in need. Wayne and Diane Tesch didn't wait for someone else to solve the problem, and we can't wait either. There is no way to fill the shoes of people like Wayne and Diane, and those of us working at the charity don't pretend to try. It's going to take all of us and thousands more we haven't yet met. And we are thankful there are thousands and thousands of adults willing to step up and join you and me in this war of love and prayer.

I am so grateful for you, the person reading this book. Whether you are new to Royal Family KIDS or one of the original camp staff, this ministry is now in your hands.

For the volunteers,

Chris Carmichael

President, Royal Family KIDS

1

WAYNE TESCH
Co-Founder

While I was visiting a camp in Michigan with a group of adults, a small, nine-year-old boy came running up and proclaimed, "Hey, me and Jesus have a lot in common!" In all my years of working with children, I had never heard a statement like that.

I knelt down on one knee, looked the boy in the eye, and asked, "You do? What is it that you and Jesus have in common?"

Excitedly he replied, "We both have foster dads named Joseph!"

Later that evening when I was alone, I reflected on the statement, "Me and Jesus have a lot in common." I was amazed a nine-year-old boy could come up with such a powerful response to his situation. He connected with a powerful truth of Scripture. He found a father.

I wondered how many other heroes of faith grew up in a home without their parents. I was surprised to discover several: Moses, Samuel, Esther, Mephibosheth, and Timothy all grew up in homes without one or more of their biological parents. I found it especially powerful that so many of the people God used during their adulthood had spent their childhood apart from the people who should have cared for them.

What insight that little boy gave me. I now have a sermon entitled "Heroes of the Faith Who Grew Up in Homes Other Than Their Own." Through the years, I've found children to be among my best teachers.

Camp has always been close to my heart. I have taught camp leadership at two colleges. There is something about the "cathedral of the outdoors" I dearly love. In reflecting on why I enjoy camping, I've come up with two reasons.

The first is that God found me, or I found God, at camp. It was a Thursday night at Lakeview Gospel Camp, on the shores of Lake Ontario in upstate New York. I was twelve years old, sitting in a Quonset-hut-shaped tabernacle, on a wooden bench with sawdust on the floor. I recall asking God what I was to do with my life. After all, in my mind, Jesus was twelve and He knew what He had to do; He had to be about His Father's business. I needed to know what I would be doing in life.

I can take you to the spot where I was sitting on Saturday, the end of my week at camp. My mom picked me up and asked, "What happened at camp?" I told her God spoke to me and that I had seen a vision of hundreds of children's faces. There were faces of children from all ethnicities: African, Native American, Hispanic, Asian, and Caucasian. I announced to her that I was called to be a minister. I would work with children, and I had to go to California to make it happen. I'm still amazed that, as a twelve-year-old, I knew in my spirit I would minister to children.

The second significant thing that happened at camp was I met Diane. That's right! I recall telling my cousin "Someday, I'm going to marry that girl!" It was during a Friday-evening all-camp banquet. I can still close my eyes and see her on the porch of the inn, wearing her dotted, Swiss, lime-green dress with her white purse and white shoes. Her blond hair flipped up, the way Jackie Kennedy wore her hair at the time. Now, to be honest, I like to say Diane was the first and last girl I ever dated, but there were a few in between.

Camp gave me the direction and purpose for my life, as well as a companion for life.

Beginning of Royal Family KIDS Camps

I was sitting in my office at Newport-Mesa Christian Church in Costa Mesa, California, when the district superintendent, Fred Cottriel, called me to set up an appointment in his office. He mentioned that Pinecrest Christian Conference Center was set to reopen after being closed for a number of years. He mentioned that I could develop a camp and use Pinecrest as a location. He thought an inner city sports camp would be nice.

I thought to myself, "I live and work in the suburbs. It would be really difficult to develop an inner city camp if I didn't live in the inner city." Reverend Cottriel said to get back to him if I wanted to do a camp of any kind. As I walked back to my office, Jill Anderson, the administrative assistant for Christian education, asked me what the meeting was about. I told her about the opening and availability of Pinecrest for a camp that we would start. Jill was working on her master's degree in social work at the University of Southern California. "What about foster children?" she asked. As soon as I heard her question, I knew what we needed to do. We would run a camp for foster children.

We did our research and found that in 1984 there were 10,500 reported cases of abuse in Orange County, California. We found one camp that was working with foster children, located in Alpine, California. We called American Camping Association and Christian Camping International to see if there were any camps specifically set up for foster children in the United States. We learned that the only camp was run by Robin and Kim Woods in California. Needless to say, we visited them. They kindly shared their model with us. We admired their excellent work with policies and procedures. We could hardly wait to begin.

On Sunday, January 6, 1985, I stood up during worship services at Newport-Mesa Christian Center and announced the beginning of this new ministry to foster children. There would be a meeting in my office after the service. I already had a few volunteers but wanted to make sure anyone who felt called to work with foster children could attend.

It was a great beginning. We started the meeting with prayer. After prayer I said, "We need a name that fits the secular community as well as the sacred. (In my mind, all things are sacred; but to include secular and governmental organizations it was important to reflect that in the name.) As we talked, someone said, "What about Royal Family Camps?" At the time, Great Britain's Princess Diana and Prince Charles were a top news item. The suggested name showed how we wanted "our" children to be treated. It included the word *camp*, but there was nothing about whom the clientele would be. Then, finally, someone said, "Why not, Royal Family KIDS Camps?" *Royal Family* was both secular and sacred; *Kids* described the clientele of the mission; and *Camp* named the place of the event. I recall the sense of accomplishment as we all said, "Royal Family KIDS Camp," and we knew we had the name.

Along with the name, we needed a passage from scripture that gave a picture of what the children had been through. I prayed for God's help to find the right verse or passage that would instill the purpose of Royal Family KIDS Camp (RFKC) into the hearts and minds of constituents whom God would call to the mission. The words of Psalm 40:1–3 were stamped into my heart and mind. As a matter of fact, we started calling Psalm 40 the "Abused Child's Psalm." Read it as a child would. Read it as an adult would.

I waited patiently for the Lord;
he turned to me and heard my cry.
He lifted me out of the slimy pit,
out of the mud and mire;
he set my feet on a rock
and gave me a firm place to stand.
He put a new song in my mouth,
a hymn of praise to our God.
Many will see and fear the Lord
and put their trust in him.

This is the anchor of Royal Family—the "Abused Child's Psalm."

Of all the momentoes RFKC has to remember, there is one that stands out. There's a trophy with a brass bus atop a walnut base that commemorates the first bus ride to RFKC in 1985. The first bus ride with thirty-seven children aboard brought me to my knees. It was like no other camp bus ride I had ever taken. As we pulled out of the church parking lot, I was shocked to see that no one was waving good-bye from the curb. At other camps, parents would be waving and some mothers would even be crying. But for this ride, there were no parents or foster parents waving.

I sat down in my seat as the bus approached the freeway when a thought ran through my mind. This was the first time I had ever been on a bus filled with foster children. Each one had a story that placed them in the social service system. I looked around and saw the scars of cigarette burns. I saw one girl who had scars from her hair being pulled out. I saw six, seven, and eight-year-olds sucking their thumbs. Others were twirling their hair. I was overcome with emotion. They all had one thing in common: pain—the pain of separation from family and the pain of being hurt physically and emotionally.

There was a fearful look in many children. We were taking them to the mountains, an unfamiliar place. We were telling them it would be fun. But they really didn't trust what we were saying. They were afraid and worried about their safety. They had been lied to before. Fights broke out among the boys. As I walked to the back of the bus, one camper looked at me, his eyes flashing with anger. "There is nothing you can do to hurt me!"

The usual, "How much farther?" was never asked. There were three of us adults on the bus with thrity-seven children. I was already beginning to wonder if this was a good idea.

The bus ride took a toll on my excitement to begin a new ministry. I thought it was a good idea, but the severity of the pain that exploded in anger and outbursts of vulgar language was overwhelming.

As we came into the camp, the staff and counselors were cheering and holding up signs with the campers' names on them. One camper looked at me and asked, "Who are these crazy people?"

Crazy? We were—twenty-three adults and thirty-seven campers at the beginning of Royal Family KIDS Camp.

My heart was breaking. I heard too many stories, like: "Pastor Tesch, I love my mom and I hold on to her legs saying, 'Mommy, I love you.' But she still beats me with a belt." Or, "Will you stand guard at the bathroom door so no one can come in?" Or, "I've been in eight foster homes, and I didn't like any of them!" Or, "My dad's in jail for drugs. I don't know where my brother and sister live. Can you find them?" It was overwhelming for a man who grew up in a loving home.

The first two years the camp went from Monday through Saturday for the children and from Sunday through Saturday for the adult volunteers. I know. We were crazy! We noticed that the counselors and staff were exhausted. When the last day of camp was changed to Friday instead of Saturday the adults were thankful for the extra night at home on the weekend. They were drained physically, but even more so, emotionally.

On Wednesday of that first week, I had just separated three boys from fighting at the drinking fountain outside the dining commons. I was having a pity party as I walked down the road at Pinecrest Camp, telling God how unfair it was. I am giving up a week of my vacation and these kids can't begin to appreciate all that is being done for them. They aren't even thankful for the camp. They are rhyming my name with four letter words. They are cruel kids who need to be disciplined. All of a sudden a brown Volkswagen Rabbit came driving up the dirt road toward me. I recognized it as my prayer partner, Glenn Rouses' car. He got out of the car with his big infectious smile on his face. "Hi, Bud!"

I couldn't believe my eyes. "What are you doing here?" I asked. He had taken a personal day from work to drive the two hours up the mountain to tell me a message he had received during his devotions that morning. He then said two short statements that have been branded into my heart and mind ever since: "Wayne, remember God has everything under control!" The second thing he said was, "You are doing what you have been called to do." I remember him parking the car, and together we walked to the archery range where we spent some time in prayer. As we walked away from the archery range, I knew that, as Bobby Clinton had said, "When your past and future collide in the present, convergence takes place. You have found your calling." As I write this, I'm still amazed at how God gave my friend a message He knew I needed to hear. He arranged that I would hear it at just the right moment, when I was overcome with feelings of failure and loneliness.

The first week of camp was a true adventure. It reminded me of my own childhood, playing in the sandbox with my trucks. However, instead of toys, the backhoe, a bulldozer, a road scraper, front-end loaders, and dump trucks were real. They were driving in and around buildings, digging trenches, leveling the land, and hauling dirt to another part of the camp. All the while we were attempting to conduct camp with kids who were behaving wildly. The food that week was hauled up from San Bernardino, thirty miles away. The camp's kitchen was still under construction. Cold cereal in the morning, sandwiches for lunch, and some form of mystery meat for dinner. Most of the time it was hot dogs slathered with beans served on paper plates with plasticware. Oh, the nightmare!

On Thursday of that week, I called the church office and asked if we could have a meal in the fellowship hall on Saturday for the volunteers as we returned home. My administrative assistant and her friends had transformed the hall with decorations. They had set the tables with fine china, not paper plates; stemware, not plastic cups; silverware, not plasticware; tablecloths, not paper placemats. It was such a wonderful thing for our twenty-three weary and worn volunteers to be treated with such care after a grueling week at camp. This dinner, born out of negative circumstances, became RFK Camp tradition and is now known as the "Welcome Home Dinner." It was needed royal treatment for "war torn" volunteers upon returning from a week of exhausting work.

At the end of the dinner, we stood around the borders of the room, and, joining hands, gathered in a circle of prayer. We prayed that the week made a difference for the kids. We prayed for strength to return. We prayed for the futures of the children. We prayed that God would raise up more adults so we could bless the foster children in Orange County. We were grateful for the week and the impact it had on each of us. We all sang "Jesus Loves Me" in a chorus of benediction.

We hugged each other and walked out of the room with our hearts broken, knowing that these are the things that break the heart of God. As I entered our home, I reached for my daughter, Renee, holding her and weeping. I reached for Diane and continued to weep. Later Diane told me she thought I was going through a mental breakdown. She had never witnessed me sitting on the couch in tears over the news, hearing reports of abuse. Every time there was a news story about an abused child, I was haunted, wondering if it could be one of our kids. Were our kids being exposed to more abuse?

Sunday was an emotional time for me at church. Normally. I am positive and upbeat while sharing the announcements at the pulpit. When I stood to walk to the pulpit, I began to weep. It was difficult to talk about the mundane activities of the church when those of us who had been at camp the previous week could think of nothing but those precious children and their pain. Concern over how our campers lived their lives in horrifying conditions consumed our thoughts. We could not forget their stories about the treatment they endured during the formative years of their lives.

Monday I went to the office, closed the door and cried. I cried for three days. My mind was mush. My heart was broken. I finally went to the office of the senior pastor, Dr. George O. Wood, of Newport-Mesa Christian Center. I told him I was finding it difficult to concentrate and accomplish even the simplest tasks. I recall only two parts of the conversation. One: sharing how there were more than one million reported cases of child abuse in the United States and we took only thirty-seven children to camp. I told him it was so unfair for me to have come from such a loving, caring family and these kids are clueless about the love of a mom and dad. I briefed him on the stories of the children, the conditions of the camp, and how proud I was to be part of that amazing group of volunteers.

When I was through, George was succinct. He didn't empathize with me or try to pump me up. Instead, he said, "Many great God movements begin small." He then told me the starfish story.

On the southeastern shore of Australia, thousands of starfish had washed ashore, left to dry up and die in the heat of the sun. Early in the morning, a man who was staying nearby was out jogging along the shore. He came upon a young boy frantically trying to save the starfish by throwing them back into the ocean. The jogger, curious, stopped and asked the boy, "I see what you're doing, but do you really think it will make any difference?"

The boy paused for a brief moment and replied, "I don't know, mister, but I think it will make a difference to this one."

I walked back to my office and started to cry once again. All of a sudden my desk became my altar. I felt the Lord ask, "Are you going to cry, or are you going to do something about it?" It was then I traded my tears for intentionality.

The team began planning for another year. I could hardly wait. We held team meetings evaluating the week at camp. The major observation we all made was that when the children were in groups of only six or eight, many negative behaviors dissipated. The schedule of camp consisted of large group experiences such as breakfast club, chapel, group recreation, crafts, and swimming at Lake Gregory. We had a schedule. The camp bell would ring and we herded these volatile kids to the next activity. It seemed that because they were in large groups so much of the time, their tempers sometimes flared and chaos prevailed. I will always remember Bethany Bennett's suggestion to decentralize the camp into smaller groups rather than keeping it a large mass experience for everyone.

This was new to me. Centralized camping for children was all I had experienced. Having never done a camp with a high percentage of volatility all in one place, I knew we needed to do things differently. This was how the activity centers began. We found that they were the key to the program's success. The smaller group format minimized the opportunity for angry outbursts. The activity centers provided opportunities for campers to do things they enjoyed. There would be many options, and they could pick for themselves rather than being told what they had to do. These kids rarely had the chance to make their own decisions. They also learned to work with a camping buddy, so they could find ways for everyone to be happy and do what they wanted. Whether using an artist paintbrush or hammering nails into a birdhouse, the kids could go from place to place around the camp. They could do archery, listen to a story with Grandma and Grandpa, or go fishing. I mention this because I believe activity centers made replicating the camps more successful. It was a brilliant idea in 1986 to decentralize the camp experience for the child.

I have talked about the struggles of putting together a camp for foster children. From those humble experiences, Royal Family KIDS is now the biggest network of camps for foster children in the United States. This happened because God calls incredible individuals to expand the vision to reach more and more children. The pages of this book are the result of men and women sensing a call to help children in the foster care system. In every church, there are men and women who are devoted and dedicated followers of Jesus Christ. They are making a difference! As you read the stories of Royal Family KIDS, be aware that those men and women are the real heroes. They have given between 250 to 500 hours each year volunteering for the camps. They are the ones who impact and influence the lives of the children. They plan. They pray. They are the incredible people of Royal Family. As you read their stories, make sure you have tissues nearby. Your heart will be moved. You will experience the "royal weep." You may even want to get involved. Please do! You'll never be the same!

2

DIANE TESCH
Co-Founder

In twenty-five years of developing Royal Family KIDS, I have learned many things, but this is foremost: God wastes nothing from our past, and he enhances it and re-gifts it in His plans for our future. Looking back over these incredible years is a stroll through tumbling brooks, rushing rivers, calm paths in quiet woods, hundreds of crowded airport terminals, and treacherous mountain trails. Most of these were unmapped and unnavigable, but they were always conquerable with God holding our hand. Friends who knew us forty years earlier in our lives came to the forefront and lent their support once we declared we were going "all out" on this endeavor for the sake of abused children. God took things that were huge disappointments in our past and salvaged them, making them fodder in developing a program that has now gone viral in answering a critical societal need. When we stuck our toes in the water of this vast ocean of hurt, we had no idea a rip tide would engulf us as we reached out to children screaming for help. When we thought we would sink, His strong arms held us firmly and brought us safely back to shore, dusting off the sand that irritated us and wrapping us in a towel of confidence that spurred us to keep going.

Condensing more than twenty-five years of history and memories into one small book is no easy task. We can simply capture a few snapshots that were mile markers and God-induced bolts of affirmation that He was walking beside us every step of the way. Many of our memories are of things we hadn't even prayed for at the time God interjected them into the story of Royal Family. It's in those times one knows this truly is God and not we ourselves. I am so grateful that God gave both of us a conscious awareness and a capacity at those times to appreciate and acknowledge from whence those blessings came. My favorite scripture is Psalm 37:4. "Delight yourself in the Lord and He will give you the desires of your heart." Throughout the years, I have tried to make this a pattern for my life. Royal Family has been a series of delighting and receiving; delighting and receiving; and so on. I have found that usually, one follows the other in proper order.

Prior to 1990, some significant things took place in my life, preparing me with the opportunities I would eventually need to grow and duplicate the Royal Family KIDS network of camps. In the late 1970s and early 1980s, I had the opportunity to help launch a quick-serve food company known as Spaghetti Pot Take Home Restaurants. It was delicious food, prepared ahead, reconstituted, and in three minutes working moms were out the door, on their way home from their work day with a hot meal for the family. I was in on the ground floor and for four years we developed a prototype, refined the operation, and began franchising stores. My responsibilities included operations and training the franchisees. With several franchises sold, consisting of more than one hundred stores and thirteen of them open, a major investor infused capital for the first fourth of an option to buy the company. We were flying high and poised for rapid expansion, and I was a shareholder. Then a number of things began to happen: First, the early 1980s ushered in the highest interest rates we had ever known in this country. Potential operators stopped buying franchises, and that source of income dropped off. Who could have predicted that? Second, existing franchisees stopped borrowing against their assets to expand their territories and build out additional stores, thus our second form of income began to dry up. Third, the suitor for the buyout changed corporate direction and no longer needed an outlet for its Durham Wheat pasta, withholding any future capital. Once the first and second happened, royalties from the franchisees diminished. Eventually, all three combined to put us out of business. Had the full buyout taken place, I could have funded Royal Family singlehandedly for years to come. Instead, my dreams were dashed, and I was devastated. How did God take this "lemon" and turn it into "lemonade" in my life? I wouldn't be able to see the reason for another four years.

Shortly after closing down the company ("first one in, last one out") a friend, Hap Byers, recognized my capabilities in developing start-up practices and offered an opportunity to do research in the small luxury bed and breakfast hotel market on the West Coast. His company had purchased a parcel of land on the coast overlooking the Dana Point Harbor. They thought they might develop an inn on the property. It was tough duty to visit many of the prime luxury B and B's up and down the West Coast, gather as much input as I could glean from some of the finest operators in the business, and take the best of all their operational knowledge and condense it into one property. It was a delight to imagine such a property.

By May 1987 we received approval from the city of Dana Point to proceed to build a twenty-nine-room luxury B and B, and the plans went into the county for review and approval. There would be a lull in my duties for a few months while we waited for approval. Summer was just around the corner, and by this time, we were embarking on our third week of Royal Family.

Those were the early days of RFKC, and we were tweaking and changing things at every turn, making the camp model stronger, safer, and better all the way around—for the kids and the adults. I had taken the week off work to be at camp at the end of June. Hap and his wife, Marilyn, had been in our church for a number of years. For the previous year, while I had worked on the B and B, they had heard me talk about this emerging "call" on our lives, and they were genuinely interested. During that week of camp, unbeknownst to us, Hap showed up one afternoon. We were shocked. What was he doing here? We walked the grounds with him, talked about our dream of more camps, and gave him a glimpse of the kids. Seeing how their behaviors were a direct result of how they had been treated and why they were now in the foster care system, he was moved emotionally.

Camp ended on Friday and we returned home, drained physically and emotionally. The children's stories were gut wrenching, and seeing the real faces and bodies that bore the pain was almost more than we could bear. We had never been prepared for what God was leading us into. Nightly I went to sleep asking God how He could allow this to happen to innocents. It simply wasn't fair. I never have resolved the answer to those how and why questions. But I did resolve to devote my life to making a difference for the better. God had to take care of justice in their lives.

We did our best to recuperate over the weekend, and Monday came all too soon. But right on time, I was back at my job on Monday morning. As usual, I went into Hap's office, where he sat behind his beautiful, imposing carved wooden executive desk. I sat down and we shared our usual Monday-morning greetings and summaries of our weekends. Knowing he had been to camp to visit the week before, I knew he would be poised to pounce with a barrage of insightful questions. He was a deep thinker and let no grass grow under his feet! After I responded to several of his questions, he finally leaned forward and folded his hands on the desk. Then he asked a question that would change my life, Wayne's life, and the life of Royal Family forever.

"Diane," he said, "I really enjoyed finally seeing what it is you and Wayne have been talking about for over three years. I now get it. But you and Wayne seem frustrated, like you want to do more and can't. What do you need to get this thing to the next level?"

"We have other churches asking us to teach them what we are doing," I said. "But from my background, I know what it's going to take to develop and perfect a model, write training manuals, and then train other people to duplicate what we're doing and to do it in another location without us being present. You know I put in an honest day's work for you here at the office, and every ounce of my creative juices is used up working on this inn. When I go home at night, I am mentally spent. I don't have any more creative energy left. I need time—a big block of time—where I can focus and concentrate on the task at hand and take all this information that's rattling around in Wayne's head and my heads and get it down on paper."

Sitting back in his chair once again, he said, "Okay. Here's what we can do. Those building plans are going to sit in that county building department for two to three months, and you really won't have a lot to do here in the office during that time. You know the bonus we agreed on that you would receive when we open the doors of the inn? Well, how about if you take the next three months off, stay at home, and sit at your typewriter and get everything that you know about this unique camp operation out of your head and down on paper. I'll take the bonus you would receive when we open the doors of the inn and keep your biweekly paychecks coming while you sit and type on the manuals at home. Don't come into the office, unless it's to use the copier or the other machines. Just stay at home and *write!*"

I was ecstatic! You tell a writer she can have three months off to write *anything* and be paid for it, she gets *really* excited! Much less, this was something I knew in my spirit was God ordained and would be the key to launching this ministry into the future. We were only taking forty kids at that point. This would mean we could reach hundreds—thousands! If Hap had leaned over his big executive desk that morning and placed a gold brick in my hands, he couldn't have given me anything more valuable than the gift of time. That's what I needed. God knew it, and He provided it. There weren't cell phones back then, so I couldn't even call Wayne from my car. I couldn't wait to get home and tell him.

Immediately, the following week, I set up shop in our den and began typing. I had made many sketchy notes about things we needed to change or things we needed to remember to tell someone else if they were to do what we were doing. But I use the term *sketchy* loosely. It literally had to come from my head. The product of those three months of effort became the original *Directors' Training Manual* from which we began teaching directors' training classes the following summer, in 1988. That summer I realized that the huge devastating disappointment of the demise of Spaghetti Pot had not been in vain. God redeemed everything I had learned in developing the franchise and was putting it to use as I began the detailed task of documenting all we were doing, making it possible for someone else to understand and then duplicate in our absence. I was reminded, "What Satan meant for evil in destroying my life, God meant for good" for abused children.

Soon after that momentous day in Hap's office, he sold the whole project to an investor. We never built the inn ourselves, the investor did, and it operates today as the Blue Lantern Inn on Street of the Blue Lantern in Dana Point. It looks just as we designed it, with all the amenities we planned. On two occasions Wayne has been so sweet to take me there for Valentine's Day. It's a beautiful respite.

It has been said by those whom Wayne has enlisted in ministry, "Never accept an invitation to go to lunch with Wayne Tesch." All those who have were given "opportunities" to put in many hours of volunteer time, beyond their normal work weeks, but be enriched beyond their wildest expectations. Wayne always has a wonderful plan for your life.

By 1990, I had been having breakfasts and dinners (and a few lunches) with this man for forty-three years, but none rocked my world quite like the one at which he proposed the "opportunity" for me to join him in leaving his eighteen-year stint at the church and launch a full-time ministry to abused children. Wayne also had "a wonderful plan for *my* life" too! Being a visionary, he could quickly jump into something like this with gusto; but not his calculating, conservative, cautious planner, wife. Was he having a midlife crisis? What could he possibly be thinking? It did turn out that this wasn't an impulsive decision on his part. In fact, we had pondered what it would be like if we had to do this with changes at the church being beyond our control.

God's prompting was undeniable. So in September, Newport-Mesa Christian Center launched us into fulltime ministry for Royal Family KIDS Camps in a wonderful, memorable farewell event. It was done with such class and dignity, with our lives of eighteen years as senior associate pastor being passed before us in review. Fifty percent of the love gift we were given would have gone to Uncle Sam had we accepted it for ourselves. We were smarter than that. So to preserve all 100 percent of it, we opened Royal Family's checking account and began immediately buying supplies, office implements, software, a desk and chair, and anything it was going to take to run a nonprofit office. We are eternally grateful for the gift and the ongoing support that was raised in that service—a huge vote of confidence as we stepped out with little but an idea and four weeks of camps behind us.

At this point, I was working fulltime at Southern California College (now Vanguard University) to provide our daughter's tuition—critical to a solid beginning. I was also our household bookkeeper and overseer. I knew all the columns on that green accounting paper had to add up each month if we were to survive. To suddenly become dependent on church offerings and donations to provide a salary for Wayne was more risk than I wanted to take. So while I agreed we needed to do this, it was with much anguish and worry. My "faith walk" would certainly be "stumbling baby steps" for quite some time.

I continued working for another ten months until I no longer could handle the load of fulltime work weeks, *plus* all the office operations of a new growing nonprofit. I could not take care of it in my "off" time from work. Having our first Royal Family office in the back bedroom of our home did make it easier to work sporadically in my free time. Many nights I remember laying my head on the pillow saying to myself, "Till the printer ceases to whine into the night, these mailings will go out to our friends and donors, keeping them informed of the progress of Royal Family KIDS Camp, Inc." (We changed the name to Royal Family KIDS, Inc. in 2011). Without the dedicated hours of my mom and dad, Art and Alice Jermy, and two or three of their dear friends, these mailings wouldn't have happened. Paying for them was out of the question.

In July 1991, I resigned my job even though we couldn't afford the decision, and now the "trust factor" kicked in. Little by little, God began to reassure me that this was His plan for us. But the reassurance didn't make it any less difficult. In my journal on September 24, 1991, I wrote: "The first miracle was finding out our daughter Renee would get $1,570 in staff benefits from my two-and-a-half years at the college! What a surprise! In addition, she received half tuition as a missionary dependent with our denomination—after petitioning for it through our local church! And, as resident assistant, she gets all room and half board plus $90 a month on her bill. So we owe $1,200 for the semester! All this *after* I had resigned. God has been good!" We were amazed and Renee had seen God provide miraculously on her behalf following a life-changing decision in our family!

The following weekend we drove to Brawley, California, to speak at a church service. It was three-and-a-half hours away, just north of the Mexican border. The area was heavily populated with migrant farm workers who worked the many produce fields in our economy. Driving up to the church, I exclaimed to Wayne, "*What* have *you* gotten us into?" The building was so tiny, it looked like maybe 50 people could fit inside, and what kind of an offering could that possibly provide? Having seen many missionary speakers as a youth, I didn't foresee myself being a missionary wife in my future. But here I was, trying to act like one and not offend anyone who might place something in the offering.

As I set up our materials in the back of the church, a little silver-haired elderly lady approached me with intentionality. She said, "Now, honey, I want to ask you a question. Do you wear panty hose?" I righted my shoulders and, trying not to insult her, (thinking, if she's into panty hose this morning, I might as well get the right kind) I said, "As a matter of fact, I do. I wear Leggs panty hose." Unabashed, she continued, "Well, in my devotions this week, the Lord reminded me of those panty hose that I've been planning to take up to the missionary room at the district office, and I keep forgetting. God said, 'If that missionary wife this Sunday morning wears panty hose, you need to give those to her. So I have them out in my car, and if I forget after the service, you remind me and I'll go and get them." YouTube wasn't around back then, but it would have been a great place for a video of the look on my face when she finished talking! I kindly thanked her, and she took her seat. Judging from her age, I figured she would soon forget we had ever had the conversation (interesting, my perspective on the latter, twenty-five years later in life). And far be it from me to remind her to go and get them. Thinking later, I realized God had me in mind the week before she would meet me and prompted her to provide for my needs—an awesome thought!

Following the service, I was again back at the information table and soon the church emptied out. I looked around and the little lady was gone. I was sure she had forgotten about the panty hose, and I was actually relieved at the thought, as I didn't want to be embarrassed. I packed up our stuff and was turning around to leave when the back door of the church swung wide open and in she walked, with the same purpose and abandon as the first time she entered. But, now, she was carrying a brown paper bag, which she pushed toward me.

"Here you are. I told you I would get them out of my car!" she said like a proud little grade-schooler bringing flowers to the teacher. "God bless you" she said and left. I sheepishly put the bag in our box of materials and waited for Wayne to emerge from the pastor's office.

We walked out to the car and drove out the driveway. His first question was, "Well, did God speak to you this morning?" We were continually looking for any assurance or confirmation we had done the right thing.

I said, "Well, I don't know if He said anything, but a little old lady certainly did."

"Well, what did she say?"

So I told him the exact conversation and what had transpired. He said, "So what's in the bag?" I reached into the box in the back seat and retrieved the brown bag. I pulled out a box of L'eggs panty hose! Not one-pack but a *six*-pack! I had never seen a six-pack of L'eggs panty hose. Nor have I seen one to this day—and believe me, I have looked. They were my brand, my size, and my favorite shade. When God takes care of you, He gets it right!

If God Himself had sat on the seat between us that morning straddling the console, it couldn't have been more clear than if He had said, "Diane, if I can take care of the thing nearest to you , your panty hose, can you trust me for the big things in life with Royal Family: your household budget? Your needs? Royal Family's budget? Publishing curriculum? Producing videos? Buying plane tickets? Rental cars? I nodded my head yes.

Later in October, I wrote another journal entry:

We received a letter stating that General Motors was settling a $13.5 million class-action suit of which we were a part, having owned one of their diesel-powered vehicles from 1981 to 1985. This was a total shock to us as a way, once again, God met our needs. Our settlement was $981, helping to pay Renee's school bill. PTL.

God even takes the lemons in our lives and turns them to lemonade if it means using it to meet our needs and encourage the steps he has prompted us to take. Again, we were amazed at His provision. It had been six years since we had to scrap that vehicle. A class-action suit was certainly not on our radar when we calculated whether or not we could afford to leave secure jobs to start a non-profit.

On November 19, 1991, Tyndale House began the conversation with us to publish our first book. They were convinced that we were the only Christian ministry at the time doing anything proactive in the area of social need. They saw Wayne as "young" and in his prime to "ride this one up." They wanted ten chapters with the first due to them in January 1992. I wanted to cry and tell God to slow down, and to shout with joy, all at the same time. The last thing I needed was to author a book in the next five months. But I was reminded that week to "Commit your works to the LORD and your plans will be established. . . . The mind of man plans his way, but the LORD directs his steps" (Proverbs 16:3–9). While we recognized God's hand was leading us, we had to trust Him to provide health, energy, rest, vision, and favor among the churches we were recruiting to duplicate the camps.

It was encouragement like this and reading in my devotions that would remind me God was with us. At this time, I was reading devotionals from Chuck Swindoll's book *Come Before Winter*, in which he quoted a verse from Fanny Crosby's song "Rescue the Perishing," remembering the dozens of times I sang this missions song while growing up:

Touched by a loving heart
Wakened by kindness
Chords that were broken
Will vibrate once more

I was reminded that this was what was happening in the hearts of the children we were serving. The hearts of broken children were being mended through the loving, caring adults serving them in the camps in Christ's name, and we were a part of it. God kept leading, and we kept following, but it wasn't without setbacks.

The day after meeting with Tyndale, Wayne was returning home from speaking in Fullerton, California, when the crankshaft on our beautiful navy and red Chevy Celebrity went through the engine on the freeway. Determined to be a unique problem in this engine and maybe a "silent recall," it left us with no reliable car to drive the many miles necessary to spread the word about Royal Family, *and,* it was paid for! That was all calculated in the decision to resign our position at the church and my job at the college. Like Job, I almost shook my fist at God, asking Him what He thought we were going to do now!

On November 23, we drove our not-so-reliable used car to Lancaster, California, to speak. It was thrilling to see the new team of trainees meeting for the first time and seeing the materials they had copied from what they had been given during directors' training that summer. They really wanted to do it "by the book." All the hours I had poured into writing our manuals were paying off. The scene was overwhelmingly pure joy. At this service, we set up our booth, as this was a mission's emphasis weekend. Wayne shared in the morning service. Following the service, we talked to folks at the booth, took signups, and encouraged people to get involved in their new camp endeavor.

As we were taking down the booth, a lady came up to me and put paper money in my hand. "I don't know what your needs are," she said, "but I couldn't sleep last night. Now, the Lord doesn't wake me up very often, but I kept waking up thinking of you. I know mom's always buy their underwear last, so take this and do something for yourself—not the ministry—something for you."

I broke down crying, speechless, as if God *again* said, "I know all your needs. If I care about you personally, I'll take care of a car for you too." I quietly thanked her and slipped the money in the pocket of the light yellow wool blazer I was wearing.

Once in the car and leaving the parking lot, Wayne again asked his typical question, "Did God say anything to you this morning?"

"Well, I don't know about God, but a lady did. She said, 'Mothers always buy their underwear last, so use this for something for you, not the ministry,' and she put paper money in my hand."

To which he said, "Well, how much?"

I unfolded it, and it was two one-hundred-dollar bills.

"Victoria Secret, here we come!" Wayne exclaimed. He always seems to find the humorous side of our worst down times, and the Chevy Celebrity blowing up was certainly one of his lowest moments to this point in Royal Family. We had a good laugh and headed down the freeway back to Orange County.

These miracles began to be almost laughable in that the more I worried about our needs and Royal Family's needs, the more He kept heaping blessings upon us, just enough to let us know He had not abandoned us and He would be our provider. And so, we continued.

Later that month Wayne had coffee and donuts with another longtime friend from the church, and among their "guy talk" was the subject of our car blowing up. Wayne mentioned that with the growth of Royal Family, there was more and more stuff to haul around and what we really needed was a van, but that would be a stretch for our budget. Wayne's friend agreed it was a nasty break. It would be one more opportunity for God to intervene in our ongoing saga of faith in the life of Royal Family KIDS, and he offered to pray with us for a miracle.

In December, this same friend and his wife invited us to go with them to hear Ronald Reagan speak at a fundraising banquet at a local hotel. They also invited their two married daughters and their spouses. We all dressed in formal attire and everything about the dinner was beautifully done.

During dinner, he told us, "You're leading a fundraising organization now and you're going to have to do events like this, so we wanted you to see how it's done."

It was a five-course meal and, of course, there's always a lull between the courses. I was seated next to the host when, while we were waiting for the main entrée to arrive, he very casually threw his ring of keys out into the center of the table. Considering the atmosphere, I thought it was quite crude for him to do such a thing. Being very good friends and knowing I could joke with him, I picked up the keys and said, "What's with the keys?" Of course, by now Wayne had leaned forward on his seat to see what was going on at the center of the table and the key ring. Our host then explained that they had just rotated some vehicles out of the fleet at their company and they had a van to donate to us for Royal Family.

"We've put all new tires on it, repainted it, and all the maintenance is right up to date. It's yours!"

Wayne and I were both speechless and our eyes were leaking. We had *never* been in a position where people's generosity was poured out on us in such ways. We are very self-sufficient individuals and can usually take care of any of our own needs. At times like this, you just don't have words to express what's in your heart. But we've learned that, while we are overjoyed at what the gift meant to us and the ministry, it was probably nowhere near the joy the givers received when they gave it. I took our host's advice and did learn from that evening: Ronald Reagan was a miniature figure far, far across the room from where we sat. There is definitely a strategy as to who sits where among two hundred tables at a fundraiser. The long-standing, potentially largest donors are seated closest to the speaker. Well, they may have been in the "seats of honor" with the best view that night, but *we* were the happiest people in the room. God had smiled on us!

During these early years, it seemed like God placed certain children in the camp who just grabbed my heart so deeply I could not walk away from them in spirit. Understand, Wayne and I continually looked for signs that we were on the right track, always making sure this truly was God and not us. On more than one occasion, we went home from the week of camp and asked ourselves if we should become foster parents and then adopt a child. But in searching our hearts and emotions, we knew Wayne would not be free to do the kind of recruitment travel needed to expand the number of camps if we had a young child at home. It was one child or thousands. We chose the latter.

Matthew was six years old, with a slight build, beautiful copper skin, and the softest curly black hair. I had become attached to him during the week. He was a child with a glazed-over look in his eyes. He would zone out, and you didn't know if he was even cognizant of what was going on around him or what was being said. He was a good boy, and kind of just floated along with the pack. Fridays are always so difficult and gut wrenching when it comes time for the kids to say good-bye to their counselors and favorite staff members. Back at the church parking lot, the counselors and staff hold back their tears at the final good-byes; they cry later, once the kids are gone. Matthew was deeply moved and having a very difficult time handling all of it. I saw him far away over on the grass, crouched down, and hovering over his sleeping bag, very quiet. This would be typical of his behavior. I squatted down and held him, assuring him *we would try to find him the next summer and bring him back to camp.* I couldn't promise anything, as these children move frequently from one foster home to another, and it's difficult to track them in the system. Finally, someone arrived to pick him up in an old rattle trap of a car, and the driver, as she talked incoherently, assured me Matthew had been to this camp before. I knew he hadn't. My heart sank, knowing he was going back to what appeared to be a "not good" situation. All I could do was hug him and assure him we would try to find him. We don't promise anything with these kids. They don't need one more broken promise from another adult: "I'll be out of jail soon." "I'll be there for your birthday"— never to show up. "I'll be off drugs the next time you see me." Endless broken promises. I didn't want him to see me crying as, walking away, my eyes blurred. A simple wave was all I could give him.

Wayne and I had said yes to God's prompting to do Royal Family, based on Wayne's knowledge of developing camps—*not* our background in child abuse issues. Neither of us had a background in social work or psychology. As we began to unwrap the whole concept of what was entailed to succeed with these children, we began saying, "*What* were we thinking?" But as God would have it, He brought individuals across our paths, most of whom we didn't even know. Some were acquaintances of friends and others were friends from our past with whom we hadn't associated for many years. Each one had the expertise we lacked and began to fill the gigantic hole we could not fill on our own.

That fall Wayne met one such individual, the Rev. David Delaplane. An acquaintance suggested Wayne meet with him over lunch. Remember what I said earlier about having lunch with Wayne Tesch? Well, David was one such person, and what a gift he and his wife, Anne, were to us. It would turn out that Wayne had a wonderful plan for *his* life too! David opened his Bible right there on the lunch table and began reading scriptures to Wayne, assuring him that Royal Family was God's answer for hurting children whom Christian ministries were not even addressing in those days. Back and forth, they shared various scriptures that had helped each of them to this point in the area of child hurt. He read verses that would soothe us as we began to grapple with the children's stories that broke our hearts. He helped us feel assured that what we were planning to do was ordained of God and would be the answer to children's deep physical, emotional, and psychological wounds. We were simple folk, but David saw this camp resource as far beyond what Wayne and I could do in our own strength. Others would team up with us and extend our hands. One such verse was, "The LORD makes poor and rich; He brings low, He also exalts. He raises the poor from the dust, He lifts the needy from the ash heap to make them sit with nobles and inherit a seat of honor" (1 Samuel 2: 7–8). How fitting that we had chosen Royal Family KIDS Camp as the name, and scripture was talking about these children being elevated to "seats of honor." This is hope given to our campers who have been made to feel like the trash of the world. David reassured Wayne that as much as we wept for these children, God loved them immensely more, and it was the adults in their lives who had made horrific choices.

He went on and read another abused child's assurance: "For my father and mother have forsaken me, but the LORD will take me up" (Psalm 27:10). It would surely be the arms of loving, caring adults who would reach out to them through Royal Family. David's words were like salve to our hearts. We read them over and over, and, later, we read them to director trainees who also wrestled with God's hand in all of these children's lives.

Another meaningful verse was Psalm 34:18: "The LORD is near to the brokenhearted, and saves those who are crushed in spirit." If anyone was crushed in spirit, it was the desperate children slowly slinking off the bus with a wary eye of distrust but really wanting to run to waiting arms of counselors and staff members who were there to greet them. Their countenance would change 180 degrees by Friday.

By the following year I couldn't wait to see if Matthew was signed up and coming to camp. Sure enough, he was there. In these early years, I was always silently doing my "research" to see what, if anything, these weeks meant to the children. Or were we just making ourselves feel good about serving them? So on Thursday night, as the children were exiting the chapel, I found Matthew "hanging out" just outside the doors. We stood under the huge spotlight that flooded the area like daylight.

I took Matthew's face in my hands as he looked up at me, his beautiful copper skin glowing in the light, and I asked him, "Matthew, do you remember after camp last year down at the church, we talked?" Matthew shook his head yes. Then I said, "Do you remember what I told you?"

Without being prompted he looked up at me and said, "You told me, *if you could find me, you'd try to let me come back to camp*—and here I am." He was smiling from ear to ear, and he rarely smiled.

My "research" was working. Here I felt that nothing was getting through to him. But behind that glazed-over look, he was taking it all in. And when it appeared to me that my words at the parking lot on Friday were like darts ricocheting off a block wall, they weren't. They were a lifeline that Matthew held onto for twelve months, a ray of hope that I meant what I said, and maybe he would get to experience one more week of that glorious time he was leaving behind. I could continue for another year, knowing it meant something huge to the children.

We continued for about a year to operate the organization daily from the back bedroom of our home. But it soon became obvious that with Wayne, the "people person," booking services and appointments on the phone in our ten-foot-by-ten-foot office and me doing detailed check entries, ordering, and bookkeeping at the same time, something had to change. He had to move down the hall into our den, which now became our second office. My dad had completely lined our garage with cabinets in which to store Royal Family's supplies, brochures, the booth, and other "stuff." Royal Family was taking over our home!

In February 1993 we received a call from, again, our friend Hap. He had taken up a ceramics hobby that had consumed his garage, and his wife told him it had to go. So he rented a warehouse with two offices in the front, but he had no use for the offices. He was inviting us to come down and look at the space. Wayne's schedule was taking him out of town so frequently that it was June before we could arrange to do so.

At about this time, we realized we needed to hire a part-time bookkeeper. Wayne laughingly says, "It was a little awkward to say to a lady, 'Would you like to come and work in our back bedroom?'" It just didn't sound appropriate for a ministry office.

Finally, we scheduled an appointment to meet Hap at the building. When we drove into the parking lot, we saw white buildings with purple pillars and a four-foot band of purple trim around the top of the building. Wayne shouted, "God's into *purple!*"

We couldn't believe our eyes. The building was just waiting for us to move in! We went inside with Hap and looked around. It was *just* what we needed: two larger offices, a restroom, and some warehouse space. It was perfect. We could get all the stuff out of our garage and set up real offices. By July we moved in and hired a bookkeeper. Again, God had provided exactly what we needed. And the best part? It was donated space and we hadn't even made it a big matter of prayer yet. He just dropped it in our lap exactly when we needed it—truly overwhelming!

While at these offices, we grew from five camps to thirteen in a year's time. Up until this summer, between January and June, *I* had shipped all the camp supplies, including apparel, to all the camps. But in June 1994, for the first time, we assembled a group of four volunteers and set up an assembly line on the parking lot outside the office door. It was a momentous occasion as we stacked up the boxes indoors. When we were done, the six of us joined hands and prayed God's blessing would be unleashed on the camps and especially on the children as the cartons were opened all around the United States over the summer. It had been a team effort, and we were exhausted and exhilarated at the same time.

We only operated out of these offices for eighteen months, then we outgrew them. But where would we find donated space to replace them? We certainly couldn't afford to pay rent. Well, God knew where the next ones were and He moved on the heart of the same individual who put us in our first donated offices—just three blocks up the street! Not only did Hap make four offices, a reception area, shipping, and a storeroom available, he offered a warehouse offsite, and we soon occupied that space too. It was in these offices that we could hire an administrative assistant to coordinate the activities of the thirteen camps. Hap also needed a place to "store" a beautiful retrofitted Victorian piano that could serve as a reception desk. It was a choice piece of furniture, and what could have been more fitting for a "royal environment" than a Victorian piano?

That same camp season we added a second directors' training site, in Bellingham, Washington. Over the course of twenty-five years, Wayne and I have said numerous times as we walked into the many campgrounds, "We have been in some of God's choicest places on earth—in the cathedral of the outdoors. From the San Bernardino Mountains of Southern California to the rambling corn fields of Nebraska to a hillside lake in New York to a sprawling village of thatched huts in South Africa. It doesn't get any better than this!"

These are the places where people go to take their vacations, but we get to come here and implore adults to team up with Royal Family and lead other adults into one of the most fulfilling experiences of their lives—being God's image of love to devastated children who need to know caring adults want the best for them, not the worst.

What a gorgeous training site Bellingham turned out to be. It's named the Firs, and when the camp is quiet and the wind blows through the statuesque fifty-foot fir trees, it creates a soft whisper and smells like a Christmas tree lot—a glorious place of quiet to bring children who only know the haranguing clatter of the city, the smell of crack cauldrons, and noisy, tumultuous households devoid of peace. These camps brought tranquility amid children's despair. These training sites became the "birthing rooms" of Royal Family— where we gently unfolded the swaddling clothes of our "baby" and held it out for other adults to cuddle and touch it, most of whom we only knew on paper in our files. It was a huge "entrusting" process, probably more for me having a mother's heart than for Wayne. But we knew that if God meant this gift to be shared to bless thousands of foster kids, the only way to do it was to open the training manuals and impart the knowledge to others and *trust* them to carry it out as we envisioned it to be. It was scary. Judging a book by its cover was my way of sizing up the individuals around the table at the opening orientation sessions, and I wasn't always sure God had nudged the right person sitting in the church pew. Looking back over twenty-five years, He got the right people most of the time! So we've spent the better part of these twenty-five years giving away the "child" we birthed and raised only for a short time. It wasn't always easy—but it was always rewarding.

I distinctly remember our trainees in one of the Bellingham classes, Ted Bernie, from Bremerton, Washington. Ted is a "man's kind a man"—a big, bulky guy, well suited for the football coach's position he held, and two other fellows. Now, I could have been borderline nervous breakdown status by this time and experiencing menopause all at the same time—in any case, I would get about two sentences into a SOTO ("Story of the One" as we have named the campers' stories) and I would be so overcome with emotion that my voice cracked. I was hardly able to finish the SOTO. Gradually, at about the same time, you'd see these massive men push their chairs back from the desk, fold their arms across their chest, and set their jaw. They weren't *about* to cry over hearing a gut-wrenching camper's story of abuse. It almost became comical by Friday as their tough shells gradually began to cave, and we could see God was moving even these tough guys to action. They couldn't walk away from what they had come to do—launch a camp for the foster kids in their cities. My most memorable, and certainly, my most favorite times at Royal Family, have been in these learning labs at the bench of the Almighty God, seeing Him carve out a personal vision and impart a dream to adults who had no idea what they were getting themselves into.

In November of that year, a few months after we moved into the four offices, Wayne went to lunch with a longtime friend, Mary Ann Manifold. You know what happens to people whom Wayne takes to lunch! He was asking her to come and work for us. Her response was that she was very content where she was working and didn't want to make a change. We really didn't have anyone else in mind that had the skills we needed, so we'd have to begin a recruitment process among individuals we did not know. However, the following Friday the phone rang at the new offices. It was Mary Ann, asking if the position had been filled. Hardly able to believe what he was hearing, Mary Ann told Wayne her company was closing and she was out of a job. Does God order one's steps? Their loss was our gain, at the blessing from God's hand. We were thrilled. At this writing, Mary Ann celebrates her twentieth year on our office team, sharing the coordination of all the camps with Linda Chenot. And what a team they are. The camp directors call them heroes, as these ladies are their mainline connection to the international office and the "Royal Family 9-1-1" for all the camp directors.

By the summer of 1995 we added a third training site in Winston-Salem, North Carolina. I couldn't believe I was going to get to travel to a southeastern state—tobacco fields, trees hung with Kudzu, (a voracious vine that grows up to eighty feet tall, covering the trees, until it kills them), Southern "twang" everywhere you listened—*and* the home of Krispy Kreme donuts! What a discovery that was and it made for a great break in the week when we and the training host couple would take the trainees there on Thursday night and laugh it up as they watched donuts careening around the room on conveyor belts. (Krispy Kreme had not expanded outside their New York and Winston-Salem stores at that point.) What a kick! Now trainees could see we weren't the hard taskmasters we had seemed to be for the previous five days. We could laugh too. Each site included a host couple, a married couple that we had recruited from among our friends to accompany us during the weeks of training to take care of the social aspect of the class. They provided the "royal treatment" we wanted them to give the adults and campers in their camps. These couples were invaluable to the training program then and still are today. Expecting the trainees to work so intently for eight hours each day, it was necessary for them to just "let their hair down" during the evening. Being spent mentally and emotionally, our trainers gladly defer to the host couple to keep everyone entertained in the evenings. This also became a huge opportunity for these potential directors to become better acquainted with their future peers. We could not have done it without, initially, Joan Anderson, and then early host couples Bob and Margaret Hammond, Jim and Joyce Hunnemeyer, Carlton and Dyonne Milbrandt, and later, a whole roster of couples.

We had only been having our hearts broken for about ten years when, at Winston-Salem, I developed my own personal SOTO as I encountered the most beautiful African-American little girl I had ever seen. Her name was Shimere. She had very light bronze skin and blue eyes like the sky. For some reason, I was intrigued with her and watched how she was addressing the week day by day. Unfortunately, being confined for the most part to the training room, I don't have much of an opportunity to be with the children. We were in the camps with a mission of a different sort. However, we accompany the trainees to meals in the dining hall. It's the highlight of the trainees' days, as they could now sit near the campers and really experience how they were interacting with their buddy campers and counselors. It really brought the week to life for them to be up close and personal, interfacing with and talking to the kids. The week couldn't be *all* classroom learning, but about 75 percent of it is.

Occasionally, it is discovered on Monday morning at the church parking lots that siblings from separate foster homes are attending the camp. In this particular camp, they made a special effort to allow these children to sit at meals together, recreating a family-like setting during their mealtime. Now, ten years into it, I was still doing my "research" to see whether these camps had the impact on the campers that we thought they were having. So I would engage the children in conversation by asking questions about what they liked best about the week.

It was Friday at lunch, the last meal together before going home. I purposely sat at the table with Shimere and her brother. Eventually I asked, "Shimere, what has been the *best* part about this week of camp for you?"

She thought about it for a few seconds then quietly answered, "Being able to sit at meals with my brother all week."

You could have pierced my heart with a knife and it wouldn't have hurt any worse. Imagine, a ten-year-old girl singling out the best dynamic of camp as being something she dearly misses and longs for in her living situation the other fifty-one weeks of the year. Can you imagine?

That afternoon the knife turned within me as I witnessed both children crying like faucets running full stream, as they hugged each other longingly and finally drove away in separate cars—she relegated to foster care—her brother with their biological mother. It only took one SOTO like this to keep me going for the next fifty-one weeks of administration behind my desk in the office, always making Royal Family better for kids like Shimere and her brother.

In 1995, Wayne and I were exhibiting Royal Family's booth at the International Network of Children's Ministry conference in Nashville, Tennessee. I will never forget the moment when I walked across the lobby of the Renaissance Hotel to retrieve a FedEx package at the front desk. Opening it, I found I was holding the page proofs that Tyndale House sent for one final look at our book prior to going to press. I couldn't believe my eyes. I had goose bumps as I raced into the exhibit hall to share the package with Wayne. They were finally publishing the book we had talked about four years earlier. We had become "authors" and were so grateful for someone not only believing in us but endorsing what Royal Family KIDS was doing for hundreds of abused children caught in the web of foster care. We were thrilled!

The start-up of anything worthwhile is exhausting. But our passion for children who are the "throw-away" kids of our society propelled us through the radical change. Our worlds had been turned inside out and upside down.

Keeping the pace of 14- to 16-hour days for months on end while Wayne traveled for two to three weeks at a time and managing the household with the financial pressure that comes with growing a ministry dependent on the generosity of friends and churches began to take its toll on my health. Did I recognize the signs? Not soon enough. And besides, I was driven to heed God's call to give hope to desperate foster children needing to know that God loves them.

One morning in 1997, I looked in the mirror and noticed large ugly red welts on my face. They were painful and would last four-to-six days and then subside, but the redness didn't. Questions poured through my head. Could I be allergic to my new estrogen prescription? Was it something I was eating? Maybe it was the makeup I was using?

For the next two years, with medical help, I went through a trial and error elimination process while the condition worsened. As I asked God for healing, I prayed, "Lord, help me. Take it away. If that is not Your will, help me find out what it is, bring me good medical help, calm my fears, and walk through this with me."

His answer to me came not in the form of a miracle healing but in a dermatologist who suspected my symptoms might be lupus. I pleaded, "Lord, help us to find out what it is." Just knowing would give us a starting point in the healing process.

The answer was succinct and test results positive. Had the problem been confined to my face, it would have been good news. Instead, I had the systemic form of lupus, in which the body begins attacking its own cells. If not brought under control, it could develop into major organ damage to the heart, lungs, kidneys, and brain. This was terrifying news at the age of fifty-one to a wife, mother, grandmother, and director of operations and training for a rapidly growing international ministry.

Educating myself about the disease let me know that definite changes in my lifestyle had to be made if I was to continue by Wayne's side at Royal Family. There is no cure for lupus. Lifelong medication, frequent checkups and blood work, extreme fatigue, potential retina damage, and joint pain are its ever-present companions.

I continue to pray, "God take this malady away." At the same time, I thank Him that, as the Bible states, at the close of creation He gave the command, "Be fruitful and multiply, and fill the earth, and subdue it." I believe God works through those who devote their medical minds to healing those of us who need their giftedness. They have "subdued the earth" on our behalf.

Learning to pace myself and live my life differently every day has become an ongoing challenge and a process that is not easy for a Type A personality who is called to a ministry the magnitude of Royal Family KIDS. I must seek His wisdom to know my limits and trust Him when I have reached them. This was 1999.

As Royal Family grew, Wayne and I both realized that sooner or later it would be impossible for us to teach all the weeklong directors' training classes, especially as we eventually had to offer four or five sites each summer to accommodate the number of trainees. I began "cutting the apron strings," preparing myself for this transition more at Wayne's prompting than my own choosing. It would become an eight-year process. But deep in my heart, I knew it had to happen. We began this process in 2000 by training four additional trainers from among our finest camp directors who also had the ability to teach. They shadowed us, teaching a small amount of material for one week followed by a second year in which we were still present, but they taught the bulk of the material. This minimum two-year training process has been maintained to the present. By 2002, for the first time, one team taught without Wayne or me being present. That was a huge step for us. That same year Wayne and one of these trainers, John Van Wicklin, trained the first class of new directors in Australia. How exciting it was to see Royal Family KIDS stretch halfway around the world. Eventually there would be multiple camps on that continent.

Prior to finally "taking *off* the apron," however, I needed to begin the process of replacing myself with a new director of training. That was even more emotional for me than replacing myself as a trainer. We thought long and hard about it and prayed much for the Lord to lead us to the right person within the organization and also to lead that person to sense the call, which would not only change his or her life but the life of the person's family. He or she would ultimately relocate their family to Southern California—a step not to be taken lightly when any children could potentially go through a difficult transition. This person would join our executive team at the headquarters and perpetuate what we had formed as the high standard for training our directors.

In twenty-five years, I have found that God *really* does do "all things in His time." By now, I had lived with the ravages of lupus for seven years, and sleeping on camp beds on less-than-comfortable mattresses was not helping during the summers. Camps don't provide Sealy Posturepedic mattresses! At one site, a dear friend and trainee, Cathy Smith, who had fibromyalgia and travelled with a Costco "life foam mattress," observed my pain and *gave* me her mattress to allow me to finish out the week. She then asked our training host to go to the local Costco and pick up another one for her. Upon making this discovery of a way to get through the nights in camp settings, the last three years that we trained, I too was shipping a life foam mattress to each training site to get a night's sleep and be up at seven o'clock ready to go 110 percent the following day. I would be standing before the training classes teaching for six hours or leading trainees around the camp observing the various activities we had just lectured about in the classroom. In addition to hosting them through the evening, we would finally get to bed around ten or eleven o'clock.

Fatigue was a large part of these weeks for me. As early as 1995 and many more times, I took solace in the verse, "My flesh and my heart may fail, but God is the strength of my heart and my portion forever" (Psalm 73:26). I depended on it! I would tell myself, Perhaps someday He will answer my question: If You knew what You had planned out for me to do with a fourth of my life, couldn't you have given someone else the lupus? (Humor.)

At the same time, my knees were finally showing damage due to inflammation, and a knee replacement was in the foreseeable future. God's words were precious to me during these years, as I read, "Come to me all who are weary and heavy-laden, and I will give you rest. Take my yoke upon you, and learn from me, for I am gentle and humble in heart and you shall find rest for your souls. For my yoke is easy and my load is light" (Matthew 11:28–30).

As my pastor, Kenton Beshore, interpreted this one Saturday night, he said, "He yokes up with us and (He) carries the load." I had to believe this and allow God to do the carrying.

I was comforted by scriptures like Psalm 41:1–2: "How blessed is he [she] who considers the helpless; The LORD will deliver him [her] in a day of trouble. The LORD will protect him [her] and keep him [her] alive, and he [she] shall be called blessed upon the earth." Psalm 63: 7-8 says, "For You have been my help. And in the shadow of Your wings I sing for joy. My soul clings to You; Your right hand upholds me."

I have learned that God is the strength of my heart, soul, mind, and body. I do His work and trust Him with my health.

I loved imparting to new camp directors the vision of what a week of leading a camp could be. It was like being a conduit through which the Holy Spirit flowed to draw people into this unbelievable experience. Wayne and I could teach textbook knowledge about Royal Family all day long, but we could never have wooed these incredible volunteers into an experience that would: require them to interrupt their families' schedules for nine months a year, work four hundred hours beyond their normal work week, learn to ask people to part with their money to support their camps, recruit and train thirty to one hundred volunteers, and ask Social Services to refer children in the system to a camp put on by their church. We poured ourselves into these people physically, emotionally, and intellectually for six solid days and *loved* every minute of it immensely! The training rooms were literally "birthing rooms," and trainees walked away holding "our baby." *God* made this happen, but I couldn't keep on.

So in 2006 we brought one of our finest camp directors with extensive training experience in his professional career onto the team. Jeff Juhala shadowed me as I gradually began to pass off the baton to him. He was a college track guy, so he knew how delicate the handing off process really is. Through a two-year process, I was finally ready to hand over all the manuals, textbooks, and documented systems of our training that had become the hallmark of Royal Family—something of which I was very proud. I even bequeathed my *purple* suede training shoes on top of the stack of manuals; I had no doubt that Jeff could fill them! By this time, more than 160 camps worldwide had been opened, and by 2008 we had enough trainer replacements so that in 2011, Wayne and I taught our last class. The site was in Kearney, Nebraska, and it was one of the most fun experiences we had had over the entire twenty-one years of training new camps. It was time; my heart wasn't ready, but my body surely was! The Lord reminded me, "I know that everything God does will remain forever; there is nothing to add to it and there is nothing to take from it, for God has so worked that men should fear Him" (Ecclesiastes 3:14). I could let go with a solid peace that it was in good hands. God *does* do all things in his time—and His timing *was* perfect!

Many people ask me, "How do you know God called you to work with children of abuse, abandonment, and neglect?"

Two moments of childhood are very vivid in my memory. Though God's voice was not an audible one, I know the influence of two individuals greatly impacted my life and my work with these special children. First, a third-grade teacher named Mrs. Hamilton in a K–12 brick school building in Corfu, New York, and a little boy named Johnny Clark.

Johnny was a neglected child of severe proportions. One of several siblings in an alcoholic family, he never had enough in his lunch bag to be called a "lunch." He brought ketchup sandwiches—except there was no meat between the bread, just ketchup. He never had an extra dime for an ice-cream sandwich—like most of us did—even occasionally. His ragged pants were always too short—about six inches above his shoe tops—and his shoes were "high tops" and always worn through with holes. He never wore socks, even in the dead of upstate New York winters. He wore a ragged bomber jacket, outgrown by two or three older siblings and way too big for him. The brown polish of the leather finish on the jacket was all worn off and the knit cuffs on the sleeves were raggedy. The stretch was all gone. It hung on him like a scarecrow's coat out in the field. Johnny's teeth were rotting out of his head, and his breath smelled of a sick odor.

No one wanted to be Johnny's friend. No one would even stand in line next to him; and no one ever chose Johnny to be on their team at recess time on the playground.

I think, somehow, Mrs. Hamilton had a special sense of my compassion for Johnny. I truly felt sorry for him. I could hardly stand to think how little he had at home or to survive on at all.

Being a precocious third grader and unable to keep quiet after I finished my schoolwork, I would begin talking to anyone nearby who would join in the conversation. Mrs. Hamilton enlisted my chattering and my obvious compassion on Johnny (the fact that I would *talk* to him must have given it away) and quietly appointed me as a "teacher's aide" for Johnny (long before school districts enlisted teacher's aides, by title).

She managed to orchestrate the seating chart so that I would *always* sit across the aisle from him. She knew instinctively that as soon as I finished my work, I would naturally turn to Johnny and start talking, asking if he needed help. Inevitably, he did. Thus, I "tutored" him through his lessons. (Perhaps God was calling me to be a teacher and I missed the call!)

I believe there will be a special place in Heaven for teachers like Mrs. Hamilton who are sensitive to a child's need to shower compassion on a very needy child and, thus, spawn the development of a compassionate heart for abused and neglected children in a third grader.

A second vivid memory from childhood is of spending the night with two girlfriends at their home. Their mom, Eleanor Lowe, was widowed when her husband, our pastor, died in a tragic, wintry auto crash.

When I would visit them overnight during the holidays, she would read us "The Little Match Girl," by Hans Christian Anderson, the sad saga of a little unnamed girl who was forced to sell matches on the streets to make enough money to take home to an abusive father. If her meager day's sales didn't meet his demands, she would be beaten. (William Bennett in *The Book of Virtues* describes him as her "foster father.")

In the story, the little girl sees visions (probably hallucinations) as she feebly strikes her matches one-by-one to keep warm in the frozen snow. In the glow of the match's flame, she "sees" a huge feast with a beautifully decorated table of food, a Christmas tree bursting with presents and lights, and finally, a vision of her deceased grandmother, the only person on earth she felt loved her. Wanting to spend a few more glorious moments with her grandmother who had already preceded her in death, the little girl lit the whole remaining bundle of matches. Just before the matches burned out, she was swept up in her grandmother's arms to join her in Heaven. She was free of the winter chill, bare feet in the snow, tattered clothes, and a father who beat her.

As a young child, I would listen to the story, and because I could not identify with her life of abuse, I could only imagine the plight of this emaciated, shoeless little girl freezing in the winter night, and I would cry and cry. I could relate to cold winter nights in upstate New York, but I had a warm bed and could sleep in a warm house.

I am of English descent and love fine china tea cups. I have a tiny, china cream pitcher with a fine hairline crack in it—not so damaging as to break it wide open but enough to be noticeable. I believe my experiences in that third grade classroom with Johnny Clark allowed a fine, hairline crack to form in my "teacup of life" (my heart), not so much to ruin the "cup" but enough to break my heart wide open when I encountered the weight of the need of abused children some thirty years later.

Though her intent was simply to read us a bedtime story, Eleanor Lowe was the second sensitive adult God used to allow a measure of compassion for abused children He had placed in my young heart to widen and grow, allowing hundreds—and now thousands—of children's stories (much like "The Little Match Girl") to make me cry, still today.

But more than crying, He turned my tears of compassion to tears of joy as we see these "children of plight" given hope, through Royal Family KIDS, of a life in Heaven—free of "winter's chill," free of pain, neglect, and heartache.

As trite as it sounds, it hardly seems possible that twenty-five years—nearly a third of my lifetime and exactly half of my adult working career—have flown by. So much of the time it blitzed by so fast, I can't even recall much of it. We grabbed the tail of a wild horse and are still taming it, holding on for dear life, all the while inviting hundreds of others to do the same crazy thing! And they have grabbed the reins and held on!

By this writing, our team has grown to twelve people in-house (and at one point fifteen) and five others in the field, including three ambassadors, John Schwider, Scott Murrish, and Laurie Fenneuff, plus two on our shipping team at donated offices in Springfield, Missouri, Danny and Jacinda Warren.

In April 2013, I retired and have never looked back. It was the culmination of twenty-five years spent "delighting myself in the Lord" and Him "giving me the desires of my heart" to be free to enjoy some of the many things I had put on hold: enjoying my daughter Renee and son-in-law, Paul, our three "grand angels," McKenzie Marie, Katie Joy, and Abby Faith, and using all my creative energies to enhance our home and other people's lives. I am so grateful that I am part of God's answer to restoring the lives of beautiful children who are the products of uncaring, brutal, selfish adults. May the children consider themselves "royalty," because we sure do!

3

ALEX ROJAS
Former Camper

I was first placed in foster care when I was in kindergarten. I was very young then, but that was around the time I can remember my earliest memories. My parents were going through rough times. My father was an alcoholic and had trouble maintaining a job. He was usually getting arrested by the police. My mom tried the best she could, but she was a drug addict. I went in and out of foster homes from the ages of five to eight. During those years, I was usually mad that I had to move around so many times with so many strangers. But in my mind, I always knew that somehow I would go back home to my parents. The last time I was taken away from my parents, my dad had asked me if I thought calling a social worker was the best thing to do, and I agreed. The police came and took us away to the police station, where our social worker picked us up and separated the four of us away from each other. Since I was the oldest, I was usually placed alone in a foster home so that my brothers and sister could be placed together in the same home.

I felt lonely during those years, but I knew that, sooner or later, I would be reunited with my family. When I found out that my dad had died and my mother had taken off back to Mexico and abandoned us, my heart sank. Even in my young nine-year-old mind, I was starting to grasp the big picture. We would be stuck in foster care indefinitely. I was a tough kid by this point, and sucked it up and maintained as best as I could in every foster home where I was placed. I was moved around to as many as thirteen foster homes in my life. My last foster dad adopted me when I was thirteen. He gave me and my second oldest brother, Randy, a good home. I still maintain a good relationship with my adopted dad. He encouraged me to think ahead about my future and what I wanted to do with my life. I told him that I wanted to leave on my own and join the Army. He agreed that it was a good idea to serve my country and set up a foundation of success for later in my life.

I first came to RFKC in 1993 from St. Andrews Church in Newport Beach, California. I was nine years old at this time. I had lived in a group home in Anaheim Hills from 1992 to 1996. My first impression of RFKC was that this place was full of very nice people who honestly cared a lot about us. I didn't have any role models at this time in my life. All the staff members in the group home were women. I grew attached to Uncle Ken and Aunt Kerry. They were in their mid-twenties when I met them. I thought Ken was an awesome guy, and I liked hanging out with him at camp. He was the "uncle" for my first and second years at camp. He finally became my counselor in my third and last year at camp.

Every year I wished I could go back to camp and live there forever. I used to go to bed thinking about it all the time as my happy place. I even thought that the camp counselors lived there all year long! Ken began to visit me every week and took me to church on Sundays at St. Andrews. We maintained our relationship even through the many moves that I went through in my life. I still go to his house and visit him and Kerry and their three kids. He has been a big brother to me for most of my life, and we will probably be friends for a very long time. I still look to him for guidance whenever I am not sure of what to do.

RFKC was a place full of good people who wanted to make a difference in young kid's lives. Before camp, I had never gone to church before and did not know anything about God. I was given my first Bible and was taught Bible stories. I think that this camp made a huge impact in my life.

Everyday my camp counselor and my roommate camper would get up early and go hiking with the other guys' cabins. It was such a relief to get away from the group home and the yelling and screaming going on there every day. Our first camp was situated past Six Flags Magic Mountain in a huge campground. It had hiking trails in the hills, big flat grassy fields, a basketball court, and, my favorite, the big pool. It was hard to say good-bye at the end of the week and know that we were going back to our foster homes.

This summer will be my fifth year as a camp counselor. I have never met so many good people in my life. Everyone volunteered vacation time to come to camp. I thought that since RFKC had been such a huge impact in my life, I should help keep that tradition going strong. I had never known Jesus until camp, and now I have helped kids learn about Him for the first time too. It is a good feeling to know that unconditional love has been introduced to them.

I love hanging out with the kids and other counselors and staff members. Everyone is so friendly and is there to have a really good time. I still wish I could live there all year long!

Someone once asked me if I could go back in time and be back again with my real parents, would I do it? I thought about it seriously, and replied that I would not give up my current life to start all over at eight years old. I have met so many good people, had so many good experiences with my friends, co-workers, and family that I could not dream of giving away all my good memories. God gave me my life for a reason.

The only week that I get off every year I spend entirely in having the privilege of being a camp counselor. I get to help spread the love of Jesus to kids who really need Him in their lives. I try to tell them to hold their heads up high, because someday you will have the opportunity to become a person who can make a difference in someone's life. There is no other better feeling in the world than to see a young and abused kid happy again, to give him or her hope for a better future is indescribable.

For many years now, Royal Family KIDS has been spreading across the country and the world, reaching out to foster kids and giving them the experience of getting to know who Jesus is. It is a great organization full of very caring people. I hope to continue being a camp counselor for as long as I can. I love going to camp and being a kid again. I hope that you enjoyed my story and can spread the good news about our camp.

4

DARREN AND MELINDA EDWARDS
Camp Directors, Fort Worth, Texas

Beauty for Ashes

"To all who mourn in Israel, he will give a crown of beauty for ashes, a joyous blessing instead of mourning, festive praise instead of despair. In their righteousness, they will be like great oaks that the Lord has planted for his own glory" (Isaiah 61:3).

Isn't it true that our Father can take difficulties in our lives and orchestrate triumph and great glory for His name?

Twenty-five years ago, the Lord blessed us with a baby boy. We were devastated to learn that our newborn had Down syndrome, guaranteeing a lifetime of taking care of this young one. At the time we couldn't foresee the beauty of God's plan for us.

We already had a love for the Lord and His work. Through the years, He used Tom, our sweet baby boy, to make our hearts tender and compassionate for less-fortunate children. God was laying the groundwork for our lifework.

At just the right time, the young-children's minister at our church attended a conference and heard about a camp for abused and neglected children. He was moved to pray for someone to make the commitment to start and direct such a camp for the North Central Texas area. He knew it was a task only the Lord could make happen. While his heart still burned for this cause, he happened to run into us on a Wednesday night as we worked in the children's ministry at church. He asked me (Melinda), and I said I was willing if Darren said yes. I had previous experience with church camps and camping in general with my family.

Darren, busy with work and raising a family, was a harder case. He just couldn't imagine adding anything else to his already full plate. The children's minister asked several times that night as he wasn't ready to give up. With me onboard, he was only encouraged to keep talking to Darren. His persistence paid off. Darren finally agreed to watch a video, and he took the book written by the founders. Darren later admitted doing this so the minister would stop asking.

After his children were bathed and tucked in for the night, Darren sat down and fulfilled his promise. As the video ended, he knew in his heart this was something God was asking of him. He told me, "We've got to do this."

So we got in touch with the national office to sign up for directors' training. However, all training camps were over for the year. That meant waiting another year. Darren told me this will really be a "fleece" of confirmation— confirmation that this was meant for us to do if we still desired to go to training a year later.

In 1998, we and three others from our church attended a training camp in California. By Wednesday night after training and fellowship had ended, our group stayed up past midnight discussing who back home could fill all the staff positions for camp in 1999. The group was determined to have camp that year. The biggest obstacle now was finding a camp facility and funding.

After returning home from the training, Darren spoke to an elder committee, the mission's group, and several ministers about starting a camp in 1999. The elders approved a budget for the first camp. Now it was on to finding a camp facility. We looked up close to twenty camp facilities and called each place to find out if we could do camp there in 1999. There were several rejections in the form of "no weeks available," "can't guarantee a closed camp for only your group," or "your group is not big enough for a closed camp." However, there were two camps that agreed to meet with us to discuss the possibility. One camp was forty-five minutes away, and the other was two-and-a-half hours. We first visited the closer one and left knowing we could rent a closed camp for a week in late July of 1999. We had two weeks to accept or lose the week. We were not thrilled with the setup of the facility but thought if we had to use it, we could make it work. Next, we traveled to the facility that was farther away. Upon arrival, the woman showing us around mentioned that she was unsure if she had a week available as she was waiting to hear back from an annual renter. That visit started on a sour note, but we took the tour of the facility and along the way began to pour out how wonderful this camp is for abused and neglected children. We shared some stories that had been shared with us at training. The woman was so moved that she decided to make room for us and tell the other client to come another week. God worked a miracle that day. We really did not know what we were doing other than sharing information and the needs of these children. Two days later we received a contract in the mail for a week in June. Two weeks later, we learned that the first facility had declared bankruptcy. God really had his hand in what we were doing.

The first camp in 1999 was so exciting! We were taking seventy-two children (there were six no-shows) and 80 volunteers. Camp training suggested a first camp of forty children. Camp was crazy; none of the volunteers really knew what they were doing. We were just following the manual, sometimes to a fault. By a fault, we mean we followed the exact schedule and timing as indicated in the manual, which meant organized games were in the hottest part of the afternoon in east Texas.

As a director of camp you hope you never have to send a camper home, but we had to the very first year. It was so hard on the leadership team to make that decision and then fight the doubts of our action the rest of the week. The silver lining is that the boy came back the next year and had a great camp. God was once again working where we couldn't.

Another story from the early years concerns a boy who had been sexually molested by his dad, uncles, and cousins. He came to camp and wanted to do nothing we had planned. He was very untrusting, as expected, and had very low self-esteem. We spent time with him where he wanted to that year, but the next year he came off the bus and ran up to me asking if he could be the emcee for the variety show at the end of the week. What a change! He did emcee the show, and he was active in everything planned at camp. God is so good!

After camp in 2003, a core group of volunteers came to us and said we needed to do more. We asked what else we should do. They told us that we needed to do something for the children that had aged out of camp. Following Paul Harvey's saying, we wanted to know the "rest of the story" with the children we had served at camp. Darren went to meet with a group of church elders, and he was told that the church would help us set up a nonprofit organization and we could move out from under the church umbrella. But we would need to find our own insurance, which turned to be a non-issue as God led us through that decision.

And so, in December 2003, Our Father's Children (OFC) was formed. We had the first Onward and Upward retreat for twelve- to fifteen-year-olds in February 2004. There were thirty-nine teens and thirty-four volunteers. We developed a curriculum based on character traits of godly men and women with drama, small groups, and an application session format. We grew in numbers over the next year and now average somewhere between sixty-four and eighty teens, with appropriate numbers of volunteers. The two-to-one teen-to-counselor ratio is maintained at these retreats, which happen in February and September.

Toward the end of 2004, Darren and Melinda met with the chairman of the board and discussed the strain on their family. They felt the solution was to hire Melinda as the sole employee of OFC. The chairman agreed and over the last two weeks of 2004, enough funding was received from new donors to cover Melinda's salary for 2005. Melinda left her teaching job in January that year to begin our lifework.

After camp in 2005, a group of twenty volunteers came to us and asked if we could lead a second camp with more volunteers from their church. Darren and Melinda agreed that it was needed based on numbers of foster children in our area. But it also meant another meeting with the board, because Darren could not take two weeks off from his job to lead camp. Prayer and discussion ensued about Darren becoming an employee of OFC. The decision was made to back Darren leaving his job with one caveat: Darren would have to complete a ministry curriculum offered by Ministry Ventures out of Atlanta and go to a seminar provided by Henri Moreau offered by the founders of RFKC, Wayne and Diane Tesch. Darren once again felt led by God and truly at peace. He gave his notice to leave his job and begin full-time work on his lifework.

So in 2006, there were two camps for six- to eleven-year-olds, one in June and one in July. The July camp started with seventy-five children and eighty-four volunteers. The July camp now serves more than one hundred children with more than one hundred volunteers. Darren and Melinda's lives were further enriched and blessed by all the new volunteers and children who attended that first July camp.

Toward the end of 2006, we were approached by another group of volunteers who wanted to be with the teens aging out of the Onward and Upward retreats. Upon prayer and meeting with some of this group, we decided to start Summit Retreats for sixteen- to eighteen-year-olds. The curriculum would be focus on life skills, such as money management, goal setting, and support systems. There would be a one-to-one teen-to-counselor ratio, and we would meet in May and October each year.

In our camp in 2010, we met a young man who had some limitations caused by having his feet held on a hot plate after being knocked unconscious by his mom's boyfriend. Half of each foot had to be amputated, after which he endured two years of therapy and follow-up surgeries. He was so cute, and had an infectious smile and a great attitude. He had trouble moving through camp, especially during organized game time. His feet hurt. One of our nurses got involved and, after looking at the socks he wore, decided to take action. She suggested we purchase the softest and thickest socks we could find at the local Walmart. We did and she took them to him. His reaction was tears of joy, being thrilled that we cared so much for him! But isn't that the Royal Family way?

In 2012, an RFK mentoring club was started for the six- to eleven-year-old age group. It meets every month school is in session and follows a mentee-mentor structure. Organized group meetings are held each month, and then the mentors spend two to six hours outside of the group meeting with their mentee. The club started with twenty-five children that first year.

Also in the fall of 2012, the OFC board agreed to purchase a fifty-acre site that had some buildings and infrastructure. OFC started a capital campaign to raise $3 million. OFC named the facility Camp Akiva. "Akiva" means to protect or shelter in Hebrew. The OFC leadership and board felt it was a great name for a place for the children we serve. When fully completed, Camp Akiva will sleep 360 and have five possible meeting sites, and will be rented to youth groups and businesses when not being used by OFC.

More than seventeen years have passed since that night when a minister was persistent. The camps for six- to eleven-year-olds have changed the lives of more than 3,500 hurting children. More than 3,800 people have served in various volunteer roles, many of them returning repeatedly.

Darren continues to dream about how OFC can do more for the children of abuse and neglect: "Holiday homecomings" for the children-turned-young-adults who have stayed in touch and need a place to go and a family to share holidays; a third week of summer camp for children from the counties around the new camp facility; family retreats in which both foster parents and children are ministered to and loved with a common goal to do what is best for the children. There are so many possibilities. Our prayer is that God will continue to bless and grow what He started so many years ago.

> "Now all glory to God, who is able, through his mighty power at work within us, to accomplish infinitely more than we might ask or think" (Ephesians 3:20 NLT).

5

JACOB ROEBUCK

Camp Counselor Director of Feature Film "Camp"

"We already work in full time ministry," I remember thinking, "Why do we need to spend more time leading mission trips?" Our senior pastor at Rock Harbor Church in Costa Mesa, California, had just announced that that year everyone on staff was going to lead a mission trip. Something about being outward focused or some other trendy church lingo idea drove the decision. All I knew was that as a lowly staffer my workload just increased because of our leadership's ideals.

So I did what any apathetic church worker would do: look for the mission trip that would take me the least out of my comfort zone. I found an opportunity to go to Mexico to build houses. It was just my speed. Go, work hard, and get the job done while avoiding any significant people connections. Who knows, if the group had the right personality, every night after work we could go out for tacos and margaritas. At least we would get to have a little fun.

I signed up with the mission team to go to Mexico. My job at the church was communications so I was prepping all the materials that advertised the fifty or so missions opportunities our congregation had to sign up for that summer. As I was preparing the listing for press, I read one that said, "Be a counselor for abused and neglected kids ages 7–11 at summer camp."

Go to that camp, God told me in my heart, as I was reading it.

No way, I told Him, *You know that half of the church with the nursery and playrooms and kids' stuff? I don't work there.*

Go to that camp, God repeated.

But you don't understand, I protested, *I am not* called *to minister to kids.*

For some reason at the time, this protest seemed logical. Still, it is never wise to ignore a prompting of the Almighty—and I had an out. I knew that it was too late for the mission team to switch me and my wife (who was also on staff) from the Mexico trip to the summer camp counselor gig.

"No problem," the mission administrator told me.

"What do you mean, 'no problem'?" I asked her, because it definitely was a problem for me. I was supposed to call to arrange a switch and she was supposed to say no, not yes. The only reason I called was to clear my conscience. I expected the bureaucracy would prevent me from following this prompting of the spirit. For some reason it seemed logical at the time.

The next thing I knew, my wife and I were sitting down with Mike Kenyon, our missions pastor, and Kathy Smith, the director of Royal Family KIDS Camp from St. Andrews Church in Newport Beach, California. A sixth-grade teacher who was shorter than many of her students, Kathy had a kindly disposition and could bring a chaotic room to attention without ever raising her voice. St. Andrews was an aging congregation and their camp needed the fresh infusion of youth our church could provide, hence the partnership was formed.

Kathy explained to my wife and me that since we were "leaders" from our church, we would not be counselors. Instead, we would run some sort of tea party for small groups as an activity. I felt a huge sense of relief. My wife would interact with the children. I would take care of logistics. The kids come, we do the activity, and then we send the kids back with their counselors. When we didn't have activities we could hang out in the adult-only staff lounge, or so I gathered from Kathy's description of camp. That was an experience I could manage—not too far out of my comfort zone at all. It might even be fun.

But there was one other thing to do as a leader: Kathy asked me to be a chaperone on the boys' bus to camp. There were three of us chaperones and about fifty boys, and I remember noting as I walked to the back of the bus that the last time I had interacted with a ten-year-old was when I myself was ten. When I said I wasn't called to minister to kids, I wasn't kidding. There was next to no kid interaction in my world. Also, as I worked my way back on the bus, I noticed these kids weren't the kids that ran around the halls on Sunday after church. They looked different. They dressed different. They used words that kids from good Christian families didn't use.

At the back of the bus one kid stuck out, Jose. He was smaller than the other kids, but he made up for it in toughness and charm. In a group of kids he was always the center of attention. In other circumstances I would have described him as a natural leader. But in this situation the word I used to describe him was bully.

He was that special kind of bully who would be nice to you at first and then turn on you for his amusement. He knew how to inflict pain, usually emotional, in a way that he wouldn't get in trouble for. He was smart enough to follow the letter of the law, but always found a way to bend the rules as much as possible. Because he was clever, likable, and wore the popular gangster-style clothes, the other kids would rarely shun him even though he often tormented them.

In my heart I despised Jose. I knew this kid was rotten to the core. I wanted nothing to do with him. And I was all too happy when the bus trip was over and I no longer had to deal with this conniving brat. Now I could go hide from kids at my activity for the week and make the most of the situation. But it wasn't to be.

Not long after I got off the bus, director Kathy came up to me with a problem. Apparently, more boys had come to camp than was expected. They needed a couple more male counselors, and Kathy asked if I would mind switching from activities to be a counselor.

My inside and outside reaction to this change of fortune could not have been any different. Outside, I consented saying I would do anything "for the kids," a mantra we often use when making personal sacrifices for our campers. But inside I shook my fist at God like a modern-day Jonah. I went from interacting with kids four hours a day to being *responsible* for the well-being of two kids, Tyler* and Miguel*, twenty-three hours a day (counselors get a one-hour break!). I wouldn't be bunking with support staff; now I would be in a cabin dealing with the whining and fighting and mess of ten- and eleven-year-old campers.

I found I wasn't a very good counselor. I often dozed off during our cabin activity time while the kids in my cabin ran wild. Also, for some reason, I kept calling Miguel by the name Victor. This is especially bad because we wore nametags all the time. But Tyler and Miguel were easy kids. Neither of them talked too much, and they only got into a fight once when Tyler smashed a rubber exercise ball with a handle on it into Miguel's face. Without much prodding, I was able to get Tyler to apologize. In retrospect, I realize Kathy probably gave me easier kids on purpose because I was a rookie.

My real breakthrough came a couple days into camp. I was already worn out, exhausted, and ready to quit. I had no idea why I was there, and I was sure that my "suffering" was pointless. That summer in California was particularly hot (with no A/C at the camp, anywhere) so even though counselors could take a short break at pool time if needed, I found myself getting in with the kids so I could beat the heat.

For some reason I can't remember, I found myself talking to Jose, the little miscreant I had to deal with on the bus. I don't remember what we were talking about, but I do remember Jose expressing he wasn't happy about being at camp. He was sitting on the edge of the pool and I was standing in the water, so that my eyes were close to the level of his legs dangling in.

There wasn't much to him. I remember thinking how scrawny he looked, especially when he wasn't wearing his hoodie and baggy pants. I noticed some odd marks on his legs, and I almost casually asked him what they were. But the question caught in my throat.

Cigarette burns.

There were dozens of them. In that moment God revealed my foolishness. I had put Jose into a neat little box that made it easy to write him off with words like *conniving* and *brat* and *rotten*. But I had no idea of who this kid really was. I had never experienced anything like the torture he had experienced at the hands of people who should have been protecting him. I had no reference to begin to understand how that kind of pain at that age twisted his understanding of right and wrong and even reality.

"I want you to love these kids without condition," God told me in my heart. "Love them because they are *my* children. That is reason enough."

With that request, God broke me. The tears I could not hold back went unnoticed because my face was already wet from being in the pool.

At the talent show, Jose and some of his followers did a rap. He looked angry, but as soon as he broke into his lyrics, we were thrilled:

> I love camp.
> The food is delicious.
> The counselors are awesome.
> Archery is the best.

And so on. I had no idea he was enjoying camp so much. I didn't realize the walls that these kids —God's kids—put up are a defense mechanism for survival in dark situations designed to destroy their lives and souls. And yet so many of the kids that come to camp are extremely resilient (Jose included), and like seeds they will grow when they receive water and light.

Jose came back to camp for several years, and there are two more stories that come to mind. Once when he had caused a particularly problematic disturbance, I had a chance to pull him aside. I told him he was a gifted leader. Kids would follow him. He had the choice to use his leadership for good or bad. It was his choice. He was stewing quite a bit, but I think he heard me.

The other story I only know secondhand. We had a superhero theme that year, and Jose fashioned himself as the Dark Knight. One morning at five o'clock, he was missing from his cabin and later found in costume patrolling the grounds. He was protecting his fellow campers.

As for Tyler and Miguel, I struggled to connect with them other than being a caregiver. They were both eleven years old, so they "graduated" that year and were not allowed to return. At our camp we do a late-night graduating ceremony for those kids who aged out. At this ceremony we eat treats and counselors say encouraging things to their campers.

I explained to the group that I had struggled to call Miguel the right name, often calling him Victor. Then I explained that perhaps the reason that I called him Victor is because he was going to be victorious.

"I believe Miguel is a bright kid with a bright, victorious future. And he will always be a Victor in my heart," I explained. It sounds hokey now, but at the time I think it meant a lot to Miguel.

The buses rolled away from camp. I was again on the bus as a chaperone. These kids were facing the fact that camp doesn't go on forever and that many of them would be going back into a system that struggles to give them any sort of true home. Some, like Jose, were tough. But other boys wept aloud. I had precious little with which to comfort these kids. In the end, I moved from seat to seat putting my arm around them and just being there.

When the buses got back to the church, they unloaded the kids and their luggage. One by one, caregivers picked up the kids. Soon they were all gone. I haven't seen or heard from Tyler and Miguel since then. But God stirs my heart from time to time with memories from that week, and I think of them and pray for them. It took a long while to process that week. To say it changed me sounds cliché. But let me try to capture what it meant in my life.

First, I encountered God at camp like never before. Many Christians at varying levels of spiritual maturity struggle on a daily basis trying to determine God's will for their lives. I have a lot to say on this, but at camp this question never entered my mind. For that one week there was no anxiety over what God wanted me to do. I wasn't wondering what music should I listen to, or if I gave enough money to church or if I should watch football or read my Bible. The freedom this gave my spirit was incredible. In fact, it made my "real" life feel fake and my camp experience feel real.

Second, and almost opposite, it caused me to question God in very real ways. Sure we all know there is evil in the world, but RFK camp forces you to see its ugliness up close. Why would He allow Jose to be painfully burned by cigarettes? Why would He let His children be forgotten, abused, molested, humiliated, and crushed to the point that they couldn't accept the love they needed even if they were offered it? I don't have easy answers for these questions, but I have made peace with God over these issues. Through this struggle, my faith in Christ has been refined and it has brought me close to Him. For some, I know, this is a bridge too far. But there is no lukewarm here.

Finally, and perhaps most dangerously, I was no longer ignorant of these forgotten children. Or, to put it another way, now I would have to harden my heart against them and, perhaps, God, if I did not in some way alter my life so I could help bring God's love and care to these orphans.

It so happened that right after camp that year, I left the job at the church to pursue filmmaking, which will factor in later in this story. I also got involved with the leadership of our camp. If we were really serving God's kids, then I wanted to help make the camp as amazing as possible. The same as if the president or celebrities or other important people sent their kids to our camp. Even though my idealism often clashed with the realities that Kathy, as the director of the camp, had to deal with, she welcomed with open arms my enthusiasm and passion. I wanted as much as possible for the camp and these kids. I told all my family and friends that, if they wished to remain family and friends, they had to volunteer for camp. Of course, this was for the most part tongue in cheek, but as I said earlier, camp did not leave me lukewarm.

Another amazing thing happened around this time. Of the fifty or so mission trips from that summer, ours was chosen to be featured at all seven of our megachurch's services. I was asked to share for five minutes at each of them. That may not seem like much, but, since then, no matter how much we have begged and pleaded, we have not been able to get the same kind of upfront time.

So I told the story of Jose and his cigarette burns. The response was overwhelming. We were overflowing with volunteers. I was thrilled to have been used by God in such an exciting way. The hilarious part is how God let me know it was Him, not me, who was at work. At least a dozen times when I was interviewing volunteers that year and asked why they signed up for camp, they described my presentation, but did not recognize me as the storyteller.

One of the people I interviewed was a part-time actress and substitute teacher, Emily Shubin. At that point, I had finished my first film, and we talked about the difficulty of being an actress in the film business. She related to me how she and her roommate, Kristin Wolven, (who also came to camp that year) had been cast in small roles in an indie film, but because she was a brunette and her roommate was a blonde, her part was cut when she was on her way to the set. Her roommate made the cut. I had to confess to her that I was the producer who cut her part!

Emily ended up telling the Bible stories at Camp for us and did an amazing job. While I can't remember exactly how it started, she, Kristin, and another friend named Jim Farmer (I twisted his arm into coming to Camp, and now he has taken over the director role for Kathy), began to discuss making a film about Royal Family KIDS Camp. We had all been dramatically affected by our camp experience and we wanted to do more than just volunteer. After several false starts, I wrote and directed, Emily and Kristin produced (and both had small parts) and Jim executive produced a film simply entitled *CAMP*.

The hardest thing, in my opinion, about running a Royal Family KIDS Camp is raising volunteers, especially men. From my experience sharing Jose's story, I knew the material was compelling if presented in the right way. We also knew that if we could get a volunteer to camp, chances were we would have a supporter for life. The problem was that persuading potential volunteers to even come to an informational meeting was nearly impossible. Sure, there is a group of people who are "called" to work with kids, but we wanted to reach guys like me who would never think of themselves as a camp counselor for abused and neglected kids. The film became an informational meeting in disguise. Even better, it was the next best thing to going yourself.

In the spring of 2013, *CAMP* played in eighty-five theaters in the United States to more than forty-thousand people. In December it was released on Netflix, and as of this writing, the film has been seen more than two million times on the streaming service. The film has also been distributed internationally in some fifteen countries. Nearly every camp has added volunteers who were inspired by the film. Several new camps were also influenced in part by people who saw the film and wanted to be a part of the story. Our "information meeting in disguise" continues to generate interest every day for RFK.

I could say much more about the movie and about how God provided for it, but film is only the medium and not the story itself. If you haven't seen it, watch it. As a film, it is far from perfect, but I think we captured the heart of RFK in the film. One suggestion: have tissues handy.

When my wife and I left California to move to New Mexico, the most difficult thing to leave behind was our camp. We met some of our best friends in the world at camp. Our worldview was altered at camp.

We worked with a dedicated group of volunteers to launch the first Royal Family KIDS Camp in New Mexico in the summer of 2015. It was so amazing to be able to return to camp.

In my seven years volunteering and three years working on the film I have spent a lot of time pondering what camp is, what makes RFK camps special, and why I am drawn to them. Here are my best thoughts.

Camp is God using ordinary people to do an extraordinary work in the lives of children whom the world has pushed aside and the enemy has targeted.

During the credits of the film, we show some clips from the research interviews we did in making the film. One of my favorite clips is of one of my favorite people, Peter Prietto, the lifeguard at our camp. In the clip, he says volunteering at camp feels like "You are grabbing the devil by the throat and punching him right in the nose." I believe the kids who come to camp have been claimed by the evil one. If you want to meet the next generation of homeless addicts, criminals, child abusers, prostitutes, and the like, odds are they are in the foster care system. Chances are they never experienced anything resembling a normal childhood. RFK is on the front lines of fighting evil. We are taking kids who are marked for darkness and injecting into them the most powerful force in the world: unconditional love.

Camp provides a rare opportunity in our perfectly ordered world for us to truly give unconditional love. These kids have little or nothing to offer you in return for volunteering. Very often a kid will be a complete terror for their counselor and never in the whole week shows one iota of thankfulness. I remember Randy German, an amazing counselor, had one of the most difficult kids we ever had at camp. I remember he would spit water at Randy, who would always respond to the kid, "No matter what you do to me, I will always love you." Rookie counselors struggle with this. It is natural to expect gratitude and it is emotionally difficult when it doesn't come. But the veterans know that the kids aren't there to make the counselors feel better about themselves.

We had a young woman volunteer with us who had grown up going to Royal Family. As a camper she never told her counselors thank you and was often deliberately mean when saying good bye. But she will tell you the experience changed the course of her life.

For me, serving at camp is pure worship of the One True God. This might be an even more important purpose of camp than helping kids, if the two could be separated. Without getting into the theology of worship (a discussion for which I am unqualified) I am never more properly aligned with my Creator than when I am serving Him by serving the forgotten children at camp.

6

RANDY AND KIM MARTIN
Directors/Trainers, Bakersfield, California

The year 1994 was a rocky one for the Martin family. Our marriage was teetering on the cliff of divorce, and our spiritual world was in disarray. It was a perfect time for God to intervene and show His grace and love. He did.

In 1995 the Martin family began a new chapter in its history. Both Kim and I committed our lives to following Jesus, and we began to explore serving. Our first endeavor was to attend a camp for foster children. I remember the day the children's pastor of Canyon Hills Assembly of God church approached the pulpit and began to recruit. As I sat in the pew, she challenged individuals to respond and give a "week of their life" to bless a foster child with the love of God. Being new to the church world, I did the only thing a normal person would do: I sat in my seat and raised my hand as high as I could. She saw my hand go up and said "I see that hand" and then proceeded to let me know that she wasn't asking for people right now, but I could make my way to a table in the foyer and we could talk. So, my jump into ministry was less than perfect.

At the end of service we made our way back to a sparsely decorated table and introduced ourselves. Quickly, Kim let them know I was the one going as she needed to take care of Zach (five) and Shelby (three). We were handed information and told about training. It was official—I was getting involved at the church and about ready to serve "foster kids," whatever that meant!

Now, let's fast forward to the week of camp. I am a new Christian and new to service, and I have no idea what a foster child is, where they have been, or what they need. All I know is that I raised my hand in a church service and needed to do something with this love that God had deposited in my heart and soul. It turned out that Royal Family KIDS Camp was the perfect setting for sharing God's love, as I would quickly find out.

As a side note, I should mention that our camp, RFK #24, was not the most law-abiding, rule-enforcing camp in the RFKC system. We loved on foster kids and created moments where they could experience the love of a safe and compassionate adult and just get to be a child for a week. There were a number of things we did in error those first years, but God's grace covered our lack of experience and knowledge with great compassion, care, and fun. The week of RFKC in 1995 would end up changing my life and the lives of many despite my human frailty and ignorance.

During the first few days of RFKC in the summer of 1995, I was selected as the "young man" who could reason with the children. Our staff was a skeleton crew of folks from all ages, stages, and positions in life. As such, my background as a coach, in education, and working with children became an asset. So when a behavior escalated into a punching episode, I was the guy called in to resolve the situation. This begins the story of Jerome*, and how God made everything very clear.

Jerome was a massive ten-year-old boy. He was a bit lumpy and had broad shoulders. His hair was sandy brown and covered his forehead. He had deep eyes that were filled with pain and shame. He was aggressive and, as we were soon to find out, prone to violence. Jerome's RFKC experience was bad from the moment he stepped foot onto the campground. No matter what anyone did, Jerome became frustrated, and it usually resulted in another child being punched. Our initial foray into RFKC seemed to be doomed from the onset, and it looked like Jerome was going to be sent home to Bakersfield.

The RFKC leadership had a meeting at camp and decided that I should give Jerome one last shot at staying at camp. I was briefed on only one thing, "Tell him about Jesus and that he can't punch people or he is going home." Wow! That was a tough request, especially since I was just finding out who exactly this Jesus is. Nonetheless, I gathered myself and prepared for a disciplinary meeting with a ten-year-old foster kid where my two objectives were to tell him about Jesus and keep him at RFKC.

The meeting was horrible! I took Jerome to the steps that exited the kitchen and we sat down and began our talk. I shared the rules and explained that he could not punch others. Jerome let me know that this was normally how he handled anger and frustration. As I would soon learn, Jerome had experienced many of the "talks" with others including counselors, therapists, teachers, foster parents, law enforcement, and social workers. I must have sounded like a broken record as I talked about de-escalation and breathing techniques to help him calm down. I could see I was losing him so I decided to go for the Jesus angle!

Remember, I was a six-month-old God follower at the time of this meeting, so my "testimony" skills were not in place. I jumped in and started talking. I began to tell Jerome my life story, and I mean my life story. The funny thing was that he was interested. We sat on that back porch and he listened as I spoke of my great childhood, success in business and athletics, and my young family. He really became interested when I shared about not knowing who I was, why I was on earth, and what life was all about anyway. I shared about our broken marriage and how I just couldn't figure things out despite all the "good" things in my life. I then shared about falling in love with Jesus and exactly how that happened. Jerome would ask an occasional question and we ended up at the base of the issue. That is, the love of God that was missing in my life is the same love of God that was missing in Jerome's. I needed to know my Heavenly Father and that I was loved, accepted, and made on purpose and for a purpose. Jerome needed the same information. What happened next shocked me to the core and solidified my call to RFKC and the cause of the "fatherless."

Following my "testimony," Jerome began to ask a series of difficult questions. Here is a short list: Where is your family now? How much do you get paid to be here? Why are you doing this anyway? You don't know anything about me, do you?

I was speechless. This boy was quizzing me and putting me in my place. I began to pray in my heart and ask God for help. I answered his questions and then asked him to share about his life.

Jerome's story was painful to hear and awful for him to share, but he did. He shared about cigarette burns on his legs and arms. He shared about watching his mother have sex with men for drugs. He shared about the beatings they both received from various men. He shared about a life full of violence, rage, drugs, sex, abuse, and neglect. He shared about moving from foster home to foster home and from school to school. He shared that he survives by hurting others. As he shared, I began to weep. And sitting on that back porch Jerome asked me, "What are you crying about?"

My response was tearful and choked, "Jerome, I am crying because of your life. You shouldn't have to live like this. You should be playing in sports leagues and having fun with friends. You shouldn't live this way!"

As I gazed into his deep eyes through my tear-filled eyes, Jerome extended his hand and placed it on my shoulder. "It's alright," he said. "It's going to be okay!"

Jerome, and many children since, have been game-changers in our lives. Jerome's story is one of many that cemented the call to RFK. It all began the day I raised my hand in church. It came to life on the back porch of camp that glorious summer day in June 1995. The call to the cause of the fatherless was birthed by God that day. Jerome made it through the week, and I went home exhausted and spiritually challenged and renewed. I shared the week with my wife and told her she had to go next year and experience this marvelous week in the cathedral of the outdoors with God's special children. Kim thought this decision was a definite sign from God as I promised to watch our two children while she went away for a week. Little did she know that she would have a similar experience, and fall deeper in love with Jesus and commit her life to serving Him by serving the fatherless.

By 1997, Kim and I became directors of the Kern County RFKC. That year we attended the first "Passing the Scepter" class with Wayne and Diane Tesch. We quickly became more involved with RFKC as Wayne and Diane mentored us in ministry and life. We were bright-eyed young folks ready to change the world, and Wayne and Diane treated us with grace and patience as they helped us learn to serve with excellence and compassion. And, as Wayne would say, "All I can tell you is this: I raised my hand in a church service to go to a camp." The rest is now history.

FROM ROYAL FAMILY KIDS CAMP OF KERN COUNTY, JUNE 2011

Coming home from a week at RFKC is like returning from a mission trip across the globe. I have had the same emotions and mental and physical fatigue on returning from a week at RFKC as I have had from multiple trips to our African orphan home. The spiritual highs and lows also accompany the return to "normal life," but there is one thing that remains strong, and that is hope.

Hope has no expiration date. In fact, neither does love or faith. These three components of a successful life are what make RFK stand above many mission experiences I have had. RFK is geared to produce faith, hope, and love in children who lack all three. The fact that these children are living in a "system" that attempts to replace family signals that their hope has been crushed, their love left untapped, and their faith dormant. RFKC, through the amazing volunteers who serve, encourages each child that someone loves him or her, that faith is strong enough to weather any storm, and that hope is alive!

One of the closing moments of our week with the wonderful children of RFK is a ceremony. During the ceremony, we bury two thoughts recorded on paper from each camper. One thought is something they want to take home from camp and the other is something they want to leave at camp. We then bury the notes and each person places a rock on the earth, thereby sealing the memory and the event. This is an emotional time for each counselor and child, as it is the end of an amazing week full of love, grace, and powerful relationship building. At each ceremony we have conducted over the past fifteen years, I am amazed at the depth of what is written. Below are some samples:

> "I want to leave that I was raped by my family's friend." – ten-year-old girl.
>
> "I want to leave that my dad is in prison." – eight-year-old boy.
>
> "I want to leave my sadness in foster care." – ten-year-old boy.
>
> "I want to leave leaving my family." – seven-year-old boy.
>
> "I want to take all my new friends home." – seven-year-old boy.
>
> "I want to take back the way God loves me." – nine-year-old girl.
>
> "I want to take home the great times we had this week." – eleven-year-old boy.

These are just a few of the comments that portray the despair and the hope the children experience. "Hope has no expiration date" means that each of these incredible children have the authority and permission to believe that life can and will get better. It was a privilege and honor to extend hope to children in seemingly hopeless situations. It worked!

As we came down the mountain and went back to "normal life," I noted the extreme sense of urgency and commitment that brought hope to the children. The staff and counselors worked tirelessly and with passion to share God's love, hope, and faith. This happened as children were told Bible stories, ate great meals, went on hikes, enjoyed tea parties, rode horses, or simply shared their thoughts and heart with a safe and new friend. RFKC works and it works because God's people give of their time, talent, and treasure to share hope.

That hope has no expiration date means that the children will never forget RFKC. In fact, we know this to be true because of Monica, a former foster youth in one of Covenant Community Services, Inc.'s transitional housing programs. Monica came to the Covenant office months ago and saw the handprints on the wall from children of RFKC. She became emotional and stated, "I went to your camp!" We immediately went to look through our pictures and found that she did attend RFKC, but it was in another city. Nonetheless, her memory proved our theory correct—hope lives here! Hope has no expiration date.

Monica was one of five former foster children who served at the 2011 RFK Camp of Kern County. She served as a counselor to two little foster girls that she loved, encouraged, and shared hope with just as someone had done with her more than eleven years ago. Hope truly has no expiration date.

On the bus ride up to RFKC 2007, Kim was riding the bus with our nurse and a few staff members. Bus rides are very unpredictable with fifty foster children aged six to eleven years old. We have witnessed fist fights, sickness, and many behavioral outbursts. On this occasion, we witnessed God's hand at work in the lives of two young girls.

During the bus ride, Kim took the opportunity to hand out business cards to each camper. The card had the counselor's name and picture of the counselor and a message. As she was handing out the counselor cards, she came to two eleven-year-old girls sitting together and chatting like old friends. The girls kept saying, "I hope we are in the same cabin." Kim asked why and they shared the story of spending their first night in foster care at our local children's shelter.

The Jamison Children's Shelter is the drop-off location for children removed from their homes due to domestic violence, drugs, abuse, and neglect. It is a large facility that tries, as much as possible, to be a good place in a horrible situation. The two girls ended up at Jamison from different homes on a very late night in Bakersfield. As they were dropped off, they made a connection and quickly became friends. The girls shared about how they moved their beds together that first night and comforted each other following the removal from their parents and homes. They shared about crying, being frightened, and hugging to keep each other calm and safe. They spent three days together at Jamison and were then placed in separate foster homes.

It was all Kim could do to keep herself composed as these two precious girls shared a moment of their lives with her. Of course, Kim would make all the necessary arrangements so the girls could be together for the week of RFKC. The girls were beyond excited as they were now able to create positive memories together for a week at camp.

An amazing backstory to this miracle is how the girls made it to camp. Just one week prior to RFKC, a camper dropped out leaving us short one eleven-year-old girl. As it worked out, the waiting list had one eleven-year-old girl that had just been added the week before. Isn't it amazing the way God works? We can plan, process, and execute, but God is always working through it all. As Kim was looking through the counselor cards, she was amazed to find that they were not only in the same cabin but they had the same counselor! No amount of planning on Kim's part could have orchestrated this perfect pairing. God was involved from the very beginning! As she pulled the cards out and handed them to the girls she said, "Not only are you going to be in the same cabin, but you have the same counselor!" The girls cried with joy and stated, "This is the best day ever." Needless to say, they had a wonderful camp and were inseparable.

Matthew 21:16 records Jesus speaking about children. "Do you hear what these children are saying?" they asked him. "Yes," replied Jesus, "have you never read, 'From the lips of children and infants you, Lord, have called forth your praise'?" (NIV).

At an RFKC in 2010, the "babes" of camp led a group in praise as we discussed Jesus and deep theology. You wouldn't think that a camp for foster children ages six to eleven would yield such a weighty discussion, but that is exactly what happened. The talk came during an outing just for the boys as the girls were busy enjoying a tea party.

We had just finished a hike and I was leading the boys in a discussion about the character and nature of Jesus. I asked about how pictures usually portray Jesus. The children replied, "gentle," "nice," "kind," "loving," "white," "long-haired wearing a robe," and "not mean." We came to the conclusion that Jesus is often portrayed as a "sissy." Next, I showed ways in the Bible where Jesus wasn't a sissy.

Our discussion moved from the cross, and Jesus taking our sin and shame through death, to the second coming of Jesus, when He comes back as a warrior with fire in His eyes and the King of kings and Lord of lords written on his robe and thigh. The kids got a picture of a different Jesus, and this is where things began to get very interesting.

Suddenly, questions were coming from everywhere and everyone:

"Does Jesus speak Spanish?"

"Did God and Jesus create the earth and then invite us? Who came first?"

"Is Joseph Jesus's dad or is it God?"

"Who do we pray to, Jesus or God?"

"So you're saying Jesus and God are three people put in one? How does that work?"

"When Jesus comes back, what will I do?

"What will happen when He comes back? I gotta see that!"

The questions just kept coming, with some children providing excellent answers. Still, I did not expect our discussion to become so elaborate and deep. The children drove it to an amazing level, and I felt privileged to sit on a stump and respond with biblical truth that can shape and change their minds and hearts.

Just as we were wrapping things up, one of the youngest kids at camp began a long question.

"So, if a bee lands on my leg and stings me. I hurt. Will that happen in Heaven?"

I explained that the Bible teaches that there are no tears, no pain, no sickness, and no bee stings, snakes, or evil or bad things in Heaven. The little boy was satisfied with my response and then asked, "Well, when will that happen?"

"When Jesus comes back to rule forever."

At which point he confidently said, "Well, He should hurry it up!"

I could only say, "Let's pray!"

Out of the mouths of babes. Amazing! What an honor to be with God's children and the "fatherless" who are so close to His heart. Our staff and the counselors are doing such an incredible job. They are serving tirelessly and without break to "sound the note of God's love" through their lives and lips. It is working. The children are feeling God's love and accepting His grace.

Neil Postman wrote, "Children are the living messages we send to a time we will not see." RFKC has transformed our view of children as arrows we shoot into the next generation. Children, foster, biological, or adopted, are all to be cherished and encouraged to develop into healthy and successful individuals. RFKC has taught us the importance of loving children that many have forgotten. The RFKC camper truly represents the "least of these" mentioned by Jesus in Matthew 25.

Psalm 127: 3–5 states:

> Children are a heritage from the Lord, offspring a reward from him. Like arrows in the hands of a warrior are children born in one's youth. Blessed is the man whose quiver is full of them. They will not be put to shame when they contend with their opponents in court.

RFK has taught us that the children and youth we serve are the arrows we send to the future. We may not know where they will land or what the ultimate outcome of their lives might be, but we can rest assured, with full confidence in God's hope, that He will care for them and bless their lives. RFK teaches this through experience each summer as adults serve children at camp to confront abuse and transform generations.

In our work with former foster youth, we find evidence that uncovers the trauma of abuse and neglect. As we serve former foster youth who are now between eighteen and twenty-four years old, it is apparent that most of them had no one to help process pain and healing when they were children in the system. No one talked to them about the grace of God. No one allowed them to be children. No one invested in their lives with hope and love. RFK has taught that we must address their trauma with God's love as early as possible. RFK and its natural plan of resiliency development helps children of abuse grow through and past their trauma in a positive manner. One week at "camp" has transformed our view of "how" we do things in the system and "why" we do what we do. The investment of RFK in children confronts abuse and neglect head on with the love of Christ. RFK exemplifies a movement that transforms the view of children from pawns waiting to develop to critical pieces of our community and Kingdom.

RFK changed the trajectory of our life. In 1999, after four years of serving at RFK as counselors and then directors, we knew God had more in store for us. After a period of fasting and prayer, we met with Pastor Wendell Vinson of Canyon Hills Assembly of God church and shared a vision to develop a faith-based foster care ministry. After some time in corporate prayer, we launched the ministry under the guidance of the Family Care Network in San Luis Obispo. As a Family Care Network sub-office, we began to recruit, train, and certify families to take foster children into their homes. We followed the RFK model we had learned over the past four years: find great people who have a heart for children, invest in them through training, pray, and stay in unity. This model served us well at RFK and God showed up every year to bless the children and every volunteer. This was the model we knew would help us fulfill the vision God provided and help change the face of foster care.

In 2003, we launched Covenant Community Services to better serve Kern County and expand services beyond traditional foster care. Through the mentoring of RFK, spiritual leaders, and Jim Roberts of Family Care Network, we developed a holistic and multifaceted ministry to foster children and former foster youth. The background of the ministry remained RFK "purple people" as they signed up to be our first foster parents, mentors, and adoptive families. In fact, in 1999 it was Billy and Christy Abney, a counselor and coach from RFK, who would become our first foster parents and first adoptive family. Since that time, Billy and Christy have followed their own path and opened a group home for parenting foster teens. So RFK has not only impacted our life, but every life we have touched through the leadership and execution of RFK.

Fast forward to 2014 and Covenant now has eleven unique programs and services to foster children aged birth through twenty-four. We have a thriving social enterprise in Covenant Coffee, which God is using to disciple, train, and mentor former foster youth for success. There is an African orphan home in Tanzania. We still serve in foster care as a licensed foster family agency, and we also serve over eighty-two former foster children each day through transitional housing programs. God has truly blessed Covenant, and it all began with raising my hand to attend RFK.

In addition to the vocational and purpose blessings RFK has been to our life, we have had direct family blessing due to RFK. Years into directing RFK, we felt compelled to take in our son, Jovan Paige. We call him our son because he moved in with us at age fifteen and remained until he was twenty-three. We did not adopt Jovan, following his wishes, but have always loved him as our own. This dynamic completely changed our family. Our children received a new brother and learned about sacrifice and compassion. They would soon turn this into action and all three served at RFK while we were still directing. RFK doesn't just change the children we serve; it transforms every person who becomes involved.

Today, we continue to serve in the field of the fatherless. Our children continue to serve in foster care ministries. We continue to advocate and raise the banner of love of foster children and former foster youth. At Covenant, we restore lives and transform generations following the blueprints and foundation laid through our work with RFK.

In 2011, Kim and I retired from directing the local RFK to join the National Training Team for New Camps and Passing the Scepter. It has been a tremendous blessing to use our years of experience to engage others to fight for children by confronting abuse and making memories at a week of RFK. It is an amazing feeling to be in the "birthing room" for new camps. It is an honor and privilege to witness God's move in a soul to fight for children and to enlist others to do the same. We have spent many days travelling this great country and crying with leaders over the plight of foster children. We have also shared tears of joy as new leaders complete their first camp and begin their own journal of "stories of the one."

Celebrating twenty-five years of RFK is a wonderful milestone to witness. Our time serving with RFK will grow to twenty-five years in 2015. By 2025, we will have dedicated more than one-half of our lives to this great ministry and God's children. The next decade will be a one of great expansion and development as God's people respond to the call to serve at RFK and move from the pew to purpose. What an exciting time to be a part of a ministry with such an impact.

7

REBEKAH COLE
Former Camper

A World of Opportunity

When a single topic fills so much of your life, you might think turning out a few pages about it would be easy. Actually, it's not that easy.

I have found myself confounded by how I could possibly sew many of my Royal Family KIDS stories into one cohesive story. The same event takes on so many different facets when you experience it at different ages. I have the unique insight (luckily becoming less unique as the years pass) of having experienced RFK as a child, an adolescent, and as an adult.

I know that it is ideal to hear a story of transformation. Everyone likes to hear the story of how lives, viewpoints, and hearts can change overnight with one single encounter, a positive memory, or a radical experience that shakes the protagonist to the core. I would be lying if I said that those are not some of my favorite stories; there are certainly plenty of those when it comes to the impact that RFK has had on so many lives in the last twenty-five years.

My story, however, is not a magical transformation of the heart. I haven't had any big whirlwind experience through RFK where my personal inner life changed in an instant. I could, in all truth, share a series of positive memories in these pages. There have been many. But when it comes to moments that matter—a life-changing encounter—I would have to say that in my experience, the "moments" that I would consider life changing, all have one thing in common. When I strip down all the different moments, and various encounters, and ages at which Royal Family KIDS has been a part of my life, there does seem to be one word that rises out of all of my stories: opportunity.

I can tell you that the aspects that were truly of monumental influence at any given age were not just the positive memories but the incredible opportunities that RFK constantly afforded me. Looking back, all the moments that matter that I can recall were not just moments at all; they were actually bridges, windows, and open doors.

I went to camp as a foster kid for the first time at the age of nine and attended camp up until I graduated out at the age of twelve. I played dress up. I learned how to dive. I got to spend a week with my younger brother, Andy. I experienced the awesomeness of camp cobbler back when the dessert was worth eating. I made worm cups, Orange Julius drinks, and consumed way too much sugar back before anyone thought twice about it. That's just what camp was for. I gave several people the coolest hairdos they have probably ever received in their lives. You're welcome, Ms. Mary Lou.

But the life-changing moment that came for me at camp came in the form of RFK creating an opportunity where my path crossed with the woman that I now call Mom. I didn't even know it at the time. My relationship with Shirley began largely after I had graduated from camp, and I was sure I was never going to see anyone from Royal Family again. To outline here all the sacrifices that this incredibly obedient, strong, determined, larger-than-life, tiny woman I have come to know as my hero have made in our journey is significantly more than this chapter allows. I will have to settle with just saying that she is my rock, my strength, my guiding star, and the most generous and fearless woman I will ever know. Shirley was also single, recently concluding a divorce, between living situations, living on a frugal income, and had already raised one grown daughter of her own. So what could possess her to open her heart to a complete stranger with the baggage of the foster care system and who was embarking on all the wonders of "teenagerdom" is completely beyond me. But she did it. And she did it with nothing but love in her heart the whole way through—love and a good set of lungs (I was a strong-willed teen, the Lord must have known what I needed). God bless her.

My childhood was not changed by a moment as much as the opportunities provided through RFK. My encounters as a child at camp opened the door to a new chance at family, at being a part of a new unit that God was creating with the fragmented pieces of both my life and Shirley's. This also influenced my adolescence by opening the doors to the idea of community.

Shirley and I attended church regularly. The Stone Church became a centerpiece in my life for several years. I went to junior high school at the academy there and attended the youth group, where I made lifelong friends, (albeit with a rocky start, as I wasn't used to living in one place for very long or dealing with friendships that would last more than a few months). I went on youth group outings and missions trips that I never thought I would have ever experienced. I got to go to one school for the entirety of high school—something that was unfathomable, given that I had moved twelve times before my placement with Shirley.

My mother is a collector of people; they are drawn to her. So she made sure I was filling the gaps that we had in our stitched-up family with influential people who would play important roles in my development. Even though I had no foster dad to speak of, I received the opportunity to have a godfather who lived just down the street. Pastor John Schwider (PJ) and Shirley were part of the team that launched the first Stone Church Royal Family KIDS Camp. In the years that followed, I would spend several hours with PJ solving the secrets of the universe either in his garage while he tinkered on automobiles or soaking up the warmth of a campfire in his backyard. As a matter of fact, PJ helped me buy my first car at the age of sixteen. By this time, I was old enough to go back and volunteer at camp.

Once again, a fresh opportunity was afforded me by RFK in the form of getting to experience camp as a volunteer support staff. To be on the giving end of creating the positive memories, to return to the land of kept promises, to experience the heaven that was the adult snack room—Glory! I also got to experience camp with friends I had made in youth group, other crazy teenagers I managed to talk into volunteering with me. I got the opportunity to interact with kids who were on the road that I had traveled, some of whom even lived in the group homes where I had lived, or had my same caseworker. I got to connect with them in a way that few others could.

The opportunities born out of RFK being a part of my life continued throughout high school. Getting to live in one place meant enough stability to focus on my grades, catch up, join in on extracurricular activities, and find a niche. By the end of my junior year, I had people asking me where I was going to go to college. This question was outrageous considering the fact that just a few years ago, I knew there was no way someone like me was ever going to college.

Opportunity through RFK knocked again when I was invited by my godfather to a breakfast where Wayne Tesch was going to be in town and wanted to meet. The exact reason why he wanted to meet was fuzzy to me, but I was willing, plus I love breakfast food. Wayne asked me at that breakfast if

I was considering going to college. Sure. He then asked me if I would ever consider going to college in California. He said he knew a guy and he knew a school. Over the course of breakfast a new world was born. A world in which I, a foster kid from the Midwest, was all of a sudden standing on the cusp of crossing the country to go receive a university education, one for which statistically I should not have been in the running. Even now, looking back I cannot say how all the pieces worked together to allow me to receive a private, West Coast education. Somehow, between the willingness of Wayne's connections and a few other academic scholarships strung together, I was able to graduate with two separate degrees. Go big or go home, right? That experience of picking up and going away to school later instilled me with the confidence to take a semester at sea my senior year. I got to visit fourteen different countries on a circumnavigation of the globe.

The fact that camp has been around twenty-five years has afforded someone like me the unique opportunity to have seen and experienced camp in a way few others have, I think.

Throughout my college years and early adulthood, I had the chance to experience the awesomeness of being a counselor. Specifically, I was blessed with the chance to be a counselor to Kimmy, who had the same caseworker as I did. But to take it a step further, I have also had the privilege of seeing Kimmy return as support staff, to work with her, and to see the amazing young woman that she has become. Camp has opened up doors for me to take on new positions and to experience and influence RFK as support staff, counselor, child-placement coordinator, leader, training coordinator, and dean of support staff. All of these roles have come with their own challenges, but they have also come with their own insights and vast opportunities for growth.

Finally, I can honestly say that RFK has provided a forum for new family memories.

I feel as though I have stepped through the looking glass and come full circle. Ironically, Royal Family KIDS Camp has quite literally turned into a collection of my family members. Last year, a fifth of the staff at camp were people I was related to: my mother, my husband, myself, my mother-in-law, and a few childhood friends were all on staff together. By the same token, burgeoning opportunity is knocking again as RFK has become a platform for me and my husband to see the needs of foster children, a mirror reflecting back to us a possible calling in what the future holds for our family.

RFK has not only been a place to create and experience positive memories but it has quite literally been the conductor and connector to several life-changing opportunities that I may not have otherwise received. Twenty-five years is a milestone, and it's important that we look at RFK not only for the positive memories that have been created but for the opportunities that this organization at large has produced. RFK and organizations like it are developers of new chapters and next steps. They cannot only spark wonderful moments of long-lasting memories and happy experiences, but these organizations can quite literally provide the bridge to some awesome new adventures that we didn't even know we would be offered. That's really the testament to something that started out as the brain seed of one couple and is now a nationwide program twenty-five years later. There is power in connection, in connectedness, and what we can do for each other. RFK is a strong, living organization of people with the capability to offer their time, education, talents, and networks.

We see the evidence of opportunities in all walks of life at camp. We see counselors become directors, pastors become ambassadors, volunteers become foster/adoptive parents, and campers become graduates. RFK is not just a place where positive memories are created; it is an environment where opportunities for a better tomorrow are formed. Not just for the campers, but for everyone involved.

8

JOHN SCHWIDER
Regional Ambassador

A child, more than all other gifts
That earth can offer to declining man,
Brings hope with it, and forward-looking thoughts.

—William Wordsworth

Camp week 2004 had just ended, our eleventh year of hosting a Royal Family KIDS Camp. The campers were returned to their foster parents, the welcome-home dinner was done, and the volunteers returned to their lives and the silence of the camp memories. I was overwhelmed at the smallness of the Stone Church Royal Family KIDS Camp. We had made a life-changing difference to thirty foster children, but there were so many who were not there.

Currently, twelve thousand foster children's lives are managed by social service agencies in the second largest county in the Unites States. Cook County encompasses all of Chicago and the majority of its suburbs, and is more populous than twenty-nine US states. I was overwhelmed by all those missed camper opportunities. The morning following the 2004 camp, I strode into lead pastor Bob Maddox's office lamenting the quandary of being unable to reach more foster children. At the end of my misty-eyed monologue Bob said, "I'll make some calls."

I did not know what that meant, and would not know for four months.

The following October, Wayne Tesch called to invite me to lunch. Although it was common for Wayne to phone me when he passed through Chicago, there was something different in his voice. As soon as the call ended, I asked Pastor Maddox whether, if I was offered a position with RFK that allowed me to stay in the area, whether I would still be able to attend Stone Church. His affirming response was a relief. I did not want to leave my church.

Stone Church was my home, my family, my rescue from alcoholism, and my discipleship into the faith by Pastor Owen Carr, Cecil Swanson, and others. At that point in my life, I did not want to leave the church where I committed my life to Christ, where I married the love of my life, and where I was introduced to the importance of children's ministry through the influence of children's pastors Ed and Sonja Corbin. There were only two episodes in which Marlene and I were not involved at Stone; they were while we attended North Central University in Minneapolis, Minnesota, and when serving as children's pastor at Journey Church in Kenosha, Wisconsin. The desire to stay at Stone was a major consideration regarding a potential ministry change.

The day before my lunch with Wayne, Bob called me into his office. It was always a good thing to get called into Bob Maddox's office. He reserved the difficult conversations for hallways and staff offices; his office was a good place. Once there he handed me a memo of understanding that outlined the dream of my life. He said the coming January I would go to work with Royal Family KIDS. Stone would keep up the cost of salary and benefits for a year while I raised my support. I would be able to stay in my home and attend my church while working for an organization 2,500 miles away. Once fully funded, I would be able to start camps, not only in Cook County, but anywhere in the world. Wherever on the planet I had relationships, there would be a possibility of starting camps and clubs. It was, and is, a dream come true.

The dream began a decade earlier at Stone's very first Royal Family KIDS Camp when I met Brandy. I did not know the first time I met her why she was so afraid of me and every other man at camp. I did not know what drove her night terrors, which required us to reverse the RFK two-to-one paradigm. Instead of having two campers to one counselor, Brandy had two counselors. One would stay up all night while Brandy tossed, turned, and screamed; the other slept to have the wherewithal to walk with her through the camp's daytime activities. Nights were heartbreaking as support staff member Shirley and I stayed up all night outside Brandy's cabin listening to the screams, ready to rush in if needed. Never in my life had I met such a troubled little girl, scarred inside and out by years of unspeakable abuse.

As an adult in her twenties, Brandy could recall in detail what men did to her. Three-year-old Brandy and her five-year-old brother became the currency to support their mother's drug habit. Although fear of men and night terrors marked her first few days of camp, by week's end she was calling me *Daddy* and wanted to go home with me. I can honestly say Brandy broke my heart. The pastoral position I held at Stone Church became a means to an end. All I wanted to do was camp, year after year, for the rest of my life.

Ten years passed when Pastor Maddox recognized that my vision for the redemption of children like Brandy far exceeded the scope of the Stone Church, and he released me to fulfill a larger purpose. He passed the keys of ministry leadership over my life to Wayne. I was in for the ride of my life.

With God's help in the nine years working for Royal Family KIDS, I have raised more than three quarters of a million dollars and created positive memories for more than one thousand five hundred children in camps I started myself or partnered with the team to help get them off the ground. I became a product of Wayne's visionary, entrepreneurial spirit, and he mentored me into becoming an ambassador, speaking on behalf of the thousands who have no voice. But RFK's is not a story of thousands. We are the story of the one.

Bekki was the one.

Bekki got off the bus looking like a very ordinary member of some disinherited race, for that is exactly what she was. Common brown hair and brown eyes, nothing to indicate an extraordinary life was in the offing. She was nine years old, living in a group home after eleven placements in only three years.

At camp she met people divergent from her experience with adults. These camp volunteers were forthright and honest. She met people who loved her, who took vacation from work just to spend a week with her, play games with her, and listen to her. Summer after summer she returned to us for another camp week. When Bekki was twelve, she was aging out of camper eligibility. Shirley, who had been an annual volunteer since the very first camp Stone Church hosted, was walking past dress-up, an area where campers donned costumes. Bekki was in the wedding dress. Shirley casually whispered a quick prayer, "God if there is anything I can do to make that happen, let me know."

He did. After camp Shirley began the nine-month process of becoming Bekki's foster mom. The following March, Bekki moved from the group home into Shirley's house. Her first Sunday at Stone Church, the greeter at the door was none other than Doc Roebuck, the camp grandpa. Bekki was home.

Camp directors John and Debbie and the volunteers from camp gave Bekki a familiarity to begin her new extended family. The church maintenance man became Uncle Mike, kids in the youth group became her brothers and sisters, and I became Pops. Even though she had a biological father, she needed a daddy. It was my privilege and honor to fill that position through Bekki's high school years and young adulthood.

While in college she met a young man named Josh. He was the one. Josh was the real deal. He treated her royally and loved her for who she was. I've been told I can be pretty intimidating to a dating young man, but not with Josh. Bekki's admonition, "Pops, don't scare this one off" was unnecessary. In fact, it was impossible anyway. It was my joy to officiate their wedding—a thirteen-year answer to a three-second prayer at a summer camp for foster children.

Marlene and I have one daughter, Kelsey. She is the joy of our lives. I was privileged to be her daddy from birth. And, although on her wedding day I gave her to Bob, a young man of character and integrity, I am and will always be her dad, her safe place, and her cheerleader through life. We also have two sons, Josh and Joe, each a man of God in his own right, and I could not be more proud of them. Each of them have been involved in camp at some level. Kelsey the most involved as a leader in music and drama. Through the years of children's ministry and Royal Family KIDS, God has allowed me to fill a substitutionary dad role to others moving into their adult years. I am so proud of each one and want to tell you all about then, but I will limit that desire to tell you about only one more—Kimmy. First, a word about foster care.

Foster homes have changed the course of many lives in turmoil, and some have had incalculable historical impact. Biblical characters such as Moses, Joseph, and Esther each lost their home of origin and stepped into a larger role of race preservation in the face of impending genocide. Modern day foster parents are for the most part, heroes. To take a child into your home who is not your own is an exercise in selfless giving. Granted, that does not apply to all, but, I believe, to most. Kimmy had both. Her first placement was not a place of selfless giving. That all changed when her Aunt Ruthie provided a loving home where she could grow during the tumultuous teenaged years.

Like Bekki before her, Kimmy came to camp at the age of nine. In fact, Kimmy was Bekki's camper, as by then Bekki was an eighteen-year-old serving as camp counselor. To our surprise, they had much in common. The most surprising was Javanna, who each of them had had as caseworker. Think of that. In a system of twelve-thousand foster children, we paired up two who shared the same amazingly loving, caring, and dedicated caseworker. Kimmy was the best camper ever! She was quiet, compliant, and obedient. All the female counselors wanted Kimmy. She aged-out at twelve and returned at sixteen to be part of our camp's teen staff.

The first full day of camp featured lunch grilled outside. Kimmy filled her plate and sat down next to me as we looked over the campground where she spent three summers as a camper. Curious as to what was going through her mind, I asked if memories were coming back to her. She only nodded a simple, "Uh-huh." I probed deeper to ask what specifically did she remember about being there as a child. Her eyes filled with tears. She set her plate down and walked away. One of the female volunteers accompanied her as she processed through those difficult recollections. Later that evening I found a letter addressed to me from Kimmy.

The letter was full of appreciative words regarding the difference we made in her life at camp. She recounted that her only happy childhood memories from that time were her three summers at Royal Family KIDS Camp. We did not know that she was having a very difficult time in foster care. Prior to her Aunt Ruthie providing a good foster home, her experience was not good. We did not know that under that camper's quiet little exterior was a life filled with turmoil.

After camp, Kimmy became part of the Stone Church family, like Bekki before her, like Marlene and I before Bekki. Beyond that she has become part of my own family, a sister to my son Joe and his wife, Holly, and part of the lives of their three children, Amber, Lucy, and John.

If you grew up like me in a home with a mom and dad, fatherlessness would be a difficult concept to fully grasp all the complexities. On the other hand, a daddy who loves is equally difficult for the inexperienced to conceptualize. I always knew when my dad was coming home and where he was when out of the house. I knew what to expect of him; I watched him my entire life. I was never so honored as when he said I was the son he always wanted and had become the father he wished he could have been. Both of my sons have become great fathers. Jenna, Josh, and Jess's daughter are blessed to have parents who love them. I cannot imagine life absent of such—the life lived by children in foster care.

Imagination is a curious thing. It is a creative force that leads the will to explore that which it does not know. In a child's world marked by abuse, neglect, and abandonment, meeting godly men and women at camp can spark imagination in incalculable ways. The camp in which I have volunteered for two decades serves children whose relationships are predominantly female. For many of the five hundred children who passed through our camp, their female caseworkers, single moms, and grandmothers were their primary caregivers. Saying that is in no way a criticism but only to show a contrast within the camp environment that includes playful, caring men.

For example, Daniel was nine years old. In the activity field lay a wide assortment of Frisbees, soccer balls, Wiffle balls and bats, kites, baseball gloves, and footballs that one would consider normal in any home with children. Daniel picked up the Wiffle bat. Vince mechanically picked up the Wiffle ball and tossed it Daniel's direction. He took a girlish one-handed swing-and-a miss. It was clear he had no experience. And this is what I love about having godly men at camp.

Without critical comment, Vince simply said, "Let me show you something." He stood behind Daniel, showed him how to grip the bat, how to stand, and how to swing. It was the first time Daniel ever held a baseball bat. For the next couple hours Daniel ran Vince ragged as he pitched and chased the Wiffle ball with shouts of encouragement. Daniel not only learned how to play baseball that day, he learned the pride of accomplishment and what it meant to have a daddy, even if only for a couple hours.

As my life changed from being a volunteer at one camp to becoming an ambassador for RFK, these stories of a child's transformation drive me through the difficult times. When asked what changes the position has had on me, trusting God fully pushes its way to the forefront. There is no safety net; ambassador is not a budgeted position. If God does not come through, there is no travel money and no paycheck. The change on me was small compared to the impact it has had on my wife of nearly forty years, Marlene.

While I was associate pastor of the Stone Church, she fit the role of pastor's wife and ministry leader effectively and purposefully. In one decision the rug was pulled out from under her. She had been displaced from her ministry life and had no place in the Royal Family. My wife, who loves predictability and consistency, had entered an unpredictable environment where things would be constantly changing and evolving. A previous revolution in her life would give her the wherewithal to move into this new arena.

A decade earlier our church went through a period of extreme conflict as discontented church members began what they called a "housecleaning." Accusations against the pastoral team ramped up to an unholy level. Some of the charges were true. There were character flaws and missteps that needed correction, but with every closeted skeleton discovery a host of false accusations were hurled our direction. Marlene's health deteriorated as we grasped for anything that would help us survive the next assault. We did not know where it would come or from whom, we just knew it would come, and it would hurt.

In the end God's grace prevailed as the housecleaning effort failed. The malcontents left and the graceful began the restoration. Pastor Phil Epperson remained steadfast and immovable through the battle, and God began healing through him and the faithful members of the Stone Church, the real church. During that time, Marlene's spiritual renewal was transformative. She would not describe herself as such, but out of the ashes rose a prayer warrior. To this day she does not begin her day without spending time with the Restorer of Broken Walls. And that is where her story and the story of Royal Family KIDS intersect.

One does not have to spend much time around Wayne before you hear the story of Nehemiah. Nehemiah's story from the fifth century BC recounts a Jewish second exodus from slavery to freedom, prosperity, and hope. Nehemiah begins a process to rebuild the broken walls around Jerusalem and reinstates temple worship. It serves as a fitting metaphor for children of broken relationships, bruised, neglected, and abandoned, as they discover hope. It serves to illustrate my wife's newfound faith in the God of love. As he began his rebuilding process, he restored her through worship. It is a restoration that elevates the individual and reveals the futility of earthly props. She faithfully serves the children at the Stone Church RFKC as assistant director to our amazing leadership team, led by Bob and Carolyn, our local heroes.

My job description could be summed up in three words that Wayne has said often: *make it happen!* Wayne has been an inspiration and a godly coach. As such he was not going to come to my rescue. Instead, he would graciously and appropriately toss the Psalm 40 grenade my direction.

In referring to that particular Davidic psalm, my context and David's share little similarity. I am not being pursued by someone who wants to kill me. I'm not living in caves and holes in the ground, and do not find myself mired in quicksand. For each of us, whatever our state, our hope, and redemption lies in a vertical relationship. No human enjoys difficulty, but life can be difficult. When we think anything important will come through ease, we set ourselves up to be disappointed.

The biblical writer James begins his epistle speaking about trouble with the words *when trouble comes*, not *if* it comes. Endurance is the path to growth and ultimately joy. James goes on to say when endurance is fully developed in a person, he needs nothing else. Wayne knew that if he came to my financial rescue, the process would be hijacked, leaving an incomplete person in its wake. It is in the pit, unable to see our way through, where we discover who we are and in whom we trust. God is faithful. Each of us has to remember for whom we ultimately work.

Another change is that this big blue marble on which humanity lives has become smaller. When an opportunity arises, such as starting camps in Ireland, possibilities rise to overwhelm thoughts of impossibility. The precursor to that change was, again, Wayne. Early in my RFK experience, when I pitched an idea to Wayne, he would often respond, "John, that's a great idea. Raise the money and do it!" The result of such coaching manifested when the Ireland opportunity rose. I didn't pitch it; I raised the money and went. The caveat is that in reality "I" did very little.

There is a big, brave, courageous, empowering God behind it all. He inspires the idea and calls willing humans to make it happen. At Royal Family KIDS we work with the most generous people on the planet, people who will use their hard-earned funds and limited time to propel this transformative work. God is trustworthy and dependable. He is faithful even when we are not. And as the work rolls on, new opportunities open.

One such opportunity is that we've begun recruiting foster parents for the state of Illinois. Camps and clubs have become on-ramps to fostering and adoption. Every year we hear of more camp and club volunteers who enter the licensing process to become foster parents. We have only added intentionality to the process by working with resource specialists and licensing representatives to lead and support people who enter the process.

If I were asked to sum up the story of Royal Family KIDS, it would be: God doing extraordinary things through ordinary people. Marlene and I are nobody special. All that we do is merely participate in the unending spiral of redemption begun, processed, and completed by God himself through human cooperation. It is through His grace, revealed in people who accept the challenge, who are unabated by difficulty, and who are willing to do whatever needs to be done to confront the abuse and change the trajectory of children in foster care.

ABOUT THE SCHWIDERS

John Schwider has served in ministry to children since 1975. He created a neighborhood kid's club in a government housing project in Minneapolis, performed a character role in the television show *Toddler's Friends* in Chicago, and served as children's pastor in two churches in Kenosha, Wisconsin, and Chicago Southland. He is currently an Ambassador of Vision Fulfillment for Royal Family KIDS. John is an ordained minister and holds a BA in pastoral studies from North Central University of Minneapolis. At the time of this publication, he and his wife, Marlene have shared nearly forty years of marriage and have three adult children, two daughters-in-law, one son-in-law, and four grandchildren. John has been involved with Royal Family KIDS since 1993.

9

RICHARD TIZZANO

Former Camp Director, Federal Way, Washington

As far back as I can remember I have always enjoyed helping kids. I have also always enjoyed going to camp. I knew Wayne and Diane Tesch from their pre-camp days. So when the Royal Family KIDS Camp idea rolled out, I did what I could to help. I prayed a little and I gave a little. A Royal Family camp for kids was something I could get behind and I did.

Then one day I got the idea that my church should sponsor a camp. I arranged a lunch meeting for my pastor and Wayne Tesch. Wayne gave a very enthusiastic introduction to RFKC and showed how God uses a week of camp to pour His love into needy kids through an all-volunteer staff.

My pastor took the bait and said, "I think we should do it." He then turned his smiling face in my direction and said, "If you will lead it."

I heard myself saying that I would direct the camp. My level of support for RFKC suddenly took on a whole different dimension.

That first experience as a camp director was a big step on my journey from a self-centered life to a Jesus-centered life. I remember meeting Eric at that first camp. Eric was a nine-year-old foster child. I was sitting next to him during the birthday celebration for all of the kids. Gifts were handed out to each child. Eric had placed his gift box next to him and was slowly and carefully peeling back the seal on the envelope that was attached to the top of the gift. He pulled out the card and stared at the front of it for a long time. He then slowly opened the card and stared at the inside of the card. When he closed it and began staring at the front cover again, I grew anxious.

"Eric," I said, "Don't you want to open your present?"

He never once took his eyes off that card. He just said, "This is a birthday card. I have never had a birthday card before."

His words brought me up short. In that moment everything seemed to slow down. In fact, Eric's words led to some serious soul searching. I realized that things didn't always need to move at my pace or at my direction. I could be in the scene, but I did not need to direct the scene.

A short time later, I moved to a new city and a new church. In a rare moment of déjà vu, I arranged a lunch with Wayne Tesch and the pastor of my new church. You would think I would have learned my lesson by that time, but the meeting ended with me agreeing to direct a new camp.

I can remember getting up in front of the congregation on a Sunday morning to announce that volunteers were needed for a week of summer camp for foster kids. I was fighting back the tears as I said, "You may be sorry that you came to church today. The Holy Spirit is going to reach into your chest and grab your heart, and you won't be able to stop yourself from serving God in this way." I told them that "moments matter" and that a week of camp can have a huge impact on a young person's life. I also shared how the impact was beginning to show in my own heart and life.

In truth, every act of service to these broken kids encouraged me to do more. Looking back over the twenty years that have passed since that first camp, I can see that God used my camp experience to give my life direction and meaning. My wife, Gloria, was a counselor at one of the camps, and she fell in love with her two campers. Shortly thereafter, we found ourselves speeding down the on-ramp into the world of foster care, a shortcut to the heart of God, a world where Jesus worked. Here are the poor. He came to preach the gospel to the poor. Here are the brokenhearted. He came to heal the brokenhearted. These are kids who are blind to their possibilities and trapped in their circumstances. Jesus came to proclaim sight to the blind and set the captives free. The more I began to appreciate what He wanted to do for these children, the more I understood what He had done for me. As my heart was overwhelmed by His grace, my sense of gratitude increased and my desire to serve Him heightened. Gloria and I chose to become licensed foster parents. From there, God began to grow our family through adoption.

Recently, as one of my children ran away for the third time that week, he slammed the front door on his way out. The sudden vibration knocked a plaque off the wall, breaking the frame. The plaque, written by Maryanne Radmacher, reads:

May you always know.
May this be the place from which you launch your dreams.

May this be the castle from which you go forth and conquer and return to celebrate and rest.

May this be the dance at which you learn to craft a confidence and ease.

In these rooms may you discover the tools to build your vision—or may we have the grace to seek that which you need so your spirit may soar.

May you always know your family as your safe and good home.

I glued the frame back together and rehung the plaque on the wall.

I have shared a bit of my story, but each of our children has a story too. Their stories are still very much "in progress." We play a part in each child's story, but it is *his* or *her* story. They play a part in my story and, let me tell you, they play a big part in shaping and bending and grinding down the rough edges of my story, but it is still *my* story. What drives us is the desire to see all of our children participating with us in His story.

In Scripture, God says:

> I'll give you a new heart, put a new spirit in you. I'll remove the stone heart from your body and replace it with a heart that's God-willed, not self-willed. I'll put my Spirit in you and make it possible for you to do what I tell you and live by my commands. (Ezekiel 36:26-27, Message)

I praise God who makes all things new and who puts His own Spirit within us to empower us to do His will. I am so very thankful for both the joy and the lessons that RFKC continues to bring into my life.

10

RHONDA MONTGOMERY
Former Camp Director, Madison, Alabama

I believe God calls ordinary people to do extraordinary things for His kids. My name is Rhonda Montgomery, and I was the director of the RFK camp in Madison, Alabama. I am *very* ordinary and this is my extraordinary story.

In 1998 I was the children's coordinator at Asbury United Methodist Church in Madison, Alabama. As I attended a national children's pastors' conference, I was looking for a mission project that an entire family could work on together. In the exhibit hall, I stopped at the Royal Family KIDS Camp (RFKC) booth and soon knew I had found my answer in their Birthday Box Program. The representative explained that the birthday boxes would be sent to a church, filled with new presents by its congregation, and then mailed to an RFKC camp. Every camp has so many great experiences for the foster children, one being a birthday party for *all* of the kids. I was stunned to hear that there were kids out there who had never had a birthday party or present. I just kept thinking, *Wow, what if they were my kids*. I immediately knew this was going to be the mission project for children's ministry.

As the representative started taking down my basic information, I was calculating in my head how many boxes to commit to, so that when asked this question I was prepared with an answer. I figured that Asbury could easily do two hundred boxes. But when asked, my response did not go as planned. "I think we could easily do four hundred." That number just popped out! I was in shock, but I stayed calm and did not show any emotion. Then again I said, "Actually, I think we could easily do . . . four hundred." It happened again! What was going on?

I decided to excuse myself for a quality heart-to-heart with God. He showed me that even though we could easily do two hundred boxes, He had four hundred children who needed Asbury's love and kindness. I was still a little nervous about doing four hundred boxes, but I was excited too!

When the boxes arrived, I got up in front of our congregation and told several stories about these precious children. The congregation was excited to be a part of this mission. We ran out of boxes to sign out, and the rest of the people in line chose to donate money to help with the mailing costs. (I had no idea where that money was going to come from, but I was trusting God.)

I imagined that children would come with their families to sign out one box, but families came up and signed out four and five boxes! One family signed out twenty boxes, Boy Scout and Girl Scout leaders signed out ten to twenty boxes, even retired couples signed out boxes. God was showing me that my vision to help his kids was too small.

The boxes all came back filled to the rim with new birthday gifts that the children would love! We put rubber bands around each box because most of them were so full the lid would not stay on. When the last box was collected we received another surprise. UPS only charged us half the shipping cost because of the purpose of our packages! We had enough money left over for thirty-five more boxes and (surprise!) a camp in Massachusetts needed just that number!

The ladies in my Thursday morning Bible study helped weigh and package all of the boxes to be mailed. The boxes were prayed over and mailed to thirteen RFK camps all over the United States.

The next year we upped our commitment to five hundred boxes. Our church always went above and beyond to get boxes to these sweet kids. Over the five years helping with the birthday box program, Asbury showed God's love for these kids by giving a total of 2,435 boxes filled with presents to these sweet kids. Throughout those years, I received many emails, phone calls, and letters thanking us for providing the boxes, but my favorite thing was getting letters from the kids. Letter after sweet letter, the campers thanked us for their gifts in their own handwriting. One would write that he had never owned a watch and how cool it was, while another would tell me her Barbie has the same color hair as hers. The RFKC birthday box program was a wonderful way for our church to come together and love on these kids throughout the country.

During the fifth year of the program, senior pastor Alan Weatherly said he felt that it was time for Asbury to start its own camp for Madison County. I was in total agreement. I knew someone needed to step up and do this for our local foster children. Pastor Alan asked me to get a team together and go to the director training. Wait, what? Thoughts started running through my head. *I can't do this, I'm not qualified. I haven't ever even been to a camp, and I don't know anything about children who have been abused.* I knew I wanted to be a part of the camp, but the thought of directing it had never even crossed my mind. I prayed constantly about it. One day as I was praying, I felt an overwhelming peace and excitement about taking this step and I knew this feeling had come straight from Jesus. The next summer Mary Williams, Linda Case, Beth Ryberg, Charlie Brown, and I went to director training. We had no idea what we were in for, but we were excited.

The first night we had dinner with the RFKC founders, Wayne and Diane Tesch. We were so blessed to hear their heart and vision for RFKC. I came away from this meal realizing the peace and excitement I had felt was in fact a calling from God to help His children in Madison County.

The following day we dove headfirst into our training. We were so very blessed by our great trainers, Larry and Mitch, and our amazing host couple, Bonnie and Keith. Before we arrived at training, I wondered what we would be doing the other four days because I was sure training would only be a few hours. I was very wrong! We would be training for a week at a host camp that also hosts director training. Within the first day, our training group felt like family. We learned everything from what to look for in a campsite to what signs to look for when a child is abused. We laughed, cried, and played jokes on each other, like all families do.

The best thing about this training was that we were allowed to observe an RFK camp in action while going through our training manual. We watched the kids get off the bus and heard all of the cheers from the counselors. We observed coach time and saw the kids laughing and playing games. One of the most impacting moments for us was watching the campers during their birthday party. They were on cloud nine. The night began with a pizza party, continued on to a carnival with games, and ended by receiving a birthday box full of brand new presents. I wish I could describe to you their faces that night—full of joy and shocked with the amount of love shown them. This concept was so foreign that many campers kept asking, "When do we have to give these back?" I had no words.

During the training, they gave us the statistics of the number of foster children in the United States and within their own county. I was curious what the number was for our county, so during the break I asked if we could research it. I was shocked to find out that we had approximately 450 kids in foster care within our county! I kept thinking it had to be wrong, because that number was too high. I checked the next week and confirmed that the number was correct. I could not believe it. It made what we were learning in training much more real for me.

I have been to many training sessions, both secular and nonsecular, and I can confidently say this was the best training I had ever attended. It connected what we were learning to real-life experiences. From observing a camp to having wonderful trainers, we learned so much that week. Not to mention we had an amazing host couple who loved on us all week and a training group that felt like family. It was a truly great experience.

After training, we came home and immediately started looking for a campsite. We visited several scenic places with cabins and a lake. I will never forget when we toured one site with our guide, SnakeBite. I had to ask him why his name was SnakeBite. He told us it was because a large snake that lived under one of the cabins bit him. Um, next please. Not a fan of snakes. But, honestly, as we were visiting campsite after campsite, I never felt a peace. So we decided to expand our search to college campuses. We toured two different campuses. The second college we visited was the same college that I had attended many years earlier.

When the Bret, director of university events, was giving me details of costs, he stopped and said, "Tell me what type of camp this is." I explained this was a camp for children in foster care who have been abused and neglected. He sat quietly for a moment and then explained, "I was a foster child. In fact, my father was a foster child too."

At that moment, I knew this is where God wanted us to have camp for His kids!

Our first year, I asked one of our campers, Danny, if he liked having camp on a college campus. He exclaimed, "Yes, I love it! It's really pretty and it makes me want to go here."

I told him that he definitely could attend this college one day, but Danny said he couldn't because his foster parents told him he was about to flunk out of fifth grade and would be flipping burgers for the rest of his life. For the rest of the week, we really worked to build up Danny's self-esteem. A few weeks later, a couple from our camp became his foster parents. He immediately went from getting D's and F's to receiving A's and B's. It was clear that in order to succeed, Danny simply needed people in his life who truly loved and supported him. Today Danny is married and is a US Marine in the Special Forces. He visited us at one of our RFK trainings a few years ago to see everyone and thank them. God is doing wonderful things in his life.

Ever since our first year at our college campus, we have been treated not as just one of the camps on their campus but as family. They go out of their way to make sure the kids have an amazing week of great memories. Every year we ask one of their coaches to play ball with the boys. The coaches talk to the boys, play with them, and then give them an autographed ball. This is a treasure to the boys. But while the boys are hanging out with the coach, the girls are having a lovely tea party. (No boys allowed!) The girls pick out a dress from our dress closet and then get their nails painted and hair curled. Then our "Camp Uncle" escorts them across the stage one by one. As they walk across the stage, the emcee introduces them and talks about how beautiful they are.

One year I was waiting with the girls in line, and one little camper, Josie, turned to me and said, "No one has ever done my hair, don't I look pretty?"

In that second, my heart broke. I told Josie that she looked absolutely beautiful, and her smile lit up the room. I don't think she stopped smiling the rest of the week.

Another fun day during our week of camp is when we go to the lake. The campers absolutely love swimming in the lake. There is a lot of splashing, giggling, and beach balls flying through the air. We also have fishing poles ready to go if the campers decide they want to fish. Most of our campers have never been fishing, so this is a thrill. Of course, the girls always have someone else put the worms on, "cause they are squishy and yucky." The boys love the worms. It is hard to describe their faces when they catch a fish; it's shock, disgust, and laughter all at once. They yell for the camp photographer to take their picture, so they have proof they caught a fish. Then, they call over someone special and have that person kiss the fish before letting it go back into the lake. Yes, I said *kiss* the fish. It's funny what we will do for our campers. The camper laughs and laughs and runs around telling everyone that they caught a fish and someone kissed it. It truly is another day full of fun.

We also have so many fun activities that the campers get to do every day during activity time. This could be anything from tie-dyeing, fuse beads, sand art, dress up, painting, or woodworking. Throughout the years, I've seen many campers enjoy expressing themselves during activity time through craft or song or drawing. One of my favorite activity time memories is of woodworking with Johnny.

Johnny's name brings back memories. He was one of our campers who had lots and lots of energy, but most of the time he hid behind a wall he had constructed so that no one could get to know him. Many of our campers have this wall. One day Johnny ran up and said, "Ms. Rhonda, come with me and make something in woodworking."

"OK, Johnny, let's go," I said.

Johnny ran straight to the woodworking table and started gathering his supplies. Our woodworking expert, Charlie, told Johnny that he would get the supplies and help him make the stool.

Johnny looked at him and said, "Ms. Rhonda and I are going to do it by ourselves."

Johnny placed all of the wood on the table, grabbed the nails and the hammer and said, "Hold the nail, Ms. Rhonda, and I will hit it with the hammer."

I quickly said a silent prayer, before he started hammering: *Dear Jesus, When he hits my finger with the hammer, please don't let me scream and scare him.* He hammered and talked, talked and hammered. Ten nails later, the stool was constructed without a single accident. He painted it and then wrote on the front, "to Rhonda, from: Johnny." He presented it to me saying, "Look what I did, Ms. Rhonda!" And then, he ran off to do another activity.

During the week he would come up to me and talk about our time making the stool. I began to see his wall coming down. That stool is sitting on my shelf as I write this as a constant reminder to pray for all of my RFK kids every day.

Another wonderful camp tradition is when our camp grandma and grandpa go around to each camper at bedtime and give him or her a quilt. The quilts are handmade and prayed over by sweet ladies from our church who spend months and months choosing the perfect material and sewing each quilt. They truly are made with love for these campers. The campers never can believe someone took the time to do this just for them and that they can keep them! Many of the little girls drag their quilts everywhere they go during camp.

One of my favorite moments at camp is on Friday. The campers are given a sheet of paper and asked to write down something to give to God.

With the help of their counselor, many of them write things like: my anger toward the person that hurt me, being scared, worrying about what happens next, and so on.

After they write these down, they receive a helium-filled balloon and attach their sheet of paper to it. Next, we take the balloons outside and explain that we are going to give what we wrote down to God. We are going to let Him handle it, and we don't have to worry about it anymore. We say a prayer over all of the balloons and the campers release their balloons. It is very powerful to watch them let go and watch their balloons go up.

Later on Friday, the campers get several items to take home with them. One of their very favorite items is the photo album. We have a photographer who takes many, many pictures during the week, then fills photo albums for each camper. I love watching them look through their pictures. They have pictures of everything they have done at camp, from their day at the lake to the tea party to hanging out with the coach to pictures of the birthday party. The photo album also contains notes written to them from their counselors and camp staff. These notes let the campers know that they are loved and being prayed for every day. One of our campers just a couple of years ago was having a hard day with his new adoptive parents. He pulled out his photo album and started looking at it, as he had done every day. As he flipped a page, a note fell out. He had no idea that notes were behind the pictures. He started reading the notes from everyone and started crying. His new parents said this was his turning point, and they thanked us for writing those sweet notes to their son.

Our return to the church with the campers on Friday is bittersweet. As soon as they get off the bus, they sing several songs with their counselors for their foster parents and social workers. The campers are having a blast performing, while their foster parents and social workers watch with big, proud smiles and tears in their eyes. Then we all sit down to watch a video that shows funny pictures from the entire week of camp. We cheer every time we see a camper on the video. They love seeing themselves on the video and hearing our cheers. After the video, the RFKC staff helps them carry their luggage to their cars. We share hugs and tears. We let each camper know that we will be praying for them every single day. This is the hardest part of camp—giving them back. We have been with these sweet campers for a week, and we truly love every one of them. After we have said our good-byes, we have a debriefing time to lift all of our campers up to Jesus in prayer.

Afterward we enjoy a dinner together, celebrating all that God has done throughout the week. We enjoy good food, give funny awards, and share moments where we saw God work in the hearts of our campers. We pray for all of our campers and then we go home for much-needed rest. But, of course, that is not the end of our time at camp. Many times we will run into campers not even one day after we get home. It is a sweet blessing to get a hug from a camper outside of camp and get to meet their foster family.

One of our campers, Billy, attended an elementary school down the road from me. His teacher was a good friend of mine. One day she called and asked me to come to her class. When I arrived, the class was finishing a presentation. The class had been asked to bring their most prize possessions, invite their parents, and explain why this is so important to them in front of the class and parents. Billy walked up to the front of the class and pulled out his RFK camp photo album. He went through every single picture and explained what he was doing and how much fun he was having. He told everyone that this was the best summer of his life, and he wanted to go back to this camp next year. It was the best presentation because it was presented with such heart. Not a dry eye in the house. At the end, every one of his classmates asked if they could go to his camp. The parents knew what RFKC was and were shocked that Billy was a foster child. This was an eye-opener for the parents in the classroom. Many of them told me that they had no idea there were any foster children in our elementary school. I gave them the statistics for our county and let them know that a large number of children are in foster care in each of our local elementary schools. They were very surprised and asked what they could do within our local elementary to help. I walked them through some basic training to help them understand what these children are going through and how to respond. My youngest daughter, Mary Beth, attended this elementary school and decided to have a "can drive" for RFKC. She asked the teachers and students to bring their empty soda cans to the school. Hundreds of cans were donated to help send foster children to camp. It is amazing to see how this ministry has affected my family. My own kids have helped in every aspect. When they were little, they helped pack the birthday boxes and organize them. As they got older, they helped us get ready for camp.

I can still remember asking my kids when they were little, "What do you want to do at camp when you get older?"

Ellen said, "I want to be a counselor."

Andrew said, "I want to be a counselor too."

My youngest, Mary Beth, said, "I want to be the director!"

Now, they are all volunteers at our camp. It is a huge blessing to serve beside my children and watch them show the love of Christ to our campers.

This ministry has not only affected my family but also our church. Because of our growing love for foster children, our church has started a new ministry called Embrace 127, based on James 1:27. The mission of this ministry is to be a church engaged in orphan care by meeting the immediate needs of local and international orphans, supporting families involved in orphan care, and creating and nurturing a culture of expanding families through adoption and fostering. The number of Asbury members who are becoming foster parents and/or adopting has increased significantly since Embrace 127 has started.

I am amazed and humbled to say this coming summer will be our twelfth camp. I look back to our first year and remember how excited I was about what I knew God would do through us. One of the biggest blessings I have seen throughout the life of our camp is having campers come back to camp to be counselors in training. It is truly amazing to see God use them at our camp to show the campers that He loves them. Many campers start asking how they become counselors too. It is so powerful for them to see people who can say, "I have been where you are and now look where God is using me."

Recently, I received an email from an ex-camper, Tiffanie. She just turned twenty years old. We went to lunch that week to catch up. She told me that years ago, she was adopted and now she was in college. We reminisced about camp and her counselors. Tiffanie, like other campers, talked about her photo album and how precious it is to her. She told me that her little brother, Michael, had been adopted too. I let her know that the birdhouse she and Michael made for me was still in my office. She was shocked and happy.

Tiffanie said, "Guess what, Ms. Rhonda—I am engaged."

I could not believe that our little Tiffanie was engaged and I congratulated her. Then she said, "Guess who I am engaged to."

Well, Tiffanie lives outside of our city now, so, I was surprised she wanted me to try and guess. I just said, "I have no idea, who?"

"Matthew."

I said, "Oh, that's great," though I had no idea who Matthew was, which she could tell by my expression.

Then, she said, "You know, Matthew. Matthew from camp."

I sat there for a moment, and then asked, "Matthew from our camp?"

She said yes with a very big smile!

I asked if they had kept in touch after camp. She said no, that she didn't even remember if she met him at camp. Then she told me her story. They both went on the same dating website, started talking, and talked for weeks before they even went out on a date. She said once while they were talking, Matthew said he had been to a camp as a kid and really enjoyed it. She said she had been to a camp as a kid too. He then said, "It was called something like Royal Camp." She asked, "Was it Royal Family KIDS Camp?" He said yes, and they soon realized it was the same camp they had attended the exact same years! They both got out their photo albums. One picture stood out. It was a picture of Tiffanie's little brother, Richard, and Michael.

I just love how God works. Tiffanie told me that she would love to write a book about her experiences in foster care and Royal Family KIDS Camp, but she didn't know how. She is now working with one of our volunteers and writing her own book. One day you will be able to buy it.

I'll conclude with this last story. Several years ago, Laura attended our camp with her little sister. The year that Laura was over the age limit for camp, she wrote a letter to everyone at camp and sent it with her little sister. Her words show very clearly what camp means to the children we serve.

> RFKC Counselors and Staff,
>
> Royal Family KIDS Camp is a memory full of joy. The reason I'm writing this note is because I wanted to thank you all. So many kids are blessed just to get to go to kids' camp. I really love the way counselors act with the campers, so much love and care is expressed when that is done! The CITs are good examples for any camper that is a graduate who wants to come back! Thank you for them because when I turn 17 this is probably the first thing I'll think of! I'm going with my daddy in three months and am really glad for that. He loves me so much and cares for me! I will be the happiest girl ever to be with him! I'm glad I can share that with

you! And for anyone else that puts RFKC together. Thanks and I love U, the only way I can put that! Love and God bless you!
XOXOXOXOXO = Laura!

I honestly can't tell you how many hundreds of times people have asked me, "How can one week make a difference with these foster kids who have been abused?" That is when I have the honor of telling a story (or ten) from camp. Just from the few stories I have shared with you, I wonder where Danny, Josie, Johnny, Billy, Tiffanie, Michael, Richard, and Laura would be today if it weren't for Royal Family KIDS Camp. I could honestly fill this entire book with hundreds of amazing, life changing stories of our campers. Yes, one week cannot only make a difference, but it can change a life forever.

11

GLENN GARVIN
VP Camps, Clubs, and Mentors

Two six-foot tables encircled with maroon plastic chairs waited for us as we entered the junior high Sunday school room. There was a smaller table setup on the side where sandwiches and sodas were lined up. This was an all-pastoral staff meeting. That day, however, we had a guest (thus, the free food). The guest was Wayne Tesch. I had heard about Wayne through our network of Assemblies of God friends in the early 1980s. The rumor was that Wayne was known for his wild ideas.

Wayne and the church in Newport-Mesa, California, had the reputation for having innovative, crazy programming that was seen as "cutting-edge" ministry. The church always offered unique and creative Sunday school classes as well as camps of all types. Wayne came to share about a program idea concerning needy, at-risk, and underprivileged children (terms that I would come to dislike because of their vagueness). I just came for the sandwiches.

Pastor Chuck Atherton introduced Wayne and said that he had an idea to help children and let him talk about how we could help. I remember Wayne sharing a couple of stories that sounded very sad, and he began to talk about this camp for hurting children. I didn't quite understand what he was talking about because I had no real understanding of the words *foster kids*.

The first thing that stood out was Wayne saying, "I am not an expert." He had only been doing camp a couple hundred hours. That's all he knew, and he was still learning. I remember that struck me because there was such an attitude of humility and a sense of learning in this new area in which he wanted us to get involved.

He wrapped up his talk with one question: Would we be interested in running a camp like his? Then there was silence. Have you ever sat around a table of staff and pastors when someone comes up with a "new" idea? To be honest, no one really wants to run with it because it means more work to an already overloaded schedule. There's a little trick we do. We put our head down or look somewhere else, but we never look the person in the eye and never are the first one to speak.

So after a couple seconds, most of the staff had their head down like we were praying (but we weren't) and then we heard our pastor say, "I think we should do this." You also need to understand that a senior pastor spells *we* as y-o-u.

My wife, Robin, was the children's pastor, and I was the Christian education pastor. So Pastor Chuck volunteered Robin to take the lead for our church (representing Life Center). The senior pastor from Norwalk, Sam Miller, would direct the first year because he and his wife had been foster parents. They were "experienced." Then the pastor offered the help of our youth pastors and our music pastor as well. Well, at least we were in this together. And because we had no idea what we were doing, Wayne came up with a plan. Robin and I would drive up to Pinecrest Christian Conference Center and spend the day with Wayne at their Royal Family KIDS Camp. We would observe how they did camp and Robin would take notes.

Looking back, Robin was the only realist among us. She knew this would be the most difficult week of our entire lives. So one day in June 1988, we arrived at Newport Mesa's fourth Royal Family KIDS Camp. The plan was simple. (To Wayne Tesch, every one of his plans sounds simple—to him). Wayne had Dave Brooks take over as camp director (RFKC's first succession), and that left Wayne free to walk Robin and me around showing us the core of RFKC programming.

The Newport-Mesa camp had grown from thirty-seven kids to about fifty. Wayne told stories and highlighted why we have chapel in the morning. Kids are fresh and we don't take advantage of their tiredness, emotions, or issues. There is a reason we have "activity centers" instead of "crafts." He told us the story of one faithful saint trying to do a Sunday school-style craft with a large group of children with behavioral and medication issues, not to mention the fact that many of them had mouths like little sailors. It didn't go well.

Wayne asked Robin to do a special chapel service with her puppets. Kids love stories and dramas, and Robin's Salty puppet was perfect, until Sam made his way forward. Robin was on stage and doing well. The children were listening and laughing and behaving well. Then an adorable, blonde-haired, fair-skinned little guy named Sam started walking to the front and center part of the chapel. Robin remained focused and tried not to let him distract her, thinking that someone was going to get him and bring him back to his seat. Sam just kept coming. When he was right in front of her, and it was obvious that no one was coming to get him, Robin decided to have Salty the puppet say something directly to him.

"Hi, I'm Salty. What's your name?"

Out of nowhere came Sam's hand and he "flipped the bird" (that is, gave her his middle finger) and just stood there smiling.

"Welcome to ministry," as Wayne would say. Welcome to Royal Family KIDS Camp! Robin and I walked and listened to Wayne the rest of the day. Robin took pages and pages of notes on a yellow pad, trying to catch every element of the unique programming geared for these special children.

As our own camp date approached, we had worked hard to duplicate everything that Newport-Mesa and Wayne had figured out through three years of experience. Now, with thirty-eight children signed up to go, we would soon find out if this crazy idea could be replicated. So we left for camp on a sunny Sunday in August 1988, just a few months after learning about RFKC. We found ourselves driving down to the campground to prepare for the children's arrival. We had a group of brave adults who we had screened and tried to prepare for what was to come. We repeated what we heard Wayne tell us. This camp is different, the children are different, and we need to really love them like Jesus would love them.

Wayne told us a hundred times, *"Just bless the children!"*

I came back to the Norwalk church on Monday morning with some of our registration team. My eyes were immediately opened to the reality of foster care, Los Angeles County style. The foster parents who arrived that morning were some of the roughest, scariest adults I have ever seen in my life. Some really nice vans would pull in and seven or eight foster children would come clamoring out. The foster moms were going to school us all about LA foster care.

After a free lunch provided by our local McDonalds, delivered by Ronald McDonald himself (the kids were very impressed with that back then), we headed to camp on the *longest bus ride* of my life. Two adults and thirty-eight foster kids on a bus made for a really rough ride. I learned more about being a kid on the streets of LA than I ever wanted to know. We clearly didn't know a lot of things about the children *or* (and that's a big *or*) their LA ways. First mistake, as I mentioned: not enough adults. Second mistake: seating the boys and girls *together*. Third mistake: two of us sitting in the front of the bus. Fourth, fifth, and tenth mistake—well, you get the idea. We were exhausted before we ever arrived at camp. I think I was happier to see the camp counselors than the kids were.

You have to imagine this scene: the bus rolls into camp filled with 98 percent African American Los Angeles County foster children from famous cities and neighborhoods like Compton, Watts, Inglewood, South Central, and Lynwood. The crowd of shouting, cheering camp counselors and staff were 100 percent middle-class whites from suburban Lakewood.

It had to be a God thing that camp worked at all. We immediately learned a few things from the children. Mealtimes were stressful. I had never given much thought to words like *malnutrition*, *holding*, or *gorging*. My world didn't have children that were underfed, sugared up, or ate sporadically.

At camp, mealtimes created tension because the children were all together in one room and lacking in the social skills required for family-style service. I watched (as was featured in the movie *CAMP*) a little guy pile his plate with bacon and then consume every last piece. If you're wondering why we didn't stop him, I think the answer was that we were in shock that he would take that much food, and we were in complete denial and amazement that he would eat all of it.

Another time, I stopped a little guy from leaving the cafeteria with his pockets filled with cereal and fries. He started crying and throwing a fit. Finally he blurted out, "It's not for me, it's for my sister in case she gets hungry later!" Cleanup puddle of tears on aisle four. My world kept crumbling beneath me.

While my wife and I were walking from the swimming pool to the cafeteria, I was complaining and moaning about it being at such an exhausting camp. I was really upset because my birthday was coming up that Thursday, while we were at camp (I would turn 26).

Robin was trying to console me and confront my attitude when Jason spoke up behind me: "Hey, it's my birthday this week, too!"

Without realizing it, a group of children had been following us. I was so embarrassed. Did you know that children listen to adult conversations? I found out that they do. I spun around and got down on his level to ask about his favorite birthday gift or party (a common question I ask kids). His answer stripped away what little I had left of my worldview.

"I've never had a birthday party."

I didn't have any words. I was stunned. I grew up in a very chaotic childhood, and yet even we had birthday celebrations. What kind of world do I live in where children are not celebrated, are not told how precious they are, are not recognized at all? Oh, so this is the world of abandonment, abuse, and neglect.

Injustice consumed my thoughts, and I had a choice to make. I could play the "oh, that's sad" game and go on my way, or I could choose to make a difference to this one. I went down to the nearest store and bought a watch for Jason. I asked my wife how I should go about giving it to him. She replied back with a much more complicated question.

"What about the other children? How many of them haven't had a birthday celebration?"

I was trying to do my one "God deed" and take care of Jason, and along comes a mom who thinks about *all the children*. I thought Jason's story was an anomaly, an outlier. We asked and found out that *none* of the children had birthday celebrations, and two of the little girls didn't even know the date they were born.

What's wrong with us? We can procreate, but we can't celebrate? We can make children, but can't nurture them? Not on my watch; not while they are in our care. We had birthday celebrations for every camper. We sang the song, we ate the cake, and we had presents for each one of them. They tore into the gifts while the adults stood by and cried a mixture of joy and shame.

Oh, the children have taught us plenty. I can say that they have wrecked my world, and now I see them all in shades of royal purple. I'm a "lifer" because I am no longer ignoring our responsibility and calling to the least of these, our modern-day orphans. All we wanted to do was run a camp for hurting children. Then all we wanted to be was world changers. Now, we understand the importance of just changing the world of one.

12

DAVE AND LYNELL BROOKS
Camp Directors, Costa Mesa, California

Lynell's Memories

Having been the nurse for Sonshine Kids Kamp with Wayne and Diane Tesch for several years, I was asked to come alongside them again in this new adventure for a different group of children at the very first Royal Family KIDS Camp. I remember the planning meetings in Wayne's office at Newport-Mesa Christian Center, then talking through what we could do and how we should go about it. We had no idea what we were getting into. We thought we knew how to do kid's camps. How wrong we were!

In my home, I have a file drawer dedicated to Royal Family KIDS, and I found notes from those early years of camp in there. We reserved a week in the summer of 1985 at the newly re-opened Camp Pinecrest. It had new dorms, but everything else was old or under construction. We were a small group of sixty, and with no kitchen we ate all our catered meals in the snack shack. For recreation there was a nice archery range with new equipment and a basketball court. There was no pool, no grassy area, no playing field, and lots of construction going on. Lake Gregory was not far away, so we bussed the campers there, paying $1.50 per person admission, plus $1.75 for the waterslide.

We took thirty-seven campers and twenty-three untrained staff to this "cathedral of the outdoors." We had no idea how volatile the campers were, and there were constant fights while lining up for meals, in the chapel time, and at the games. The children did not listen to directions at story time or any other time. The techniques we had used at our other kid's camp did not work with these children. All of us were unprepared for the challenges of that week. Personally, as the camp nurse, I had never seen so many medications for children.

It was all very overwhelming and one of the most exhausting weeks of my life. After dragging myself into the house when I returned home, I told my husband I felt like a ceramic pitcher that had been totally poured out and then left in the sun to bake for a week. I was so dried out, so empty, both physically and spiritually. I had seen the challenges for Wayne too. I told my husband he needed to go with me the next summer.

"To do what?" he asked. I said, "Just be there for Wayne, just walk with him, support him, help him with whatever he needs."

David said he could do that. Thus started a thirty-year commitment for the Brooks family.

It takes a whole church to have a Royal Family KIDS Camp. Some need to go to the camp as counselors and staff. Some need to help at the church the first day when the kids leave for camp and others on the last day when they return. Others need to give; others need to pray. Still others take care of children for those going. In 1986, when both David and I were planning to go to camp, our daughters were eleven, nine, and seven. This was not the kind of camp where you just put the staff kids in with their age group. For two summers, a close friend who lived three hundred miles away kept our girls for the week. We each drove half way and we passed the kids off at an In-N-Out restaurant. That was a lot of effort for everyone. Year three I asked another friend who lived locally if she would take the girls and she said yes. When we got back, I found out her two children had been at a summer camp all week, and she had taken our girls when she could have had a week free. The next year, she asked me if she could have the "girlies," and it became an annual tradition for our children. What memories they have of "Camp Siemon." What a blessing to David and I to be relieved of the worry for our own children as we were ministering to other children. To this day, our adult girls have a lasting relationship with this wonderful family who shared a week of the summer with them for so many years.

DAVID'S MEMORIES

Flying the police helicopter over the church in the summer of 1985 on the day the campers were to leave and seeing that the children were still there because the bus had not shown up was my first realization that it was going to be a tough week.

Then my wife came home so broken, so exhausted. She had come home from many camps but never this defeated. That was when I saw the need to get involved.

That second year, the camp was still not completed and there were no water fountains where the campers could get water throughout the day. It was very hot, so I got containers and cups to place in strategic locations around the camp to hydrate the children and staff.

We also realized the counselors and staff needed a place to get away for breaks throughout the day. So keeping chests filled with ice and beverages and snacks available for them became part of my job for the week. Seeing a need and filling it.

The campers came with such limited supplies, and even those were in a trash bag. Shoes that did not fit or were so worn out they were useful only as flip-flops, torn underwear, no socks. I remember Grandma and Grandpa McNutt tracing campers' feet on a piece of paper so I could go to town and find shoes that would fit them. In later years, Grandma and Grandpa took up this task, and when the shop clerks learned that they were buying these items for children at a camp, they often gave a discount or donated the items.

There were still no real play areas for the children those first couple of years, except the basketball court. We lined them up in there for morning exercises, played basketball, and divided the area for other activities. One year we had Big Wheels, and after trying them on the road, which was too steep, we decided to make a Big Wheel course in the basketball court. It was all set up, ready for the kids. A little later in the day, I went to get ready for the kids to arrive to ride Big Wheels and found a sixty- or seventy-foot pine tree had been cut by the construction crew, and was lying across the basketball court and the Big Wheel course.

This was part of the work going on at the camp. It needed to be done, and our need for a play area came second to that. I talked with the camp staff, and they had no intention of getting that tree cut up and out of the court before the campers arrived to ride the course.

I was unhappy about this unforeseen situation. I very frankly discussed with the staff the need to get this tree out of the way so we could use the basketball court. They did not see how that could be done in such a short time.

Using my best police command voice, I looked at the tree people and said, "Roll it!"

And roll it they did! Those guys got in there and moved that huge tree off to one side of that court so we could reset the Big Wheel course as planned.

Another experience was a trip to the emergency room. In an outdoor amphitheater, new benches had been built from wooden planks. These were rough-hewn, not a sanded finish, and one of the unforeseen consequences of the new benches turned out to be a six-inch splinter in a male camper's behind. These kids are pretty tough, and he handled this situation extremely well. He was loaded up into a van, and the nurse and I took him to the hospital. This incident became the "butt" of many jokes that week from the campers and the staff.

From the emergency room to the archery range—last day of camp. Balloons are attached to the hay bales, lots of balloons so all the campers get to participate. This was a huge confidence builder for them to pop these balloons with an arrow.

One particular camper who had not been able to hit the target all week kept shooting the arrows over the bales, way past the balloons. As I was watching this, I sent up an "arrow prayer" that this camper could pop a balloon. Just then, a gust of wind came up and a balloon broke away from a bale. As it was floating away, the camper shot his arrow, piercing that balloon in midair. What a thrill for the camper and for me. Thank you, Lord, for another answered prayer for these precious children.

After my second year of being the utility man, in 1987 Wayne invited me to one of those famous lunches of his. He asked me to take the leadership of the camp, to be the director. This is Wayne's leadership model: do it one year, bring someone alongside the next year, and then hand it off to them to do it. Wayne was going to bring people up to the camp to see it, to share a vision he had for what we now know as Royal Family KIDS, Inc., but he needed a director to take it on from here. I had performed a lot of volunteer work, had worked a few summers at this particular camp facility as a teen, but this would be my first attempt at leading a team of volunteers in making memories for these very special young people. I talked this over with my wife and we knew we should do this, but would need to work together. This was not about a week in the summer time. This was a yearlong commitment. So in 1988, the baton was passed from Wayne Tesch to David Brooks, who became the second director of the Costa Mesa Royal Family KIDS Camp. That summer we took eighty-one campers, forty-one counselors, plus staff. The camp had grown considerably in a short time. My wife, Lynell, was my right-hand person, and it was a big surprise to learn I was also responsible to raise the funds for the camp. It did not take long to realize the need for an assistant director.

After bringing Bill Richardson onto the leadership team, I had an experience that changed my thinking and how we organized our camp. My leadership style is to know how to do whatever it is I am asking someone else to do. Here I was leading a group of counselors, and I had never been an RFKC counselor. So I asked the assistant director to take the lead one summer so I could be a counselor. What an eye-opening experience that was. I realized how many times one had to say the same thing over and over, and keeping track of your campers was not as easy as it sounded. Doing activities that were unfamiliar, or not necessarily my choice, but what the campers wanted, was challenging. The unintended consequences of some of the rules that had been established became clear as well. That experience led to changes in the guidelines and rules for the camp. Years later it was my joy to write a reference for one of my campers who landed a quality job that started him on a professional career path.

As I have been looking through the items in our file cabinet, I found the agendas for leadership meetings, where the training for the counselors and staff was developed.

Connie Counselor was one of the training ideas. It was a skit, using a tool box with items that the counselors would need for a week at RFKC, such as a key because "you are the key" to these campers, a funny hat with a tag with "PMA," for Positive Mental Attitude, and other things forgotten over the past thirty years that Diane Tesch incorporated into the amazing formal training available to the leaders today.

Then there was the personality assessment in the form of colored T-shirts that helped us understand as leaders that we needed the complete array of the four colors on the leadership team. Those of us like David, who is red, and me, who is blue (all organized, but no fun), needed the yellows, who loved fun and spontaneity, and the greens who did not want to rock the boat but wanted peace and calm. These skills learned and taught to the RFKC team are skills I still use today. I assess new employees with this personality test. I still need all the colors on my team. I know that humor is important in teaching adults as well as children, and so much can be caught and taught through music.

Then there were all the fundraising projects. We did a bass-fishing tournament for a number of years, garage sales, coin cans ("your change can change a life"), gift wrapping at Macy's one Christmas, and then the bike-a-thon, which has become Tour de Orange County, California, is a very well-organized cycling event. Since those years, a wonderful karate tournament funds a large portion of the Newport Mesa Church camp today.

The last notes I have are from 1995, when we realized the need to split the responsibilities up for the director of the camp. It was a heavy load to prepare and lead the camp, plus do all the fundraising. The leadership team came together and decided to add an executive director who would do the fundraising, a director, and assistant director would do the preparation and lead the week of camp assisted by the dean of men, dean of women, and the rest of the staff needed for the week. David took the executive position and I was made the director that year assisted by Jim Manifold and David and Kathleen Hayford, as the deans of men and women. I remember falling in love with the book of Nehemiah as I studied to lead this wonderful team and make memories for the campers who would be coming up the hill that summer. Years earlier when our youngest was an infant, I went to a women's retreat and had an interesting spiritual experience. During a quiet time of prayer and reflection alone, I saw in my mind's eye a woman walking in a field with a clipboard in her hand. I shared that with a close friend and later when we were home, she gave me a clipboard so when the time came that the Lord was preparing for me, I would be ready. Now years later I found myself at Camp Pinecrest again, (a place where I had been a camper and then worked for three summers during high school) walking around with a clipboard in my hand, working with children who needed a chance to be kids if only for a week, because a week of RFKC changes lives.

Thank you, Wayne and Diane, for listening to the call of God and setting sail into the unknown. Because of your obedience to God, thousands and thousands of lives have been influenced and changed. It certainly has changed mine for the better.

13

BILL RICHARDSON
Camp Director, Costa Mesa, California

I began my journey with Royal Family KIDS in 1986 when my wife, Donna, was selected to be a counselor in the second year of Royal Family KIDS Camp. Basically, I came to camp at Pinecrest Christian Conference Center four out of five days and just helped out with whatever needed to be done. You need to understand that in those early days there were no specific rules about background checks, fingerprinting, and so on. Because I attended Newport-Mesa Christian Center, now Newport-Mesa Church, and knew Wayne Tesch, I was allowed to come to Pinecrest and help out in the background.

Most of my experiences with camp have been very positive, but that first night I arrived at camp was a Tuesday. There had been a problem with one of the twelve-year-old boys who was being sent home. Gary Huntley and I were tasked with taking him home and explaining to his foster parents what had happened at camp. It was an introduction to the difficult decisions camp directors must make in the interest of protecting campers and their experience at camp. This lesson would play out as an example for me over the next twenty-five years.

In year two, 1987, I went to camp as an activity center worker. I had gone to the Huntington Beach Police Department and obtained four bicycles from their lost and found. The bikes were scheduled to be sold because the owners had not claimed them for over a year.

My intent was to have a bike repair activity center, where the campers could learn how to work on bikes: changing tires, tightening chains, and general "tune-ups" that made the bikes a little safer and made them operate better.

One of the eleven-year-old boys came to the activity center and proceeded to completely dismantle a bike, and I mean completely, right down to the cones and bearings in the wheels. He then put it all back together in about twenty minutes. After putting it together he said he wanted to "test drive" the bike, and he proceeded down Pinecrest Road toward Highway 118 and San Bernardino. Fortunately, he returned to the activity center, but not before he gave Dave Brooks, the camp's assistant director and me a real scare. It turned out his bike "repair" skills had come from a rather shady past. He had been caught stealing bikes, stripping them down, and rebuilding them so they couldn't be recognized.

Another incident related to the bike center was a young female camper learning to ride a bike for the first time. To me, this emphasized the positive, practical teaching aspects of camp and the opportunity for the campers to do something they otherwise would have to wait many years to accomplish.

In my third year at camp I became Dave Brooks's assistant director. He had now become director of the Costa Mesa Camp. A lot of truly inspirational things happened in those early years, one of which was when Dave, a police lieutenant at the time, John White, a fire captain, and I, a lifeguard lieutenant, all did some chapel time wearing our uniforms. We had heard the stories of how many of the campers had negative experiences with men in uniform, as these were often the ones who removed them from their homes.

Our idea was to share with the campers that officers in uniform are not a threat to them but that their interests are the safety and well-being of young people just like them. We shared about our jobs, our families, and our relationship with our Father in heaven. All in all, it was a positive experience for the campers and for Dave, John, and me as well.

That same year, Wayne and I had speaking engagements in Orange County during camp. Wayne went to a church function, and I went to the Hoag Hospital Lifeguard Seminar. On the ride back to Newport Beach from camp, Wayne shared his vision for expanding Royal Family KIDS Camp and developing more camps in order to reach more kids. I truly believe that was the seed God had planted in Wayne for the future and for what Royal Family KIDS has become today.

By 1988 I had become the camp's director, and we had grown from thirty-five campers to about sixty. More defined roles had developed in camp with individuals having specific skill sets being placed in positions to use their skills to make the camp experience even more positive for the campers.

Swimming became a big part of camp, not just for the campers, but as a means of allowing the counselors a little down time, if for no other reason than to get a shower. But the commitment of our counselors has always been such that many of them give up this free time to get into the pool with their campers, just to have fun!

Sports also became a great activity at camp. Coach Ed Davis began providing athletic activities in the afternoon. The one key that Coach Ed employed in his activities was that the score was always a tie and that everyone was a winner.

I remember that the dramas had evolved into very specific messages for the campers. Johanna Townsend and Rene Davis, Coach Ed's wife, had written three dramas: *In Search of God's Kingdom,* an Indiana Jones type story, *The Sheep Fold,* the relationship of the Good Shepherd with His flock, and *The Olympics,* relating the value of running and completing the good race. Eventually these dramas were rewritten and expanded to more dramas. But the themes remained the same, and the message of hope and love remained the keys to presenting positive information to the campers.

Chapel time had become more specific in its presentation with music, drama, and fun activities to make the message enjoyable and meaningful. While we sometimes don't recognize that the message is getting through, one of my favorite stories validates that what we do makes a difference.

We were in chapel. One of the boys who had difficulty with the sound volume was sitting in the back of the chapel with no shoes on. I noticed that his feet had sores on them. When I asked what happened, he explained that his shoes didn't fit right. It turns out that he needed shoes nearly two sizes larger than what he was wearing.

I immediately contacted our "camp go-fer," Nate Molstad, and had him make a special trip to buy the proper size shoes for this camper. One of the miracles in this incident was that the shoe store had just closed when he arrived, but the manager, who knew of our camp and what we do there, opened the door so the purchase could be made.

When Nate got back to camp with the shoes, he went directly to the dorm and the camper's room. When presented with the new shoes, the camper got really excited, and couldn't believe that the new shoes were for him. We wrote his name in them so he would know they belonged to him.

But the story doesn't end there. The camper gave his old shoes to Nate and asked if they could be given to someone who needed them. The next day one of the young female campers soiled her shoes badly, and while they were being cleaned she needed another pair of shoes. You got it! The boy's shoes, which had been cleaned up by our nurses, were a perfect fit. And they matched her counselor's shoes, which made it "totally cool." It was another small miracle.

In the early years of our camp, we had to beg, borrow, and rely on difficult fundraising tactics to pay for our camp. We did garage sales, used cans to collect coins, and a myriad of other things to try to pay for camp. Our church often helped to underwrite the cost of camp. In all the time our camp has been in existence, we have utilized an estimated $1.9 million, making maximum use of kingdom dollars in serving more than two thousand campers, bringing our average camper attendance to ninety-four in recent years.

Today, we have two very specific fundraisers that are dedicated to raising funds for our camp and club program. The Bob and Barbra White Invitational Youth Karate Tournament (BBWI) and the Tour de OC (TDOC) Bike-A-Thon provide for our every need as a camp and club. The BBWI alone has raised more than a half-million dollars for our camp in nine years of putting on the tournament. The TDOC has provided more than one $100,000 in funding over the years and expects to provide even more in the future.

The relationship with Bob and Barbara White has been exceptional. Barbara is our head nurse at camp and does phenomenal work there. Their daughters have been counselors and staff at our camp, but the White's commitment to Royal Family KIDS goes far beyond just our camp relationship and the funding they provide for our camp. They have instilled in others in their Kenpo community the desire to help raise funds for camps across the nation. Their aspiration and commitment are an inspiration to us all.

In 2014, Newport-Mesa Church marked thirty years of conducting camps. We are fortunate to have been selected as one of the training camps in the western region of the United States and are honored to have both Directors' Training and Passing the Scepter training conducted at our camp. Numerous camps have been impacted by having their personnel attend training at our camp. We feel blessed to be a part of helping to continue the legacy of Royal Family KIDS in this small way.

One of the keys to our success as a camp has always been the dedicated people who come to share and display the love of God with the children. Probably the best definition I have personally heard came in a letter from one of our staff in 2013, when he was not going to be able to return to camp for the first time after serving for ten years with us. His message was so powerful I feel it is important to share it in its entirety.

His letter was entitled "The Call."

When you break down Royal Family KIDS Camp, there are two main aspects. The first is the lost and broken children that we experience and interact with.

As a member of the volunteer staff we immediately become examples of the legacy of Christ's unconditional love, the most powerful force in all the earth. A love that knows no bound.

We are called to love the "least of these." These children are societies "least of these." They are often forgotten, put aside, and unimportant. As they grow up, they struggle with their past, their future, and what they will become.

One verse rings in my mind as I think of our campers. "He raises the poor from the dust and lifts the needy from the ash heap; he seats them with princes and has them inherit a throne of honor. For the foundations of the earth are the LORD's; on them he has set the world'" (1 Samuel 2:8, NIV).

So much power is placed in our hands as ambassadors of Christ. This is the call for Royal Family to take the needy and forgotten and set them on their rightful thrones.

I will never forget a few years ago when we were in chapel and a certain camper, who was sitting in the back, was listening intently to the morning message. The whole week he had not focused on a thing that was said, except this devotional. When the speaker said, "Do you know that you are all kings in God's eyes?" he perked up and listened intently to what was being said.

Right afterward he ran outside to his counselor and said, "Do you know God thinks I am a King?"

That boy gave his life to Christ at that camp and we saw a radical change in the following years. It was not because the speaker said something so radical that it changed his life. It was because he found belonging, importance, and security. Somebody loved him! That is our job, whether we have the easiest camper or the hardest one, our job is to love.

That is the calling of camp, to love unconditionally!

The second aspect of camp is the radical life change that takes place in the hearts of the volunteers.

My family has a rich heritage with Royal Family, a legacy that carries on today. My parents made the decision to adopt me because of this camp. My life was radically and forever changed at this camp.

As I have become a man, my experiences and the heart-wrenching things I have seen have molded me into a better husband, father, and son.

Not only has camp altered my personal life, but it has seeded my place in heaven. So many years I came to camp to serve relentlessly for others. Now as I sit on the brink of missing one year, I realize that camp is so much more than just helping others, *it grounds me.*

As volunteers we get so caught up in the aspect of serving that we forget Jesus wants a relationship with us as well. This is His time to mold us and grow us into the men and women He has called us to be.

Victories are not won by mere happenstance. Victories are won by warriors. Warriors of the faith are the most feared of all.

This week history is being written, legacies are being formed. How will we leave these legacies? Will we quit when adversity rises or will we draw strength from Christ and persevere?

One thing remains, LOVE! That is it! It is that simple. Love conquers all things. First Corinthians 13 is the "Call," the answer, and the key to changing lives this week. Love leaves the ultimate legacy that will last a lifetime.

OHHHH, am I going to miss you guys this week! My heart and prayers are with you! At times people forget the sacrifice you and your families give for this camp. You two have had one of the largest impacts on my life and on the lives of literally thousands of children. We have spent many summers together. It has truly been an honor to learn from you and serve with you.

In my twenty-five years at camp, I have seen this scenario played out over and over. Our intent is to serve the children, but in the end we are blessed by them and the changes we often see in them.

We are also blessed in the changes God makes in us. Our church is fortunate to be on the campus of Vanguard University, therefore many of our counselors come from the university. The students hope to do their practicum and get credit for the time they serve. That they do, but many end up changing their majors to take classes that will lead them on a path of social work, or working with kids and adults who need the kind of experience Royal Family KIDS provides for our campers.

On our staff we have three educators who teach classes in social sciences, counseling, and psychology. Two of them are part of the five-person team we have at camp as our "camp counselors," and many of their students are counselors.

The changes in the lives of the children can be measured in what we see in their demeanor and the fact that previous campers are now coming back to camp to be able to share a similar experience with kids who were like they were, and to relate the grace and love of Christ in a meaningful way.

In the summer of 2014 we rejoiced as five former campers participated in our camp. One new former camper joined us, and three returned for the second time, along with Jason Howell, who celebrated his sixteenth year as a counselor at our camp. Jason was a camper in 1985, and Tony Choi was his counselor.

The personal impact and changes I have enjoyed include understanding my role as a leader better. With a staff of more than one hundred, I have had to learn how to work with volunteers in a meaningful and productive way, while at the same time maintaining the strength in leadership required when having that many people working with and under me.

All of us who have experienced RFKC these past thirty years wish to express our sincerest gratitude to Wayne and Diane Tesch, the staff of Royal Family KIDS, and to the members and staff at Newport Mesa Church for continuing the vision and in supporting the cause of reaching out to hurting children in our community.

On behalf of all of the counselors and staff of RFKC-Newport Mesa, and especially from the children, thank you for your continuing investment in the future of kids who are otherwise discarded, abandoned, and left without much hope.

14

JEFF JUHALA
VP of Training

OUR RFK JOURNEY BEGINS

Can a ministry that alters the direction of your life begin with a discarded dream in a trash can? Well, for us it did!

Our church's new children's pastor, Phil Popineau, had longed to be at a church where he could start a Royal Family KIDS Camp. Pastor Phil invited Wayne Tesch, RFK's co-founder, to come and speak to a group of children's workers with the intent to start a camp. After hearing the ministry explained, my wife, Janet, and I thought it sounded like a great ministry, and we would become camp counselors whenever it got started. We had both been involved with youth camps and family camps when we were growing up in church, so it felt like a great fit to take our wonderful childhood memories from our camp experiences and be able to create those same experiences for kids in the foster care system. We had both grown up in great families and safe child-hoods, so the opportunity to use camp as a ministry to hurting kids was instantly of interest to both of us.

Two or three couples in the meeting raised their hands and indicated that they might be interested in being directors and starting the ministry, so we awaited the announcement of the camp getting started, and promptly forgot all about it.

Right about the time of that meeting, my wife and I began feeling a special burden in our hearts for orphans. It was not an overwhelming instant impression, but something that we began to notice over the next eighteen to twenty-four months. David Grant, a missionary from India, came and spoke at a missions convention at our church and spoke about the hundreds of thousands of orphans in India. Somehow, his words just seemed to penetrate deeply into our hearts about those orphans. I'm sure we had heard about orphans before, but this time it seemed as if the words were meant just for us. Our church, Calvary Temple Church in Concord, California, was already supporting Angie Thomson, a missionary to the orphans in Romania. Angie had been to our church numerous times to raise awareness and funds for their ministry to orphans.

Our hearts had always been touched by this ministry, and we had given financially to help support the cause, but the next time we heard from Angie, the pictures and the stories of the orphans just seemed to hit us at a deeper level. Janet and I would look at each other during a church service as if we were each saying, "Do you think God is saying something to us right now about orphans?" Because we felt this move of God in our hearts and heads, we would occasionally talk about it and pray about it. Not knowing what to pray exactly, just telling God we recognized something was happening and we wanted to be open to wherever He was leading us.

On another occasion, I was driving to work when I heard a man speaking on the radio about the orphans he was working with in Cambodia. Once again, it just seemed to extend out of the radio right into my heart. I told Janet all about it when I got home and once again, we stopped and prayed, although we didn't know what for exactly. We both felt this burden, so we began to pray about what the Lord wanted to do with us in this area. The Lord continued to tug at our hearts about orphans over the next twelve to eighteen months. We would occasionally pray about it, wait, and wonder why we had a burden for orphans.

THE TRASH CAN

I had a meeting planned with Pastor Phil, and I told Janet I would ask him to be in prayer with us about this burden for orphans. We concluded our original discussion, and just as I was leaving, I remembered to ask him about the orphans. I was literally reaching for the door to leave when I turned around and said, "Pastor Phil, I know you have a lot of other things to pray about, but if you have any extra prayer time, would you and Barbara pray for Janet and me about orphans?"

As I walked back to his desk, I mentioned that we had been praying and feeling very strongly that God was definitely putting orphans on our hearts, but we just didn't know what to do with those strong "nudges." Pastor Phil was sitting in his chair at his desk, and he looked at me with a funny sort of look. He swung his chair around and reached into the trash can behind his desk and pulled out a book written by Wayne and Diane Tesch, *Unlocking the Secret World of Child Abuse*. He asked me if I remembered the meeting when Wayne Tesch explained what Royal Family KIDS Camps was all about.

"Yes, I remember. What ever happened with that?"

"Nothing! Nothing has happened for two years, even though several couples were interested in being the directors, it hasn't worked out for any of them."

Pastor Phil and Barbara had continued to pray for someone else to take the role as a camp director. They had talked to several other people they felt would be qualified, they handed out books about the camp, and had worked hard to find someone, but as of that time and for different reasons, no one had either been interested or available.

That morning Pastor Phil was praying in his office, wondering if he had missed something. Was he all wrong about starting a Royal Family KIDS Camp at our church? It had been two years since Wayne spoke that night and, so far, nothing. They had been sending their prayers up to God, but they had been hearing nothing. They had been asking people to be the director, but it always ended in no. Earlier that morning in his office, Pastor Phil was looking at the books on his shelf. When Wayne spoke at the church two years before, he had left a number of extra books to hand out. Pastor Phil had been giving these books out to prospective directors to get them interested in becoming a camp director. As he looked at his extra books on the shelf, he left one book on the shelf and tossed the rest in the trash can, as if to say, "Lord if it's not going to happen, then let's just move on!" There went Pastor Phil and Barbra's dream of starting an RFK camp in Concord, right into the trash can.

Later that same morning, I walked into his office and shared our burden about working with orphans. Pastor Phil handed me the book from out of the trash can, and said, "Maybe you could do something with orphans right here in this country." He went on to tell how he had been praying and asking and only hearing no from people.

As I left his office, I thought, "That was very interesting." Maybe this is why God has been giving us a burden for orphans. I took the book home and shared the story with Janet. She, too, felt like God might be up to something.

THE SILENCE OF DREAMS AND PRAYERS

As Pastor Phil and Barbara were praying, God was answering, but the answer was coming to Janet and me. I can imagine they thought their prayers were not being answered at all, because they weren't finding a camp director, while all along God was answering their prayers by speaking to our hearts through various missionaries and the stirring of our hearts whenever we heard about orphans.

As we read *Unlocking the Secret World of Child Abuse*, we read the story, the history, and the miracles of how Royal Family KIDS Camps had begun. As we read, we realized this just might be what God was calling us to do.

OUR LIFE-CHANGING WEEK OF CAMP

We attended RFK's weeklong directors' training in Portland, Oregon, with more than thirty potential directors from other churches and states. Unbeknownst to us, that week would be the start of a brand new journey for our lives. To me, it was one of the most emotional, faith-building, eye-opening, God-inspiring weeks of my life.

Janet and I both come from good Christian homes with wonderful parents and great siblings who truly care for each other. We knew there were other kids better off than us, and there were some less fortunate than us. We had never studied child abuse and never really knew anyone who had been abused. At least, that's what we thought at that time.

As I have been educated from my camp experiences, I've come to realize we all know people who have been abused, we just don't know that we know them. It takes a lot for someone to let you into their deepest secrets, and most people have learned that it's usually better to just keep it quiet and try to blend in. I remember the training exposing us to the statistics of abuse, but it was the stories of kids who had been abused, and in terrible ways, that ruined me. I guess I knew about abuse from news reports, but this training revealed the reality of abuse and its effect on children.

The story that shook my mind was the father whose son was afraid of snakes. The father attempted to cure the son's fear of snakes by putting him in a sleeping bag with snakes in it, and then tying up the end of the sleeping bag. Our trainer said, "This is not child abuse, this is child traumatization; it goes beyond abuse."

The story bothered me in class, but it was later in our room that it finally struck me that I had no clue about some things in our world. Janet and I talked that night after class, I sat on my bed and thought of that little boy in the sleeping bag. Fathers are supposed to protect their children and provide for them. That's the example that both Janet and I grew up with in our families. But my mind could not comprehend this story. I could not understand how a father would purposely bring that kind of hurt, terror, and trauma to his son. Are there really people out there who hurt their children with purpose and intent? How could someone do that? As I thought about it, sitting in our room there in Portland, Oregon, I just broke down and cried for that little boy.

AND SO THE JOURNEY BEGINS

Those may have been the first tears I shed while being involved in this ministry, but they would not be the last. Over the years, I have read about and heard so many stories of abuse. People who lock a child in a dog kennel, molest them, or find tortuous ways to cause great pain. Some of these victims have shared their stories with me personally. Even celebrities such as Chevy Chase and James Garner have endured horrible abuse. Their books describe the horrors they endured as children and their ability, or lack thereof, to overcome. In the book, *"I'm Chevy Chase . . . And You're Not,"* author Rena Fruchter describes how Chevy was abused both physically and emotionally by both this mother and step-father. The abuse was so bad that Chevy could not forgive them even after their deaths. Chevy said, "I'll never forgive them. At their graves I didn't. It was too hard for me. You would think a grown man could shake it off, as the coffin was being lowered, to say, 'I forgive you.' I don't forgive." Chevy's mother and stepfather had become monsters in his life.

The training from Royal Family was my first exposure to the fact that some children have monsters in their lives instead of parents, guardians, and protectors. How can there be such monsters?

Matthew 18:6 (NIV) reads, "If anyone causes one of these little ones— those who believe in me—to stumble, it would be better for them to have a large millstone hung around their neck and to be drowned in the depths of the sea."

If you only cause them to stumble and you'll be thrown into the sea, how much more for those who have become monsters to the little ones?

When we left directors' training, we had been trained on how to put on a camp, but we knew we could only do it with God's help. I remember saying to God, "God, I have no idea how Janet and I can raise fifteen-to-twenty thousand dollars for camp. I'll ask, but You have to make people say yes. I have no idea how we can get thirty adults to volunteer to take a week of vacation for someone else's kids. I'll ask, but You'll have to make them say yes. I have no idea how Janet and I can find the four-to-six hundred hours in our already busy lives, but we will rework our schedules and carve out some additional hours, and then we need You, God, to multiply those few hours like the fishes and the loaves of bread, and make those few hours turn into hundreds of hours."

As I left training that week, I could not help but think that that week was probably one of the most impactful weeks of my life.

JANET'S TURN

I remember our first day of training. We were excited and full of wonder: what was this whole Royal Family KIDS Camp really all about? Is this what God had been preparing us for the last two years as we've felt a burden for orphans? So, on day one, my emotions quickly turned from excitement to extreme sorrow and stunned disbelief as we heard sickening stories of horrific abuse done to precious, innocent children. My heart was broken for these kids, and the tears flowed freely. I remember thinking at that time, how can we *not* do this? These kids need love, God's love, and lots of it.

Jeff and I, at that time, had been blessed with three beautiful children we loved immensely. They meant the world to us! I could not comprehend how anyone could ever purposefully and intentionally, maliciously hurt and neglect such precious gifts.

We finished the week of training. Everything was done with excellence. We had been treated like royalty. We had been treated like family. We had been thoroughly trained and encouraged to start a camp. I was sure this was exactly what God wanted us to do, however, my initial thought was, *We don't have an extra four hundred to six hundred hours to do this.* Our kids were one, three, and five years old. "Busy" does not even *begin* to describe our lives. How in the world can we do this?

One evening, soon after we got back home from training, after we'd put our kids to bed, we were watching the news. There was a brief story about a child being harmed in some way, and it made me just want to go pray for my kids. I went to my room to pray and ask God to protect and keep my kids safe from evil people.

As I poured out my heart to God, I heard Him whisper, "I love your kids more than you do."

I felt immediate peace. I began to thank Him, and then I heard Him whisper again, "And I love the abused and abandoned kids too. They just don't know it yet."

At that moment, I knew I had been truly called by God to do this.

I also couldn't help but remember the book and the trash can. Out of the trash can, the book and the dream had been revived. Many of our future campers had been swept off the table of life and into the trash can. Now, we would be taking the kids out of the trash can and reviving their dreams too!

CAMP DIRECTING AT THE CORNER OF FAITH AND WORKS

We went on to direct the Concord, California, camp from 2001 to 2006 with the help of so many great volunteers. Through it all, we have become so much closer to God, the Supreme Camp Director. For us, directing a camp became the biggest step of faith we had ever taken, and the biggest volunteer job we had ever led. Our experience with our previous ministries simply required us to show up and work hard. But directing a camp required us to show up, work harder than we ever had before, and take a step of faith into the unknown.

Hebrews 11:1 (KJV) says, "Now faith is the substance of things hoped for, the evidence of things not seen." The "not seen" part was where we had to sign a contract with a campground, believing we would raise the money, but not "seeing" it in the bank yet. It was believing, in faith, that we could recruit the volunteers and have the time to get all the work done. The first year built great faith in us, only to have us strengthen our faith muscles each year trying to grow, or recruit new volunteers, or raise more money than we had the previous year. But that is how faith grows, from stepping into the unknown and finding God's hands under your feet.

Our faith grew, but so did our works. Directing a camp is so much work, but the work is worth it. There's a great phrase I've read in the past that states, "We never said it would be easy, but it will be worth it." That's camp directing to a tee! Hours and hours of paperwork, phone calls, meetings, fundraising, interviews, set up, tear down, loading and unloading. I remember several nights telling Janet between 11:30 p.m. and 12:30 a.m., "Janet, I've hit the wall, I can't do any more, I'm going to bed."

Of course, the kids at camp have absolutely no idea how much work it takes. How could they know? One former camper came back as a volunteer counselor and discovered how hard it was during the week of camp. The former camper remarked, "As campers we had no idea how much work this was. We just thought you guys stood around most of the day." Ha, we wish.

> What good is it, my brothers and sisters, if someone claims to have faith but has no deeds? Can such faith save them? Suppose a brother or a sister is without clothes and daily food. If one of you says to them, "Go in peace; keep warm and well fed," but does nothing about their physical needs, what good is it? In the same way, faith by itself, if it is not accompanied by action, is dead (James 2:14–17 NIV).

One of the things that attracted me to RFK was the faith and the works. It's not just a ministry of faith, it's literally doing something about the physical needs of the kids we serve. It may be providing clothes, birthday presents, first-time experiences on a climbing wall, or riding a horse. We were doing more than just saying, "Go in peace and keep warm." We were actually providing a place of peace and safety with custom-made quilts and blankets, three meals a day, and photo albums to hold onto the great memories forever. Camps and clubs are faith in action.

Faith and works also means we follow the interests of the campers. Working with the state means we don't proselytize, but we do share our lives, our dreams, and our examples of living. If the kids want to know more about faith and ask questions, then we answer their questions. I've seen some campers who have a deep theological thirst for God. And then there's the one camper who said, "Jesus, Jesus, Jesus, you keep talking about this guy. When's he coming to camp?" We follow their interests because some kids want to catch the faith, but some kids want to catch the frogs.

Applying faith and works did amazing things in us. For Janet and me, getting involved with Royal Family KIDS opened a chamber of compassion in our hearts that we did not know existed. We had a hidden capacity for loving and laboring on behalf of foster children, and RFK opened the door and let that love and labor come out.

A Place for Mary

One of the most memorable stories from camp came as a last-minute effort. Four days before camp was to begin our social worker discovered that one of the girls dropped out and we had no replacement. About the same time, a foster mom contacted the church asking if her foster daughter could return to camp. We really wanted to get this girl to camp, but there was little time and no energy to go through all the steps necessary at the last minute. I was exhausted, and most of our team was already overburdened with last-minute preparations for the camp. I stopped by the home of our camp nurse to drop off some materials for camp and before I left, she looked at me and said, "Jeff, is there anything else you need?"

She said it in such a way that it stood out, and rather than just say, "No, we've got it covered," I told her about the open spot and the girl who was interested in coming back to camp, but I didn't have the time to find the foster mom, get the forms completed, signed, and cleared by her social worker.

Nurse Diane said, "Give me the paperwork and the phone number, and we'll see what we can do." Diane made it happen, which is a tribute to our great camp volunteers, the people who get it done and have a heart for kids.

Mary (not her real name), came to camp and seemed to have a great time. She was quiet and reserved, but she loved the activity center and made several projects at the metalwork station. At the talent show, she sang a beautiful song a cappella. Nobody knew she could sing so well. Several of the adults specifically told her how well she had done, and that she had a beautiful voice. That night, we had the kids fill out a letter titled "Dear God." It allows children to express themselves to God in any way that they'd like.

One of Mary's counselors was able to see her letter when we collected them. Mary had written, "Dear God, help me try not to commit suicide again this year."

What? Suicide at the age of twelve? Here is a beautiful young lady with a beautiful voice, whose foster mom called at the last minute, when we happened to have an open spot. That was a divine appointment! We were so thankful that Mary made it into camp. And, yet, our hearts were broken, just knowing that a twelve-year-old sweetheart had tried to commit suicide. It speaks to the pain and hurt and the difficulty that many of these precious children go through, and the value and life-changing opportunities that can come when you bless these kids with your time and your heart and discuss the never-ending love of Christ.

A New Burden

During our fourth year of camp, we began to feel God stirring us to go into full-time ministry. Janet and I would talk about it and pray about it, feeling that God was definitely calling us to something, but we didn't know what. Much like the burden for ministering to orphans, we didn't feel like we were supposed to do anything yet, we just felt like He was preparing us for something. We talked about it several times and one night I drew a Space Shuttle on a launching pad because it felt like we were getting fueled up and getting ready to blast off to somewhere that only God knew.

In January 2006 I was on a business trip to Bakersfield, California, and I was listening to a book on tape titled *The Rise and Fall of Theodore Roosevelt*. I was captivated by all he accomplished before he became President, and I was feeling a little underwhelmed with my own accomplishments. Some months earlier, Wayne Tesch had also mentioned that it would be a good idea to start studying for my minister's license or get my master's degree if I ever wanted to get more involved in Royal Family. This had been weighing on my heart because I wanted to accomplish more, like Roosevelt had, but I just didn't have the time, the money, or the energy.

One night while in the Bakersfield hotel, I was in the shower, and I believe God gave me a verse, Leviticus 9:5. But then I started thinking, *Wait, was that God speaking to me, or did I just think up that verse myself?* Then I thought, *If it was me, I would have never come up with Leviticus 9:5. What in the world could be in Leviticus?*

As I was showering, it occurred to me that the book of Leviticus was all about the Levites, God's tribe of priests to the Israelites. At that time in my life Janet and I were praying for real specifics from God's Word to speak to us, I mean real specific, like saying, "Jeff, study for the ministry so you can work for RFK," that kind of specific.

Well Leviticus 9:5 wasn't quite that specific. In the KJV it reads, "And they brought that which Moses commanded before the tabernacle of the congregation: and all the congregation drew near and stood before the LORD."

Well, that doesn't say anything specific at all. So I began to read further, and discovered that this is the start of Aaron and his sons being called into the priesthood. I remember thinking, "Okay God, so if this is my sign, how can I afford the classes for the ministry, and how do I afford the time to study?" I was swamped as it was as a husband, dad, employee, and co-camp director. I had *no* extra time. I decided on the drive back home that I would check the calendar and see if there were forty days between the time I got home and the next RFKC directors' enrichment in March 2006. If so, then I would do a forty-day breakfast fast, praying for direction about our burden for ministry, the minister's license, and Janet's ongoing mystery health issues. I got home on a Friday night, and if I started the fast on Saturday morning, there would be exactly forty days until the directors' enrichment. So the fasting and prayer began.

ANOTHER INFLUENTIAL BOOK

Part way through the fast, I had been reading a book called *Seven Laws of Divine Increase*. I was reading it one day at lunchtime, and everything in it seemed to be speaking about going into full-time ministry. I called Janet and said, "Janet, we need to read this chapter tonight when I get home." That night after getting the kids to bed, we sat on the couch with the book in our hands ready to read. It was just after nine o'clock and the phone rang. It was Wayne Tesch. After a few pleasantries, he came right out and asked if we'd be willing to move to Southern California and go into full-time ministry with Royal Family.

I knew that this was it, and we would be leaving. Janet was sitting next to me on the couch, I had the phone in my hand, and I mouthed the words without saying anything out loud, "This is it." We went on to ask Wayne some questions and he said we could meet in March at the directors' meeting and talk about the details. After hanging up, Janet and I talked about it, what it would mean, and then we prayed for God's clear guidance and direction.

JANET

I too felt that "knowing" you sometimes get when God is trying to tell you something. I knew we'd be moving. However, there were also several ways that God confirmed to me personally that this was, in fact, what He was asking us to do. After the phone call from Wayne, even though Jeff and I felt confident that we would be moving to Southern California to join RFK full-time, I called my mom to ask her to be praying with us. We lived only about fifteen minutes from her, and we have a very close relationship, so I wanted her to know right away, because I knew it would be tough on her. The very next Sunday, as we sat together in church, one of the first scriptures the pastor read was in Genesis 12:1: "Now the Lord said to Abram, go forth from your country, and from your relatives and from your father's house, to the land which I will show you." My mom and I just looked at each other, with tears in our eyes, knowing.

At that time, I was in a women's Bible study at church. A week or so after Wayne's phone call I sat listening to the well-known, anointed, powerful speaker on the video, I could hardly believe what I was hearing. I felt like there was no one else in the room, like she was talking directly to me. I even looked around the room at the other women to see if they were hearing it like I was. The speaker was talking about when God was leading the Israelites into the Promised Land.

As she looked into the camera, it felt like she was looking directly at me, and she said, "God is leading you into the Promised Land. He will make the path, but you must take the path." Again, it felt like God was saying that He was making a path for us to move to Southern California and that we must take that path.

Nearing the end of Jeff's forty-day fast, the phone rang. When I answered, it was a recorded message from a very well-known author, speaker, and teacher of the Word. We had been regularly giving money to her ministry, but I had *never* received a call from her before. Part of her reason for calling was to say that she was praying for all her donors, specifically "praying for wisdom for decisions." Wisdom for decisions! I was blown away. There we were, praying about this *huge* decision, and I get this phone call. Absolutely *amazing!*

When March came, we loaded up the faithful minivan with our kids' gear strapped on top, and started the seven-hour drive to Southern California with our four children. We were anticipating the meeting with Wayne to find out more about this life-changing opportunity, but our kids at the time didn't know anything about it. One of our children became sick, vomiting in the van on the trip and was begging us to return home so she could be in her own bed. We had this appointment, so we had to push through to get there, sick or not. It would not be the last difficultly our kids would have to endure on this journey into ministry.

Wayne laid out his simple proposition: quit your job, find a new camp director for the Concord camp, sell your house, find a new place to live near the Southern California office, move by the end of summer so the kids could get into school, and start work in September 2006. Then, go to training to learn how to raise financial support as a missionary and become the eventual director of training for Royal Family KIDS. Yep, that was the call. We had a quiet, but godly "knowing" that this was it; we just needed to know the details.

THE CONFIDENCE IN THE CALL

In some ways, it seemed like an overwhelming job opportunity. We knew that the Lord was calling us to something just like this. It was like the time when He prepared us to become camp directors, He had also prepared us to be ready for full-time ministry. It seemed like for the last two years of being a director, God was preparing our hearts, preparing our jobs, preparing our family, and preparing our lives to be ready to move and go into ministry. One day before Wayne's call, the associate pastor had invited me to lunch, which he had never done before. At one point during lunch he said to me, "Where do you see yourself at work in two years?"

Out of the blue I said, "I don't even know if I'll be here in two years."

It was just one of those things where you felt the Lord stirring you and you don't exactly know what stirring is, but you know He's doing something.

Our house was 1,120 square-feet with six people living in it, so it was crammed tight everywhere. We had boxes and baby seats and toys and books and Christmas decorations and photo albums stacked everywhere, and a treadmill in our living room. We needed a larger house, but we were sort of stuck. As we felt God's calling increasing, we knew at that some point we would be moving. There was no scripture telling us that, no godly booming voice, we just knew we'd be moving from this house and away from family.

Besides the cramped living conditions, we were also experiencing the three plagues of termites, mold, and rats. The termites were an occasional discovery, the mold was a regular chore to maintain, but the rats were maddening. They weren't in the living areas, but they were in the ceiling, the walls, and under the house. A few times, we awoke in the middle of the night from loud thumping sounds above us; it sounded as if the rats were having a wrestling match in our attic. One day, I was crawling under the house checking for termite tubes, the ground was muddy, dark, and dank. I was crawling through the mud when I noticed something growing under the house. It looked like white blades of grass scattered about in the mud. Even with my flashlight, I couldn't tell what it was. At the opening with more light, I was able to identify the "white grass" as a fungus growing on rat feces, and I had just crawled through thirty feet of it. Needless to say, we were completely ready to leave that house. I remember telling Janet, "It won't take much to get us out of this house," because we were done with it. Not only did we know the Lord was calling us, He had started to make the nest uncomfortable so we would be ready to fly.

I remember our senior pastor at Calvary Temple Church using the eagle's nest analogy one day. He said that the mother eagle builds a safe and soft nest for the eagle eggs and for the eaglets after they are born. But when the eaglets get older and begin to grow, the mother begins to remove all the soft padding inside the nest making it a less comfortable place to stay. She knows the young eagles must leave and fly on their own, and one way to help them is to make the inner nest less comfortable. That's how we felt. God was preparing us. He was making our home less comfortable, so when it would be time to go, it would be an easy decision.

Even at work, I could tell that I was getting restless. I started my job as the safety director for Contra Costa Electric in 1991, and I was in my fifteenth year there. I started getting bored with my work, and I started taking on additional projects such as leadership training, which really opened up new avenues of interest for me. My mother, JoAnn, got me involved in a local Toastmasters group. We had some great times giving speeches. (Yes, public speaking can be fun!) The leadership training and public speaking corresponded with several opportunities to become a regular speaker at many local refineries for safety presentations. Looking back, Janet and I could clearly see God's hand preparing me for my future work with RFK. The leadership training, Toastmasters, and presentations were foundational experiences for me to become the RFK training director. I have told many people, I used to do safety manuals and safety training, and now I do camp manuals and camp training.

Once we decided to move to Southern California, we had friends over to help prepare the house to be sold. A longtime friend, Kevin Eseltine, was helping paint the house, and he asked me if it was a difficult decision to move and go into full-time ministry? I remembered something John Maxwell had said in one of his seminars: "Make your most difficult decisions early in life; then you just have to manage those decisions the rest of your life."

I told Kevin, "It was an easy decision to make. As Christians, we were ready to obey God. We wanted to be obedient and we wanted to say yes to His callings. We made that decision early in life, so when the time came, we simply had to manage that decision."

Making the decision was easy, partly because God had given us so many confirmations that we knew He was there for us, and we knew that this was what He was asking us to do. But managing the decision was going to be difficult. Managing the decision meant leaving my employer of fifteen years to whom I was very loyal and who had been very loyal to me. I had made great friends and had a lot of success there. Managing the decision meant leaving our church of fifteen years, where we made great friends. Managing meant selling the house and trying to buy a new home in Southern California. Managing meant telling our kids we were going to move four hundred miles away from their family and friends, the only home, school, and church they had ever known. Managing meant that we were leaving both sets of our parents and several of our siblings as well. So the decision was easy to make, but it was certainly difficult to manage.

DIFFICULTY IS RELATIVE

Of course, difficulty is all relative isn't it? One year after camp was over, we brought all the campers back to the church to be picked up by their guardians. There was a set of siblings we had taken. Prior to camp, their home had burned down. When their guardian arrived at the church to pick them up, the siblings received the bad news that a new home had not been found and they had no place to go. We also discovered that their guardian was in no condition to take the kids. Our social worker had to make the difficult decision to send the children somewhere else right then. One of our great volunteers stepped up and agreed to open her home and take the children on a temporary basis. The temporary basis lasted six months.

When we talk about difficulties in our lives, it's always a good perspective to remember the difficulties in the lives of the kids we take to camp and club. Their difficulties always seem to outweigh whatever difficulties we may be experiencing. Their home burned to the ground, then they had a great week at camp, then they discovered they had nowhere to go, and their guardian would not be allowed to take them either, so there was absolutely nothing familiar for them to return to. They were put into yet another temporary placement, and even though it was with a wonderful family, it was not their family or their home. The difficulties we lived through have been pretty minor compared to most of the difficulties our campers have experienced.

SOUTHERN CALIFORNIA HERE WE COME

We said good-bye to family and friends, and we headed on our new adventure working for Royal Family KIDS and living in Southern California. Our goal had been to find a place to live in July so the kids could get used to the neighborhood, the town, a new church, and begin to develop new friends before school started. That was our goal. We looked at countless homes to find the right one for our family, but between price, size, and location, we just couldn't find the right home for us. Time was passing, school was about to begin, and we still didn't have a place to live. We decided we had to rent something immediately to get the kids enrolled in the local schools. Our goal had been a place to live by mid-July, but we finally signed a rental contract for a home the Friday before Labor Day, and school started the Tuesday after Labor Day. It was crunch time, right down to the wire. Getting the kids in new schools was really a challenge. They didn't know anybody, and nobody in the school knew them. We know it happens all around the country, but it was still difficult. Our oldest daughter stepped into her first year of middle school, her first year of public school, and she didn't know a single person out of 750 students. She wanted to be a good daughter and not complain about the move, but she was also dealing with the turmoil from all the changes. That turmoil resulted in many doctor appointments, tests, X-rays, CAT scans, and so on, trying to discover if there was anything wrong with her physically. She was having regular, extreme abdominal pains. Her first year, she missed approximately forty days of school. The teachers, counselors, and school administrative staff were wonderful in their understanding and certainly helpful. But we all had to walk through that very difficult year for her and for us. The following year, she was able to rebound and do very well. Her last year of middle school, she really began to blossom, excel with her grades, and was given the All-Around Outstanding Eighth-Grader award by the principal.

Again, it was an easy decision to make, but there was difficulty in managing the decision, even with the family. And so it goes with life. Even when God is in the decision, even when He is calling you, even when you have confidence in His plan, there are still difficult days that must be managed.

NEW TRAJECTORIES

Royal Family KIDS has changed the trajectory of our lives. We were innocently bouncing along with family, work, church, and life when the burden for foster children confronted us in the face. Many days have been difficult, but so many days have been wonderful.

Why do we stay involved when we could be doing something easier, when we could be making more money, or traveling less?

We know that God called us, and thus far the call has remained.

Isaiah said it this way in 6:8: "Then I heard the voice of the Lord saying, 'Whom shall I send? And who will go for us?' And I said, 'Here am I. Send me!'" (NIV).

Theodore Roosevelt has a great quote about the "man in the arena." Here is Jeff's RFK version:

> The credit belongs to those of us who help in some capacity with camp and club and at least try, though our faces may be marred by dust and sweat and blood, we strive valiantly, we may err and come up short, for there is no effort without error or shortcoming, but we know that with great enthusiasm, and with great devotion, we spend ourselves for this worthy cause, knowing at the best, when our time with the kids is over, the triumph of high achievement, and at the worst, if we fail to reach a certain child, at least

we fail while daring greatly, so that our place shall never be with those cold and timid souls who knew neither victory nor defeat.

I believe there is no failure in our camps or clubs; just trying is a success. It may appear in our human eyes that a certain child was not touched, but with Spiritual eyes, the Lord knows the seeds that have been planted. He will know their growth and what they produce. In 1 Corinthians 3:6, Paul says, "I planted the seed, Apollos watered it, but God has been making it grow" (NIV). At least we have dared greatly and we have not sat on the sidelines knowing neither victory nor defeat. I would rather suffer the possibility of defeat in an attempt to reach these precious children than to be victorious at watching them wither away in front of our very eyes.

We have been exposed to some great miracles of God's provision by raising funds for camp and now as home missionaries.

We have made some great friendships with the Concord Camp volunteers and by connecting with so many wonderful camp and club volunteers across the country.

We have seen our faith stretched as camp directors and as full-time employees of RFK.

We have seen our children's lives changed by the move, and through their involvement in RFK programs.

Royal Family KIDS is close to the heart of God. James 1:27 says, "Religion that God our Father accepts as pure and faultless is this: to look after orphans and widows in their distress and to keep oneself from being polluted by the world" (NIV).

For now, this is where we have been called, and foster children are whom we serve. We can't reach every foster child, but we can do our part. Our final story is of a little boy who went to camp one year.

After camp ended, all of the other children had been picked up and he was the only one left. Our team tried to be encouraging and told him, "Hey, we are calling right now and someone will be here soon."

He never looked up but said, "That's okay, everyone always forgets about me!"

He was so used to being forgotten, it didn't even faze him. He was a little boy who had been swept off the table and into the trashcan and forgotten. But, for one week, we were able to pull him out of the emotional trashcan and provided him with some fun, positive, life-changing experiences. We don't always know what environment the kids go back to after camp or club. But we truly believe that the camp and club experiences plant the seeds for self-confidence, a better life, and a relationship with a loving God.

15

JOANNE FELDMETH

Founding Director of Clubs and Mentors,
Director of International Programs

I had every reason to say no when Wayne Tesch suggested that I help his team start a mentoring program for Royal Family KIDS campers. I had admired Wayne and Diane and the RFK camping program for a very long time. But as the director of a foster family support agency, I had spent fourteen years looking for a mentoring program for the foster kids we served.

I never found one that worked for "system" kids.

One director of a top-rated mentoring organization told me, "Joanne, we aren't trying to match foster children any more. It takes us eight months to match a kid to a mentor—and most of the time a foster child moves placement within the first year. That means we have to start all over again to find a match in a different neighborhood."

With so many other at-risk kids to serve, he explained, this was a waste of resources.

Even more alarming, I had seen two well-funded programs specifically focused on mentoring foster children fail. One shut down completely and the second group matched only a handful of children. Both programs were coalitions with different agencies taking key areas: one group recruited mentors, another gave the training, and the third (a government agency) matched the children to the trained volunteers. Most would-be mentors lost heart while they were still being shuffled between agencies.

But getting matched to a child was even harder than getting approved. Social service agencies saw matching unknown (to them) volunteers to vulnerable kids as a job that added lots of liability and no extra funding. In one case, a church recruited thirty mentors who were trained and cleared by that coalition. Not a single mentor was matched to a child.

Any wise observer would figure that starting a mentoring program for foster children was just not doable. But I found I was burning to say yes.

I knew that research showed that mentors make a huge difference for at-risk kids. For some foster children, a mentor is as close as they will come to having family. When children have bounced through many homes, trusting a mentor can be their first step toward trusting a foster parent. When *mom* or *dad* are scary words, having a mentor can provide a bridge to eventually accepting an adoptive family.

I also knew that mentoring foster kids is not easy. Volunteers have to understand that these children have been deeply hurt. Foster kids don't always say thank you. They won't necessarily love you or even like you. They may be angry at everyone, especially you.

But I kept thinking that if *anybody* can do this, it will be the volunteers from Royal Family KIDS Camps, who have watched kids get off the bus hurt and frightened, angry and sullen, and have seen children blossom over the next five days.

Just as important, social services already matches foster kids to Royal Family KIDS Camps. Local agencies in more than thirty states refer campers to the screened and trained RFK volunteers in long-established public-private partnerships.

A New Call

My next question was, Could God be answering my prayers for a mentoring program for foster kids by challenging me to help RFK start one? After praying and talking with my family, I knew the answer was yes. I called the board members at my agency to give them notice that I was stepping down in two months.

Soon afterward, I began meeting with Wayne and RFK staff members Glenn Garvin, Jeff Juhala, and Glenn Howard, as well as Bill Clarkson, an experienced camp director, pastor, and strategic planner. By January 2008, I joined the RFK staff. The RFK leadership was ready to dream about what our ten thousand volunteers might be able to do *after* camp ended each summer.

One early shift was that we decided not to do "only" single mentoring. Why break up the camp team just as we were going deeper with the kids' lives? Why not use the RFK model of community and teamwork? Why not start clubs as well as a mentoring program?

So we planned a "two-track" program that stretched through the school year: (1) a once-a-month club meeting for mentors, helpers, and kids plus (2) an average of one-hour a week of individual mentoring. We also agreed that the mentoring would be individual but *not* isolated one-on-one time with a traumatized child. Our mentors needed to adapt the two-deep camp safety rule by mentoring with a second cleared adult or in public places.

A second principle was that we matched mentors *only* to kids who had gone to Royal Family KIDS Camp. We knew that five days of residential camp was an immersion experience that broke through barriers and bonded our kids to our mentors before we even matched them at club. Most mentoring programs match children to strangers; our program would match kids to friends they already knew.

But would it work? Would a five-day residential camp give us the foundation for a year-round program?

OUTCOMES

By fall 2008, our first seven mentoring clubs (then known as Royal Friends Clubs) were ready to launch. The clubs were based in six states and had matched more than one hundred campers to mentors in the first year.

From the beginning, the matching process flowed from relationships. Not every match was easy, but they all began with a shared, "I know you from camp!" foundation. Club helped—with the opening session becoming Camp Reunion Day, as kids recognized not only their mentor but their friends from the summer.

On the first day of club, one director said, "The kids ran into the room like they were returning home to family!" For a foster child, who usually feels like a stranger (even at home), that is a precious experience.

Later, another RFK director told me about a child who had come early and waited for an hour to be picked up for the first club meeting, admitting she couldn't sleep the night before. "It's just like Christmas!" she sighed.

KEEPING PROMISES

The next question about our new program was, even if the relationships start well, could they last? Could Royal Family KIDS mentors stay connected with children who were chronically bouncing between foster homes, group homes, schools, and biological family?

That cycle of chronic broken relationships sends terrible messages to foster children. I knew one foster child who, a year after adoption, still grew anxious when meeting strangers. Seeing a woman enter his home one morning, he whispered fearfully, "Is that my new mommy?"

This revolving door of foster care becomes an issue in mentoring club kids. Sometimes, mentors arrive at a group home or foster placement only to discover that the child had been moved days before. That's when a flurry of phone calls begins, and social workers begin a fresh round of paperwork.

Nine-year-old Matthew,* one of the first boys matched at RFK, was removed from his home just one month into club. He had assaulted his baby brother and was moved to a hospital program two hours away. His mentor—encouraged by his club team and determined to keep the promise to be "Royal friends until the last day of Club"—faithfully drove out to see him. The mentor was Matthew's only visitor, the only friend who came just to play games and talk with a troubled child.

"I don't think Matthew's mentor could have hung in there," his director told me, "if he had not been able to meet with the other mentors at club." The next year, Matthew was able to move back home with support from Royal Family and church volunteers.

Matthew's mentor faced a unique situation, but he was not alone in staying faithful to his mentoring commitment. Foster placement moves have been routine every year in every club. Yet by the end of our first year, we discovered that more than 90 percent of our club kids were still meeting with their mentors on the last day of club. That mentoring retention rate at Royal Family KIDS Clubs has continued through today even though we are now matching more than eight hundred children annually.

IMPACT

When a mentor keeps a promise to meet with a foster child for the whole school year, does it really matter? Yes. Research shows that a sustained mentoring relationship improves any child's academic, social, and emotional outcomes. But for a foster kid whose childhood has been filled with broken promises, it has an even more profound healing effect.

- Jenny had been in five foster homes and was afraid to be adopted. She loved spending time with her RFK mentor, Christy. However, over the year her trust grew as she watched as Christy befriended her new foster family. By the next summer, Jenny told her foster parents yes when they asked to adopt her. "She just needed one person to stand in the gap for her," Christy told me, "so she could learn to trust."

- RFK mentor Mark smiled when nine-year-old Jamal* announced that when he grew up he was going "to have a good job so I can get a house for my kids, and teach Sunday school and . . . be a mentor!" Jamal's dad is in prison, but this little boy has clearly decided to model his future based on his RFK mentor's life. Mark has now mentored him for four years.

For traumatized children like the ones we serve in club, having a mentor and trustworthy friend can be a first step both to healthy relationships and to believing that God loves them, that they are treasured "royal" sons and daughters.

A FAITH-DEEPENING JOB

For all the difference Royal Family KIDS has made in the lives of children, I have to address the difference it has made for me. My own faith has grown and deepened as I have watched God's people step up to take care of children who have been abused or abandoned.

This year, I moved from US club leadership to directing the International Camp and Club program. Some RFK leaders outside of the United States are dealing with issues like HIV/AIDS, child trafficking, and war in very different cultures. But the RFK stories from places as far-flung as South Africa or Chile have something in common with the American stories of Matthew, Jenny, and Jamal: they are always about a child with broken relationships. RFK camps, clubs, and mentors cannot "fix" everything that is wrong in a child's life. But those healing relationships can be the beginning of a child seeing herself and her future with new eyes.

RFK has given me new "eyes" too. I have watched the radical impact a local church—anywhere in the world—can have if it takes verses like Matthew 25:40 seriously and treats traumatized children like royalty. I cannot imagine more important Kingdom work—and I am very glad that when Wayne Tesch asked, I said yes to joining Royal Family KIDS.

"And the King will say, 'I tell you the truth, when you did it to one of the least of these my brothers and sisters, you were doing it to me!'" (Matthew 25:40 NLT).

* Children's names have been changed to protect confidentiality.

Joanne Ross Feldmeth, MA, is RFK Director for International Programs and was the founding Vice-President for Clubs and Mentors. Prior to coming to RFK, Joanne served as executive director for the Child S.H.A.R.E. Program. She holds a master's degree in global leadership from Fuller Seminary's School of Intercultural Studies with a focus on at-risk children. She is married to Dr. Nate Feldmeth, and they have two adult daughters and three grandchildren.

16

CAROLYN BOYD

Founding Director of RFK Australia
(Southern Cross Kids Camps)

In the early 1990s, I attended the Children's Pastors' Conference in Denver, Colorado, and first heard Wayne Tesch share about Royal Family KIDS. I was touched and thought, *What a great idea. So happy someone is working with these needy kids.*

Fast forward to 1995, and I found myself as the Bible teacher together with Sue Carpenter, at a Royal Family KIDS Camp in Boise, Idaho, directed by Tom Turco.

When I arrived at the RFK Camp in beautiful McCall, Idaho, I was not prepared for the week that was to come. I was given access to some of the background information of these children and was horrified at what had happened in their short lives. My emotions ran wild—highs and lows every day—and always the question, What difference can one week really make? Well, God was about to answer my question through a nine-year-old girl.

Crystal arrived at camp with her head hung low. She avoided eye contact and would only reply to questions with a yes, no, or a shrug. Each night she experienced night terrors and horrific nightmares. But during chapel one morning, the question of forgiveness came up. That night in her cabin the counsellors were talking about the Bible story and suddenly Crystal spoke up, saying, "God could never forgive me." And then she poured out her story.

The reason she was in foster care was because neighbors had reported her family to the authorities. Her parents were involved in occult practices and frequently made spells. Sometimes they trapped animals and used parts of them for these spells.

That night the counselors prayed for Crystal to know God's peace and for the nightmares to stop. As the sun came up next morning, Crystal sat up in her bunk shouting, "I didn't have the dream, I didn't have the dream. He does forgive me!" She didn't stop smiling and chattering for the rest of camp, and my heart was changed forever. A week *does* make a difference!

Taking that vision home, I talked to everyone about this amazing camp. I kept waiting for the person who could start this in Australia to appear, until at last I heard the Lord speak: "Carolyn, stop waiting for someone else. *You* are the one with this burden and vision. Trust Me and see what will happen."

Over the next three years I was able to convince people to come to the United States to see what I was talking about. I sold it as a vacation plan! "Come for a glorious week of camp in the majestic Idaho Rockies, then go to Disneyland before you fly home."

Over three years fifteen people made the trip, and their story was always the same: "I thought Disneyland would be the highlight, but everything paled after that week of camp. *It* became the highlight."

From that group of people, three camps eventually emerged, followed by others as people from across Australia heard and came to experience them for themselves.

The first Melbourne camp commenced in 2001, and since that time eleven more have been added. At the time of writing, there are six camps in Victoria, with a seventh in preparation, three in New South Wales with a fourth in preparation, and two in Queensland. At least two of these camps are offering club and mentoring groups. Our vision remains strong: to bring these camps to every state and territory in Australia. They run under the banner of Southern Cross Kids Camps, with a blue starfish puppet named Bluesea as the official mascot. Bluesea appears at each camp during J-Zone (chapel) to acknowledge and affirm campers who have shown good attitudes and deeds of kindness while at camp. Regardless of their age, everyone at camp loves Bluesea.

On behalf of all our camps along with our governing board, I want to acknowledge and thank God for the vision and work of Wayne and Diane Tesch and the amazing team they have raised up to lead the ministry of Royal Family KIDS. May God continue to grow the organization as it reaches out to so many children across the globe. SCKC in Australia honors you!

Carolyn Boyd
Founding Director SCKC
Carolyn joined her Heavenly maker not long before this book was published. Carolyn had a background in teaching, a decade on church staff in Melbourne, Australia, and was launched into itinerant ministry as part of Carpenter's Cross Ministries.

17

LANCE COLKMIRE
Camp Director, Cleveland, Tennessee

Life at Camp 54

Cory was one of the twenty-three kids who attended our inaugural Royal Family KIDS Camp in 1999. On Monday night during the first Sheepfold Chapel, this eight-year-old inner-city boy kept his fingers in his ears, refusing to listen. On Tuesday night, he continually made disruptive noises until we had to move him to the back wall, where he insisted on sitting on the floor. He then threw his tennis shoes across the room to make sure we knew he was there!

Next day, his behavior became so bad that we had to isolate him in a safe room. Cory snatched up some papers and ripped them in half. Our camp psychologist Susan responded by grabbing some tissue paper and throwing it into the air. This disarmed Cory, and he settled down. He then unexpectedly asked Susan and me, "Can I come back to camp next year?"

We said yes, and from that point his behavior improved dramatically. During the last chapel on Friday morning, Cory came forward and helped the music director lead a song.

Cory came back to camp again the next three summers, and always had the same "cousin" (counselor), Jonathan. On his final bus ride home, Cory wanted to give away all the pictures from his photo album—his way of coping with it being his last year at Royal Family.

THE POWER OF PRAYER

Jump ahead to 2014—the sixteenth year of the Cleveland, Tennessee, camp. It was the fourth time for our camp theme to be Sheepfold. On Wednesday morning after Breakfast Club, a third-year camper, Mattie, came to me and said, "I am going to get baptized at my church in a couple of weeks."

I congratulated her and asked, "What church do you attend?" She told me, and then said, "But I want to get saved here at Royal Family KIDS Camp."

At that moment, another third-year camper, Chase, who had been adopted recently, overheard our conversation and told Mattie, "I can tell you about that." He then proceeded to tell her about asking Jesus into her life.

Mattie responded, "I am going to do that tonight in chapel." (This would not be in response to an altar call, for we follow RFK protocol by not calling for public professions of faith.)

Later that day, a new camper, eleven-year-old Joey, saw me preparing a PowerPoint presentation with an illustration of Jesus, the Good Shepherd, laying down His life for the sheep. He asked, "Who is that?" and I realized He knew almost nothing about Jesus Christ. I handed him a Bible, and He read the story of Jesus' sacrifice and resurrection.

In those moments when children come to us with such questions, I am reminded that Joey and each of our other campers has a prayer partner from our church whom they will likely never meet, yet who is praying for them while they are at camp.

I remember being at Royal Family KIDS Camp directors' training in 1998 when I learned that an RFK camp director from another state, who I had never met, was praying for me that week. At the planned time during the week, that person's letter was given to me there in Houghton, New York. What a blessing!

In Houghton, I roomed with Jerry White, a foster parent from my church. Jerry had once told me, "Our church needs to do something for special-needs kids."

When I learned about RFK at a children's pastors conference, I came home and told Jerry, "I've got the program we need to do—Royal Family KIDS Camp."

Jerry described the week of directors' training as being even more intense than the training he had received as a soldier preparing for the Vietnam War. He became our assistant camp director and camp grandpa.

Even though I had been involved in children's ministry all my life, including serving impoverished migrant children in Florida, that first year of camp profoundly impacted me and the rest of our team.

After that year's camp birthday party, Amber gave away all her presents. Otherwise, she said, she would be forced to get rid of them once she returned to her foster home.

That night, twelve-year-old Josh, who was tall for his age, slept with the toy cars he had received.

That week, Evan told me, "I can't visit my mom and dad because they fight with butcher knives."

On the last day of camp, twelve-year-old Jessica kept unpacking her suitcase. She was not ready to return to the group home where she lived. Jessica asked her camp cousin, Sherry, "Can't we just stay here at camp? You and I—we'll live here together."

It crushed Sherry's heart to lovingly tell Jessica no. However, she promised to pray faithfully for Jessica after camp ended.

Every year, I urge our camp cousins to continue praying for their two campers, and for the camp staff to keep praying for certain children who are on their heart. I emphasize that members of our royal family are no doubt the only ones praying for certain kids.

This reminds me of something Wayne Tesch told me years ago. I had asked him, "What is the most important aspect of Royal Family KIDS Camp?"

He said, "People praying for children who have been abused, abandoned, and neglected."

We must remember the truth of 1 Corinthians 3:7: "It's not important who does the planting, or who does the watering. What's important is that God makes the seed grow" (NLT). May our prayers water the seeds we plant in the Royal Family children.

GENUINE FAMILY

Royal Family KIDS Camp has been a true family experience for the Colkmire Clan. My wife, Sharon, who is a school nurse, became our camp nurse in year one. That first year, I was reminded of a scripture the Lord had impressed on us several weeks before we were married: "Don't look out only for your own interests, but take an interest in others, too" (Philippians 2:4 NLT).

Our youngest daughter, Allison, now twenty-six, has been both a cousin and a lifeguard at RFKC. A couple of years back, one of her campers, Gina, spent the entire week trying to convince Allison that she could not stand her. However, when Friday morning arrived, Gina tearfully told Allison she loved her before she boarded the bus.

Our other daughter, April, has been a camp art teacher and a cousin. One year after camp, I received a phone call from a foster mother who said, "Can you please tell me who Cousin April is? Keisha will not stop crying for her." April was still single and living at home then, so I let her talk with Keisha on the phone, which helped.

The next summer, Keisha's foster mom told me, "When I saw how Keisha had become attached to your daughter during one week of camp, I realized that she could emotionally attach herself to someone. So I am pursuing adoption."

Yes, Keisha was adopted into this wonderful home.

In October 2014, one of our campers, Tessa, was adopted by one of our church families. Her adoptive father, Matt, is one of our veteran camp cousins. While Matt and his wife, Amber, became Tessa's foster parents before she attended our camp, his participation in RFKC helped turn the couple's heart toward adoption.

In 2013, inspired by their service, our camp coach and her husband (also a volunteer) adopted two-year-old Tyler. Coach Michelle's parents—Pam, our child placement coordinator; and Doug, our archery instructor—had been RFKC volunteers since 1999.

Always New

I've been blessed to direct sixteen summer camps so far. Also, in 2004 we started a fall retreat for middle-school kids in foster care, and I've led eleven of those challenging weekends. Twenty-seven events, serving more than seven hundred kids, with a total attendance of more than one thousand. Yet, RFKC stays fresh because we always (1) learn something new, (2) try something new, (3) serve new and returning campers, and (4) serve with new and returning volunteers.

1. Learn something new

It took us fifteen years to learn that not *every* kid wants to make a bug box!

2. Try something new

I'll mention two recent successes (while ignoring the one-and-done failures!).

- We (literally) launched a life-size Angry Birds game, using large exercise balls, a wall of cardboard boxes (with volunteers sitting strategically beneath them), and a giant slingshot mounted to two concrete-base poles. A birthday-party blast!
- Two years ago, we dropped the end-of-the-week talent show in favor of preparing kids to do skits, present music dramas, and play hand-bell songs that we weave into the chapel services throughout the week. The kids feel so special getting on stage in this manner, with their presentation fitting the theme of the chapel time. They get more focused attention than they do in being "Act 13" of a talent show!

3. Serve new and returning campers

An eight-year-old girl who came to camp for the first time in 2014 almost did not make it when her foster mom's car would not start. We arranged to pick her up safely, and she was extremely quiet and withdrawn for the first part of the week. However, by Friday her face was living up to her name's meaning, which was "shining."

Last summer, one of the first-time boys did a running flip as part of his cabin's music drama during chapel. The next morning, that ten-year-old asked me, "Who was the star last night?" The next week, his foster mother mailed me a card expressing how deeply the camp had touched Noah.

One morning at breakfast this summer, a second-year camper asked me to sign the back of her camp T-shirt. I did, and then I asked the nine-year-old girl, "What do you like best about Royal Family KIDS Camp?" Bria immediately answered, "The best part of camp is the first day; the worst part is the last day."

4. SERVING WITH RETURNING AND NEW VOLUNTEERS

Laura, who grew up in a difficult home environment, served in our first camp as a cousin. The experience set her life on a new course. She pursued a counseling degree, and today is a school counselor—and is still an RFKC volunteer.

While a stable team of volunteers is critically important to a successful Royal Family KIDS ministry (and, thank God, He has given us such a team), nothing is more exciting than raising up new and young volunteers. Last summer we had three college students and two high-school seniors serve. Who knows what the Lord might do through their lives once their hearts turn to broken children?

Lasting Expressions

My vocation is serving at Pathway Press (the Church of God Publishing House) as managing editor of publications. This has provided me with the privilege of writing about a few of my RFKC experiences in magazines and books.

More significant than my writing, however, are the written and verbal expressions from the boys and girls we have served:

- In our third year of camp, when our key Scripture verse was Jeremiah 29:11 ("'For I know the plans I have for you,' says, the Lord."), ten-year-old Bobby gave me this note: "Pastor Lance, God has a good plan for your life."

- A few years ago on a Friday-morning at camp, nine-year-old Janie left this note in her cabin: "Do you remember this bruise on my leg? Well, if you do, that is from my mom spanking me so hard. She made my bottom bleed! Do not tell anyone except for the rest of the people that work here! If you tell my mom or dad, I will be in big trouble."

- During our first year, we established the tradition of planting a tree where kids bury bad memories they have written on slips on paper. As the ceremony began, ten-year-old Andy spontaneously asked, "Why don't we sing 'Amazing Grace'"? So, as the awful memories were brought forward, we all sang, "I once was lost, but now I'm found"—led by a boy whose two parents were in prison.

As long as God continues to provide the amazing grace I need, I plan to be a Royal Family KIDS Camp leader.

18

RYAN MCANELLY
Former Camper

Ryan's Story

I was born in the heart of Long Beach, California, in the late 1970s. My parents were married a few years before that; my older sister was a flower girl at their barefoot wedding on the beach. They were a couple of carefree, young hippies getting started on an adventure for which neither was prepared. I don't think they realized the sacrifices involved in becoming parents.

From what I understand, neither of them had good relationships with their own parents, and their families are still very disconnected to this day. (I've only met my biological grandparents once in my life.) This may be a reason that things went south so fast. As we all know, marriage and child-rearing are hard work.

I don't remember too much about my father because my parents split up when I was around the age of two. My sister always thought it was her fault because they had different views on parenting and were always arguing about it. What I do remember about him was that he was a soft-spoken man with long dark hair who always smelled very nice.

The few times I did see him, he showed up in a fast car with the music really loud. He would shower me with hugs and kisses, making me feel center-stage. Unfortunately, those times were rare after a couple years. I think he had a really hard time handling my mother.

My mother was a tall, striking, strawberry blonde who was one tough woman. We had a one-bedroom apartment in a rough part of town. (Some may call it the ghetto!) I don't remember my mother ever going to work. She always had the music turned up loud and kept the house spic and span, a quality I inherited.

For a few short years, she made sure I had food readily available and taught me the difference between right and wrong. She stressed how important it was to take care of my belongings. She rode a ten-speed bike all over Long Beach, usually with me on the back. I am thankful for those few years that she attempted to make the best of a bad situation.

Things began to go downhill when she fell in with the wrong crowd, many of whom were bikers and Hell's Angels. I remember spending quite a bit of time in low-lit biker bars throughout Long Beach and Signal Hill with my mom while my sister was in school. I was three going on four, playing pool, and listening to the jukebox with huge, bearded men dressed in denim and leather and fueled by cigarettes and booze for breakfast, lunch, and dinner.

She eventually ended up finding new love for a short time with a Harley mechanic. He began living with us (still in a one-bedroom apartment) and treated us very well. I was tickled, played with, and even read to! Life was good as far as I knew and soon I had a new baby brother.

My mom's boyfriend started building Harley motorcycles from scratch in our garage and was quite successful. He was a good father to all of us kids.

Oddly enough, my mother had paired up with one of the few bikers who did not partake in the wild life of the Long Beach bikers. He tolerated her dabbling with illegal substances and over-use of alcohol for a while, but eventually it became a bone of contention. They began arguing a lot, which I'm sure was pointless because you can't have a reasonable conversation with someone who is not in their right mind. He became tired and frustrated and finally moved out. Drugs and alcohol became an almost daily substitution for the absence of whatever my mom was looking for, despite the fact that she had three children to care for.

The next block of time still seems to be a blur all these years later; perhaps because it is too painful to remember. My brother would be dropped off somewhere, my sister would go to school, and I would go along with my mother to a house where everyone would seem to me to be asleep, passed out all over the place in the middle of the day with the windows blacked out or barred. Sometimes the door jams would be splintered from being kicked in, or a dangling door would be pushed back into place once we were inside and then barricaded in place with a heavy chair. A shot gun would be laid back on the cushion. I would be sent to play in a backyard full of old rusty things and weeds by myself while my mom would be inside for hours.

After a while my mom quit bringing me to her outings and made my sister watch me. My brother would still be dropped off somewhere else, and big sister and I would be left to fend for ourselves. As you can imagine, my sister became more of a mother than a sibling. My mom's outings were short at first—just a couple of hours and then maybe a day or two. She would come home with food, hugs, and kisses, and resume right where she left off.

After a month or so of this, she began leaving us for longer and longer periods of time. Sometimes, she would be gone close to a week, then just over a week. We began running out of food and our utilities were turned off. My sister and I had to beg our neighbors for food and dig in the trash behind the liquor store for anything edible we could find. We made sure we went to school every day because that guaranteed us one hot meal.

Eventually, while we were at school, the owner changed the lock on our door and we were without a place to live. We were starving and without shelter. Luckily, we remembered that the garage didn't have a lock on it, so we used it for shelter. My mom's ex-boyfriend had some old sheets in there that he used to spread greasy motorcycle parts on, so we slept on the concrete floor in our garage and used old Harley rags for pillows and blankets. I remember satisfying our hunger by eating expired Pop Tarts from a dumpster.

One of the most painful memories from my childhood was coming home from preschool at the age of four to find our only shelter, the garage, locked. I didn't know where my sister was and found myself crying uncontrollably and wandering around in the alley. When I look back on it, I can't believe that not one of the neighbors came out to help me.

Finally, my half-brother's uncle came by, after calling and getting a disconnected message. He rescued my sister and me. I don't think I had ever been happier to see anyone in my life. Turns out he'd had my brother for quite some time and had been waiting to hear from my mom. We ended up staying there for what seems like a long time. We started having a normal childhood again and were being fed well, sleeping in a bed, and working on getting enrolled in school. Things were confusing but not uncomfortable.

Right when I started wondering what happened to my mom, she showed up out of the blue and said we had to leave immediately. She took my sister and me, but left my brother with his uncle. I was confused but happy to be back with my mom. She took us to one of our aunt's houses and dropped us off. She promised she'd be back soon but that never happened. I didn't see her for many years after that. After a few months, my aunt decided she couldn't handle taking care of us financially or emotionally. She dropped us off at an orphanage and the real trials began.

I have very few memories of the sitting home. I remember being split up from my sister, who was the only one looking out for me in the midst of all the hysteria that was happening in my life. I was allowed to see her every now and then on a playground on the campus. During those times, she would comfort me and tell me everything was going to be all right, that our mom was going to come and get us, and everything was going to be back the way it was. Unfortunately, that never happened. Instead, we went into the system.

My sister and I were placed in our first foster home together. I don't remember much about it, except that our foster mother didn't care much for us. We were only there for a few months. While she did provide necessary food and shelter, she had a dark side.

When my sister was not around, she would use me as what I have often referred to as a human punching bag. I don't remember her name, or even what she looked like, but I do remember that I feared her greatly. I was terrified of making eye contact with her and could not even answer simple questions. This, along with my withdrawn behavior, agitated her greatly, and she would sit me on the edge of her white sofa to scold me and then smack me hard for not responding. I would fly off the couch and my head would hit the wall. My sister would come home and see the welts and bruises on my little body and go toe-to-toe with the lady of the house.

Back to the sitting home we went. Because of the experience at our first home, the state had trouble finding us a home together. I was quickly picked by a new family without my big sister. I had a really hard time with that because she had basically been my guardian for several years and was the only person I trusted. She had always made sure we had something to eat, even if it was only a piece of bread with water. She always protected me and didn't allow me to get roughed up as long as she was around. She was the only one to give me hope that everything would be all right and our mom would be back to get us soon. Luckily, before I left with the new family, we were given the opportunity to sit at a swing set for an hour or so together on the campus. She gave me a little ceramic duck she had made and painted for me. I remember her crying and telling me everything was going to be okay, to be strong, and that our mom was going to find us and everything would eventually be made right. I was about five years old by that time, and deep inside me, at five, I no longer believed her.

The new family had a house with six other foster children, each with their own set of problems. I was very quiet, withdrawn, and shared a room with an older boy, maybe nine or ten, who used to hit me in the throat in the middle of the night for no reason. I would lay there gasping for air and unable to make any sound. I guess that was his plan since it's hard to cry when you're having trouble breathing. I would try to tell our foster mom, but she never believed me. I would promptly get popped in the mouth and told to go stand in the corner for lying. He often told me that he was going to become a police officer when he grew up and he was gonna track me down and kill me! Again, I would tell our foster mom and the same process would be repeated as before. She would slap me and send me to the corner. One of my foster brothers was named "little Sonny." He was three or four years old and had been a drug baby. He could not speak and they left him in a onesie in an oversized crib all day long. If I tried to play with him, I would again get smacked and sent to the corner. This became my life for almost a year.

Luckily, my aunt, living in the mountains of Big Bear, started the process of obtaining custody of me, so I didn't have to endure much more than a few seasons at that home. She had already rounded up my sister from a home in Beverly Hills, and she wanted me out of the lousy environment I was in. We moved in with her, and things were looking up.

I look back at my time in Big Bear with thankfulness, despite the fact that I had been very much neglected. I had never been physically abused, but I wasn't parented either. My aunt and her husband were busy with their new business and lots of recreational drug use. I was left to fend for myself.

I remember feeding myself the same thing for the entire time I was there: frozen waffles, Cheerios, and bologna sandwiches. To this day, I can't stand the thought of those foods. My aunt's food was kept locked in a separate refrigerator. We went shopping for clothes maybe once a year, regardless how my clothes were fitting or how fast I was growing. I never questioned anything and was able to endure teasing at school for my clothes because I was thankful to be away from the only alternatives I had known.

I spent my time in Big Bear running all over the mountain with no one to stop me. I skied, hiked, fished, climbed trees, and swam in ponds and lakes. No one cared what I did so long as I stayed out of trouble. My sister wasn't around much, as she started to get involved with drugs and boys—I was living with relatives but very much alone.

In the summer of 1988, I went to a camp near my house in the San Bernardino Mountains called "God's Family KIDS Camp." God had a hilarious idea: Let's take a lonely, anti-social, abused little boy and stick him in the middle of a group of people who are going to tell him he is loved, give him way too many hugs (there is no such thing), and celebrate him in all ways for a week. It worked! I was a sponge and soaked it up. I could not get enough. I had a great counselor, named Jeff, and he made the week a blast. He gave me my first Bible, which I still have today.

When the week was over, I could not wait to come back the following year. In the meantime, I went straight home and decided to go to church regularly for my "nice people" fix. I got plugged into the closest church in the area. I found loving people who were always smiling and hugging me. They even missed me when I couldn't make it one week.

Although I loved going to church for the people, the part about God loving me and Jesus dying for my sins did not go over too well with me. How could a God who loved me allow me to endure the past ten years of my life? I didn't think I had any time to sin between getting pummeled and moved all over the place.

I decided to read my new Bible from cover to cover to disprove it. It definitely didn't turn out how I planned. The Bible made sense, had answers, and helped me understand what made nice church people act the way they did. I carried this Bible with me for the next ten years. I even brought it the following year when I went back to RFKC.

My second trip to camp was as wonderful as the first. I was treated like a king, hugged, told I was loved, and learned more about the seed that was planted the year before. I got it, but not completely. The seed was watered, though, and camp again was the watering can. I believed God was love, and that was good enough for me the next few years.

Unfortunately, I was too old to return to camp the next year, and I was crushed. Besides church, it was the only place where I felt truly safe and loved and where I could just be a normal kid. I was just too old at that point. I began a new crusade to find another camp. I ended up at many different camps over the next few years. Summer camps, winter camps, beach camps, but none could compete with the time I spent at RFKC or the gift of love that was given to me, as well as just the opportunity to just be a kid.

Back at home, the drama continued. My sister had a falling out with my aunt and her new husband and ran away. She contacted the state to try to get custody of me and informed my caseworker that there were drugs in the house. I had no idea. I guess I spent more time outside exploring and being free of beatings than testing my guardians for illegal substances. I was yanked out of the place I called home for almost seven years and was back to being confused and in the middle of a mess. I stayed with my sister and her boy-friend for a short time while the courts helped me figure out the next chapter.

My little brother had been adopted by his aunt and uncle at whose home my mother had dropped him off almost seven years earlier. Apparently, they had been trying to get custody of me also. I was now at the age when I could decide where I wanted to go and live, and I did not have to be forced into a home or situation that I did not want. I made the decision to let my sister, who was only eighteen, have her own life and went to live with my brother and his adopted family. After all, she was just a kid herself, but she still felt the need to protect and shelter me from the all the garbage we continually seemed to be facing. My sister, who had always been a solid crusader for my safety and well-being was crushed, but I knew deep inside she had a life of her own to live.

My decision to live with my brother's adopted family proved to be a bad one. Over the years, I had experienced tons of physical abuse and neglect, but the assault on my psyche from the verbal abuse for the next six years was almost too much to bear. I think sometimes you can adapt to physical abuse and learn to hide your vulnerable side from your abuser as a way to prevent them from receiving the satisfaction of striking you. You can even get used to being alone by getting lost in books, living vicariously through movies, and doing whatever it takes to fill the days.

While in their home, I was constantly told in harsh terms that I was going to grow up to be a loser like my parents. I was told that I was not bet-ter than them because I went to church on my own and that I was a hypo-crite. I watched my brother get knocked around and was powerless to stop it. If I tried to defend him, I would get wrath turned on me for an hour in a lecture about how lousy of a son I was because I thought I was better than they were. Their "lectures" lasted anywhere from one to three and sometimes four hours. Their screaming and frothing mouths would let me know over and over that I was all wrong, all bad, and a screw up. I never questioned or challenged them in any way. I did as I was told, I was not a troublemaker at school, and miraculously had no trouble with the law.

The pain of their verbal abuse was more prominent than any physical pain I had ever known. It knew no boundaries, was much more relentless, and could even keep me from going to a study or church function. I found myself questioning many things about who I was, about my past, about my new faith, and about how strong I could be. The seed that had been planted years earlier was still being watered by youth groups and Bible studies. I was lost at times, but never without hope! I never questioned God, just myself.

Unfortunately, I had very few adults encouraging me or just loving me for the mess I was. I had no one to mentor me and teach me the right thing to do from day to day. I was on the brink of an emotional collapse at the age of fifteen.

I spent a lot of time lost in my head and drowning in waves of confusion as I had been for so many years already. I decided it was time again to go to winter camp with our church youth group. It was always great to be in the mountains, away from all the craziness of life and hysteria that kept me from peace and sanity. Again, I went for my nice people fix, to feel loved. I looked forward to hiking, polar bear swimming, archery, and reading my Bible.

God had another plan for my weekend. For years, I did not fully understand God, but He was drawing me to Him. I read the Bible I received from RFKC almost six years earlier every day, even more than my schoolbooks. Finally, the seed that had been planted years earlier at God's Family KIDS Camp bore fruit. I gave my life to Christ in the midst of that peaceful place snuggled back in the mountains. I was a vine bursting through the top layer of soil on which so much garbage had been littered for years. It was a perfect place and perfect time. I was now a new creation—a saved soul who was coming away from this camp experience with real meaning, and, finally, real peace!

Because of the constant state of war in my head back home, I needed a real relationship with Jesus more than ever. I had no idea where my life was going, but at that point I was just completely amazed that so much of what I had been striving to understand for so long was made known to me! The nice people at church I loved being with all these years actually had a relationship with a true and living God who promised to love all of us unconditionally and to never give us more than we can handle, because if we truly let Him, He would be the one to bear the load for us!

I came back home feeling fresh and renewed, but my real life was waiting for me with a vengeance. Persecution became a regular part of life at home for another three-and-a-half years. Anytime I was not at home, I could be found at Bible studies, youth groups, leading worship at church, and performing in a Christian punk rock band. The second I stepped outside, I surrounded myself with fellow believers to help and encourage me and to prepare me for whatever wrath may be waiting the moment I arrived back home. Nothing ever changed, and I eventually moved out a couple of weeks after graduating high school. I had Jesus, two boxes of belongings, and a guitar.

Emancipated into a big unknown world and not knowing how to do much of anything, I started a long uphill journey. There were many bumps and bruises, but I knew I was never alone. Since then, I have had my Heavenly Father to constantly pick me up off my face and dust me off. I have had to figure out a lot of the things the hard way, but the Lord has always been a gentle hand on my shoulder nudging me along and a tender voice telling me that I could do it.

Some years later, while still stumbling around in life, I married my high school sweetheart, Sherry, and another handful of years after that I found myself a father to Jude and Chloe. If you ever told me I'd be married for fourteen years and the proud father of two, I wouldn't have believed you. I look back on a lot of the trials I went through to get to this point and realize they are what made me the man I am today—a hard-working man who loves Jesus and adores his family. I am forever grateful for the summers I spent at God's Family KIDS Camp. I truly believe my experience changed the trajectory of my life. Statistically speaking, I should be in jail or repeating the patterns of my parents, but God stepped in. He broke the cycle.

19

SCOTT AND TRICIA MURRISH

Regional Ambassadors and Accidental Foster Parents

Sitting at my desk on a Saturday morning, I was preparing for a full Sunday of ministry at my church. Being an associate pastor, my primary role was being in charge of the youth and children's ministries. As I was finishing off my plans for the weekend services, which included my Sunday school lesson, worship service, children's church, and a youth event, I neatly stacked the pile of classroom attendance folders that were to be handed out to our teachers the next morning. Then my phone rang. It was a *real* telephone—the kind that had an actual metal bell inside and a long coiled cord attached to the handset that you could tuck between your cocked shoulder and your ear. I had no idea that the ringing of that telephone would forever alter the direction of my life, marriage, and ministry. I will never forget it.

As I picked up the phone, a firm voice asked from the other asked, "Is this Pastor Scott?"

"Yes it is," I replied. "How can I help you?" It was a friend of mine from church who was a police officer.

"Could you come to the station?" he asked. "We have a situation we are handling here and I think you might be able to help."

The officer was calling on behalf of a social worker who was working with a young girl as she was being taken into foster care. She wouldn't speak to *anyone*. Her family was experiencing what I've come to call a "violent explosion of pain" in their lives.

I immediately left my desk and drove to the police station. As I nervously walked in, I was taken to talk to Michelle.* I recognized the girl as one who had been at our church's youth and kids events from time to time. She was seated on a cold, metal folding chair that was against a painted concrete block wall in a tile-floored hallway. The social worker was watching from nearby as I sat down in the chair next to the girl.

As she looked up at me, I was startled when she said, "Wow! Thanks for coming Pastor Scott. I didn't know that anyone knew I was here."

Michelle looked like she was about nine years old. She was small and frail with sunken brown eyes. Her clothes hung from her body, and her hair was filled with lice. She was actually fourteen years old and looked (and talked) like she had made more "grown-up" decisions in her life than many people twice her age.

When the social worker realized that I knew the girl and that she was actually opening up and talking to me, she pulled me aside to ask a question.

"Would you and your wife consider allowing Michelle to stay with you for the weekend?" She shared how there were no openings in any of their foster homes for a teenage girl that weekend. She went on about how "it usually doesn't happen this way, and it would only be for the weekend." She was confident that they would find a regular placement for her on Monday. She also mentioned that since we knew her and had made a connection, that it would be better for the moment—*just for the weekend.*

Within a matter of hours after that original phone call at my desk, my wife and I became accidental foster parents. They did a background check and a home visit, and by that evening she had moved into our home. We were considered an emergency or "temporary" placement. Little did we know that the weekend would turn into a week, and the week would turn into a month, and the month would turn into *nine months.* The whole experience turned our world upside down.

I had known about children in foster care, and had heard news story after news story about children being abused and neglected. But I had never been face to face with all the issues that surrounded the tragic situations that so many children and teens deal with every day. There are families where the pets eat better (and more regularly) than the kids. Homes where children navigate a "minefield of fear" every day, not knowing if the next step they take, word they say, or even a look they give will unleash another explosion of pain in their lives.

Inviting Michelle into our lives changed us in ways that we never could have imagined. It wasn't all lovely and nice either. Many people think that becoming a foster parent means that you are going to have a child who is "ever-so-grateful" come into your home and that you will be able to "love them through" their tough issues. But this is not the case. When a child's world is filled with venom and violence, those are the things that will likely come out of them on a regular basis. I don't want to generalize, but that is often the reality.

When chaos is normal, normal can feel like chaos. (Is there ever such a thing as normal?) I had worked with teenagers for more than a decade. My wife, Tricia, and I had read loads of books on parenting, marriage, family, and ministry. But nothing had adequately prepared us for the challenge of helping this young girl experience life without the yelling, stress, anxiety, and fear that had become a daily part of her world. What we thought would be a walk in the park would become a walk down dark paths of relational struggles.

During Michelle's time in our home, we did lots of fun things as a family. We celebrated her birthday, went on family trips, enrolled her in a Christian school, and even had family pictures taken. It was our intention to make her as much a part of our family as possible. It was difficult to send her on visits to see her mom, though. The court had not severed parental rights, so she still was allowed to have regular visits with her mother over the weekends. The dysfunction of spending time with her family spilled over into our home both in her behavior and hygiene. Five weekends in a row, she came back to us with lice. Her mom was convinced that you just couldn't get rid of them.

Toward the end of the eighth month in our home we had decided to ask the court if we could become permanent legal guardians. We didn't feel that it was our place to ask for a severance of parental rights, we just wanted to ensure that she would be given the stability she needed to prepare for a future, go to college, and get set up for life on her own. What we thought was going to be a happy day in court, turned into a day of hot tears and heated words as the judge awarded full custody of Michelle back to her mom. That evening, she moved out of our house. We were stunned.

After one day back with her mom, Michelle ran away. We had no idea she was gone because we were "out of the loop" of her life. We found out two weeks later that she was missing. We were crushed. It felt as though we had failed and that it was our fault. Our nine months as foster parents ended in a tragedy that left us reeling with thoughts of *what if* and *if only*. If we had only left things the way they were, none of this would have happened. If we had only checked in with her mom sooner, the chances of finding her would have been different.

This painful experience of loss caused us to begin searching for ministries that dealt with children from the foster care system. It was while on a cooperative mission trip with a church from a neighboring town that I first heard about Royal Family KIDS. We were laying cinder-block walls for a new church in Mexico with a team from Topeka, Kansas. While on the job site, I was telling Gregg Wood, one of the pastors on the trip, about losing Michelle. We were setting a row of blocks in place as he simply said, "You should come visit this camp that our church does for foster children. I think you would love it."

Camp! It was like bells went off in my spirit. Tricia and I had spent summer after summer taking youth and children to camp. This was something that resonated loud and clear in my heart. We knew the value of a week of camp in the life of a child. After getting home from the trip, I immediately began finding out everything I could about Royal Family KIDS Camps. We called the national office and sent for their materials. It was a months-long process for us to get clearance with the pastor and our church board to attend training. But that next summer, my wife and I were on a plane to attend RFKC's weeklong directors' training.

We were greeted with a warm reception at the airport by our wonderful host couple, Carlton and Dionne Milbrandt. They were holding a sign with our names on it and were wearing purple Royal Family KIDS Camp shirts. They drove us to meet the rest of the trainee team and our leaders for the week, Wayne and Diane Tesch. That evening we shared an amazing meal in a beautiful home that flowed with southern hospitality. We felt like we were with family.

This was one of the most professionally organized training events we had ever experienced. From the time we arrived, every detail had been thought of. From our greeting at the airport, to the excellence of classroom materials, to the built-in times of interaction with the camp that was running, everything had been orchestrated to give the trainees the tools they would need to replicate this camp model back home. I began taking mental notes of all that went into making this week happen. It was impressive.

Sunday began with a commissioning service for the camp staff at the host church. There was a special time in the service when everyone who would be working at camp was asked to come to the front for prayer. It was moving to see everyone lined up in their camp shirts—a unified "army of compassion" being sent out for the week of ministry. Again, *impressive*. After the service, the camp staff headed off to prepare the campgrounds for the arrival of the children. The trainees went to a classroom to begin our orientation for the week. This included a moving session on the awareness of the abuse, neglect, and abandonment of children. Tissues are mandatory for this part of the orientation. Tricia was not prepared for all we saw and heard during this session.

That evening, half of the class went back to the hotel. The rest went out to the camp to observe the preparations for the week. One of the components of our training was real-time learning experience, in addition to being in the classroom. Rather than just reading it from a book, we were given the opportunity to experience firsthand what we were learning in the class. Brilliant.

Tricia went out to the camp that Sunday night, and I stayed back to observe the process of checking in the children at the church on Monday morning. After all the children arrived and were checked, we got on the bus. I was excited to actually be able to ride the bus out to camp with the children. This should be fun getting to share the excitement of arriving at camp with the kids. I wasn't prepared for the experience that unfolded.

I sat down on the bus next to a boy named Charlie,* who was about nine years old. He was wearing dark blue sweat pants and a matching long-sleeved sweatshirt. Although we give every child a brand-new T-shirt to wear on the first day of camp, Charlie refused to take off his sweatshirt. He insisted he keep it on, so we put the T-shirt on top of what he was already wearing. The whole way to camp, he never took his eyes off the floor and wouldn't answer any of my "ice-breaker" questions. It seemed as if nothing could get past his shell. It was a quiet ride to camp in our row.

When the bus pulled in, we were greeted at the camp entrance by the camp staff and counselors. They were cheering for the kids and jumping up and down with excitement. The night before, they had made signs with the names of the children on them. They even included a Bible verse and the meaning of the child's name. It was a thrill to watch the children press their noses to the windows as they looked out at the celebration in the parking lot and to hear them as they noticed their own name on a sign! Charlie said to me from his seat, "There won't be one with *my* name on it. They don't know I'm coming. I didn't even find out I was coming until this morning." As Charlie stepped off the bus, his counselor walked right to the door and greeted him by name with his very own sign. His eyes lit up. They *did* know he was coming! This would be the beginning of hope for this little boy.

As the days went by, the children experienced unconditional love as it poured out from the counselors and staff. There were activity centers, group games, chapel times, fishing, archery, a grandma and grandpa—even a birthday party! But one of the daily favorites was swimming. It was refreshing to jump in the pool and cool off. This camp was late in the summer, and it was a *hot one*. Charlie, however, refused to go swimming. He wouldn't even take off the long-sleeved sweatshirt and pants he had worn every day.

Thursday, before breakfast, there was something on the schedule called the polar bear swim. This was built into the week as an extra time for the kids to get in the pool just for fun. They would even bring in blocks of ice to toss in the water to make it more "polar bear" like. The counselors did a great job of building it up for the kids to add to the fun factor of taking the plunge. Charlie still refused to take off the sweats to go swimming.

One of the counselors at camp was an amputee. His name was John.* John had lost part of one leg below the knee in an accident. He had one of those amazing prosthetic legs that allowed him to run and even jump. The children were drawn to John, as he would challenge them to races. They would even challenge him back by saying things like, "I bet you can jump high enough to touch the branch of that tree." And like the "six-million-dollar-man," John would play right along with them and take every challenge.

On the morning of the polar bear swim, all the children and staff were standing at the edge of the pool, ready to jump in. And then it happened.

As Charlie stood off to the back, John dipped the toe of his prosthetic foot into the water and then quickly pulled it out, yelling, "Brrr . . . That's *cold!*"

As Charlie watched this scene unfold, he stepped closer to the pool and shouted out, "Hey! You can't feel that!" He then paused, looking down at his sweats, and then back up at John.

It was as if the logic was playing out in his mind, *If he can have fun and be okay joking about his own wounds, then maybe I can be okay too.* He then pulled off his sweats, revealing that he had a swimsuit on the whole time. He also revealed dozens of cigarette-burn scars that marked his legs and back that he had been too embarrassed to let anyone see. I was moved to tears. Charlie's outlook was forever changed that day—and so was mine.

It was on a footbridge at that training camp that Tricia and I felt something big taking place in our hearts. Wayne and Diane had built into the end of the training week a moment for us to take time to be quiet and listen for God's voice. We spoke out to each other how all our past experiences in ministry felt like they were leading us to do this camp. We were compelled.

Our experience of pain after becoming accidental foster parents led us to this moment. Our experience of this excellent week of training led us to a level of higher expectation of ourselves and of how we would implement the Royal Treatment to the volunteers in our youth and children's ministry at church. Our experience of leading our first Royal Family KIDS Camp and how it would forever change our lives was completely overwhelming—and yet natural at the same time. We just *had* to do this!

After moving to another church and launching our second RFK camp, Wayne Tesch invited me to become a full-time ambassador with RFK. This meant resigning my position of ministry at our church and launching out to raise funding (like missionaries going overseas) and to take on the role of launching new camps and clubs in Nebraska and the surrounding states. We have not looked back as we have seen the organization grow in the number of camps, clubs, children, and volunteers. I now drive thousands of miles each year speaking in churches, schools, conferences, community service clubs, and foster care organizations to share about RFK and to find people who are willing to take giant steps of faith in serving children of abuse. What a ride!

It is truly amazing how much can change in your life with just one phone call!

20

DAN AND SANDY FONG
Camp Directors, Kearney, Nebraska

The Beginning

John Wayne. Staring up at the huge statue of the Duke, I felt a spasm of excitement as my wife and I walked through the Santa Ana Airport. I mean, c'mon, John Wayne was on the Mount Rushmore of actors at our house when growing up. Now, here we were, walking through the John Wayne Airport with the giant actor staring down at us.

But as we walked into the unknown, I don't think I had the confidence that the Duke had. He seemed to approach any situation with his chest sticking out and both guns blazing. Me? I was whispering to my wife as we waited to be picked up.

"Remember, we haven't committed to anything yet."

"No," Sandy agreed.

She knew we had enough on our plates with our careers and two small children. And we'd given ourselves permission over the years to say no, even to good things, for the sake of our family. We had agreed to go to training mainly as a way to finally see California.

But after meeting Wayne Tesch and seeing a Royal Family KIDS Camp in action, we threw up our arms in defeat. We were hooked.

CHANGED LIVES

The impact of Royal Family KIDS on the small campers is fairly well known. Glowing reports from caseworkers, foster parents, and elementary teachers reinforce what's being accomplished in only five days. But what flies under the radar is the impact camp has on the adults. As directors, Sandy and I were privileged to see firsthand the transformation of our staff and counselors.

We returned from training with an excitement that was contagious. That first winter, we recruited family members, small group members, coworkers, and longtime friends. But while recruiting and training, we only preached about the impact we'd all have on the little lives. We had no idea the life-altering decisions some of our adults would experience.

Dynae was our camp nurse the first two years. She did a wonderful job; she was knowledgeable, compassionate, and fun to be around. So we were shocked when she informed us she wouldn't be returning the next year. But it wasn't because she didn't have a great time. Instead, God had nudged Dynae and her husband to adopt two young foster boys. So we had to recruit another nurse. But Dynae had chosen to give up a weeklong experience for a lifetime commitment.

Other adults at our camp made life-altering decisions also. As a university professor, Sandy was responsible for many college students applying to work at camp. Numerous young people came to camp with one course of study, only to change to a social work major after a week with these precious yet hurting children. How rewarding it was to see young people dedicating themselves to working with children of abuse and their families. A week had indeed turned into a career.

A favorite counselor memory involved one of my closest friends. After four years of hearing me talk about camp, things finally worked out for Jeff to be a counselor. He knew quite a bit about the ins and outs of the week; for years he'd listened to me go on and on about the kids, their backgrounds, and how much fun the week was. After hearing me ramble for years and attending training, Jeff thought he got it. Yeah, right.

Jeff was there to greet Dustin getting off the bus. He held up Dustin's poster and knelt down to introduce himself and talk about the week ahead. I leaned in to listen and share this experience with my buddy. He probably expected Dustin to ask about the activities at camp, or the food, or maybe even how old Jeff was. Instead, Dustin threw him a curve.

"Can I call you Dad?" the eight-year-old asked.

"Uh . . .," Jeff didn't know how to answer. He looked at me. We hadn't covered this in training.

"Can I call you Dad this week?"

As director, I made a quick decision. I guess I didn't think it would hurt. You see, Dustin hadn't seen his own dad for years, not since his dad went to prison. For one week, he'd have a dad. For five days, rarely did Jeff go anywhere without Dustin holding his hand. And whenever they encountered anyone on the sidewalk, or the cafeteria, or the dorm, Dustin would introduce Jeff to them by saying, "This is my dad." For five days, Jeff filled the void that aches in fatherless boys' hearts.

As Dustin walked away on Friday afternoon with his foster mom, Jeff turned to me and said, "Yeah, now I get it."

GOD'S PRESENCE REINFORCED

I've heard my wife say repeatedly that Royal Family has allowed her to see God differently. She'd always had a love and respect for the Lord, but the way God provided for our camp throughout the years really changed her perception of Him. And I experienced that also with directing camp. Time after time, we'd see a roadblock only to have God lift it away. It all started when we came back to Nebraska and began looking for a campground.

I didn't know much about campgrounds. In fact, I was pleasantly surprised to discover how many facilities were in our area, or at least close enough to consider looking at them. But to our disappointment, many beautiful "Christian" facilities weren't so open to allowing us a week of camp for so few campers.

Sandy and I had an appointment with Scott at yet another facility. I purposely hadn't told him of our intention over the phone; we at least wanted to clearly communicate our dream in person.

We sat down in Scott's air-conditioned office on a warm, July afternoon. Scott let me speak first. I told him how we were looking for a facility to host a camp for abused children. But we'd only bring twenty-four children the first year, probably only about fifty people total for the week. This was the part when most people looked at us like we were crazy. Instead, Scott tilted his head.

"Are you kidding me?" he asked. "For two years my board of directors has been telling me to reach out to foster kids. We've contacted Health and Human Services, group homes, and quite a few child welfare agencies. All of them turned us down. Now," Scott continued, his voice rising, "You come in here and tell me you want to put on a camp for foster children? Of course, we're going to make this happen!"

Just like that, our wonderful relationship with this Christian facility began. And it kept getting better. Numerous times when going over the bill or discussing plans for the next year, Scott would tell me, "It's not about the money, it's a ministry."

He meant it, and his facility meant it. They had given us a discount the first year, then continued to give us that discount every year since. But just how committed this facility was to our camp was reinforced after our ninth year of camp.

It was a fall evening and I was just walking into my garage after mowing. My cell phone rang. It was Deb, the facility person we now dealt with when planning our week of camp.

"Dan, is it a good time to talk?" she asked.

"Sure," I replied, not knowing what we needed to discuss about summer camp on an October night.

"Well, there are a couple of us here, so I want to put you on speaker phone."

Now my curiosity was piqued.

"Dan, you know Royal Family is our favorite week of the year. Our staff loves what we see happening that week. We feel God works more during that week than any other.

"Well, we've been planning our budget for next year. And we feel led to decrease your rate for everyone out at camp. We want to lower your rates this next year and then continue to lower them every year. In fact, our goal is to keep lowering them until we can provide the entire week for free for Royal Family KIDS Camp."

I don't remember quite what I said. What could I say? God had once again provided, as we had seen countless times.

THE INFLUENCE ON OUR CHILDREN

When Sandy and I went to training, our children were nine and seven, the same ages as our campers. All of us were excited when we returned from California. Sandy and I were already making plans for camp, the kids were giddy because of a new puppy we picked up on the drive home.

But our children quickly became excited about the vision of RFKC and we enjoyed seeing the impact on them. Abby, our verbal one, constantly wrote in her fourth grade class about the stories we were sharing. Soon her teacher and other school personnel were becoming aware of the camp that would be impacting our area.

Since our children were the same ages as our campers, we considered them experts when planning activities and the menu for the week of camp. They soon became involved with the prayer aspect that is so important to this ministry. Also, they logged many miles in the back seat as we took fundraising trips.

After watching us in action, Abby and Logan knew what to do. Sandy's sister and her husband were working our camp and their children would join ours for that week at our house with a babysitter. Here's where their expertise also shone. They planned a "cousins camp" for that week, planning out every meal, scheduling activities for each day, even designing a shirt for each child.

When we arrived home after an exhausting week of directing our first camp, we saw a poster on the wall that indicated which child had prayed for our camp each day and what specifically they had prayed. God had indeed softened their hearts for this ministry.

One year our daughter approached us about a job she had in mind for camp. Knowing she wasn't old enough to actually be at camp, we listened intently. She told us she wanted to be the prayer coordinator. She took the responsibility very seriously and made it a priority to get more people involved praying for our week of camp. It's no wonder that RFKC had a major impact on Abby even before she was able to be a counselor.

Our son Logan was equally touched by camp. We lived next door to foster parents, and Logan became friends with the two foster boys. The boys were frequent visitors to our backyard and dinner table. And when one of the boys was adopted by the family, he raced over to tell Logan that he had a "forever family."

Sandy and I traveled to numerous churches each spring to raise awareness and funds for the camp. Our children accompanied us and usually played a role in handing out materials. One Sunday Logan asked if he could speak up front with the microphone; he wanted to inform the audience of the changes he'd seen in his neighbor since he had attended camp.

Our children felt the impact of camp at an early age. But it wasn't always a feel-good attitude. After the first two years, Abby informed us that every time we had someone over to the house, all we did was talk about Royal Family KIDS Camp. We wanted to make sure that even though our biological children were our priority, we wanted them to have a heart for other children, as we did. We didn't want our children to feel neglected because of our passion, so we came up with a compromise. We wouldn't mention RFKC from a week after camp ended until after Christmas; then we could begin the process of preparing for camp.

Each year after camp we'd have a serious family discussion. Do we direct camp another year or do we hand it over? It wasn't always a slam dunk. But as our children matured, they saw the importance of camp more and more. By the time they reached high school, they were adamant that we not give it up until we had all worked camp together as a family. Abby was a helper at camp for two years before becoming a counselor. Logan has helped with camp for a few years. Now he's ready to be a buddy to two young boys for a week of memory making. It's so rewarding as parents to see both our children have a heart for individuals who are less fortunate.

A Far-Reaching Influence

Our longtime dean of men was employed as a counselor in a local high school. When a former camper came into his office to discuss college plans, Tim asked her if she even remembered the Royal Family experience. Her face lit up at the mention of the camp she had attended seven years earlier.

She recounted memories of the week of camp and the individuals who had invested in her life. Camp had completely changed the trajectory of her life and the lives of her family members. She explained that things were difficult for her family; she would have joined a gang if not for the influence of the people at camp. She was headed to community college now, the first in her family to do so. Most importantly, though, she and her family had all become Christians. Does she remember camp?

"Royal Family KIDS Camp," she said, "has made all the difference in the world to me."

Our Takeaway

Before becoming involved with RFKC, we thought we knew God. However, after becoming directors, we gained a new perspective on who God is and how much He is involved in our lives. As new directors, we were excited to begin the adventure of making a difference for abused, neglected, and abandoned children. But tasks often seemed outside our abilities and certainly outside our comfort zone. During that initial year as directors, we learned more about God's faithfulness. Just when discouragement would start to set in, we'd receive a phone call of encouragement. When we worried about finances, the mailbox would have an unexpected check from someone who had heard about the camp. And when it appeared we wouldn't be able to register the number of campers we wanted, God again came through in a way that was nothing short of miraculous.

The primary area in which we have grown is realizing that nothing in our lives can thwart the things God has in store for us and for our partnership with Royal Family. We have often said that if God is in this ministry, we're not big enough to keep it from going forward. After experiencing a number of situations when we couldn't see how things would turn out, we've seen how God's faithfulness was there in every event. We now have a stronger trust in the loving, caring nature of God. We've always known how much God loves the children who attend Royal Family KIDS Camps, but now we have a truer understanding of how much He loves us.

21

DARREN DAUGHERTY
Camp Director, Waxahachie, Texas

What Happened to My Heart at RFKC?

When our church decided to host a camp, most of us did not adequately understand how our hearts would be affected in the process. Each child was different, coming from unique situations of abuse and neglect, and each year's camp had different dynamics, including children who enthusiastically received love and children who rejected love (at least for the first couple days).

The Littlest Camper

On a Monday morning in July, the anticipation was almost unbearable. The charter bus was finally in sight, making its way up the winding road. Waving our signs, we jumped and cheered. The bus came to a stop, and I found myself fighting off the tears. Children streamed off the bus with smiles on their faces and hands over their ears (because we were so loud). A few of them ran, with their arms open wide, to counselors holding signs bearing the children's names. I had to turn away as the tears gushed down my face.

There she was, the little six-year-old for whom I had prayed a number of times during the past two weeks. Although I was not a counselor, she was on my heart because she was the youngest child coming to camp. The sun reflected off her blonde hair, and she shone like a star. Her beautiful smile hid any signs of abuse or neglect. I looked at her and asked myself, *What could have happened to her that would make her a candidate for this camp?*

Little Gestures

On that first day of our first camp, I was about to learn the great significance that little gestures can have in the lives of children who have faced great hurt and disappointment. I sent Cindy a welcome note through camp mail, and I did not expect what followed. After running over to me and thanking me for the card, she showed it off to other volunteers as if she was carrying a prized painting worth millions of dollars. Cindy would tell people, "Look at the note I got. Read it." Her reaction touched my heart very deeply, not because my card was on display but because her actions seemed to say, "I'm welcomed. I'm loved. I'm special." She hung the card on the wall by her bed, where it stayed all week, joined by many other cards of love.

On the second day of camp, when I entered the dining hall, Cindy was waving for me to come join her table. She was saving a seat for me. We had bananas that day. She loved bananas. Cindy removed the stickers from two bananas and put one on my name tag and one on hers. I didn't know if this was a significant gesture in her mind, but I realized again that my words of affirmation on the first day of camp made an impact on her, so much that she saved a seat for the guy who sent her that card.

Little Surprises

I was the director of curriculum and club times, which means that I was in front of the campers often. Cindy sat on the front row in every Breakfast Club and Adventure Club, volunteering for everything. When I would see her throughout the week, she would let me know that she suspected I was the costumed scientist, the voice of the crazy chipmunk puppet, and the jungle professor. She wanted me to admit it. She would grab my hand and say, "I'm not letting you go until you tell me that you are Dr. Bogus (the scientist)." She was persistent, but I would not divulge my secrets.

The surprise birthday party was, without a doubt, one of the highlights of camp. Every child was enthralled with the displays of love they received from gift-givers they would never meet.

As I performed a magic show in my clown character, one child yelled out, "Hey, where's Darren." The older kids knew where I was, but I noticed Cindy started looking around for me. As the kids opened their presents, I ducked into a room, removed my makeup, did a quick change, and went back to the party. Campers showed me their new toys with excitement. When I went near Cindy, her eyebrows went up and she spoke to me with a mixture of great excitement and disappointment.

"You missed it," she said. "There was a clown here at *my* birthday party." She did not realize that I was the clown whom she helped with a magic trick.

Later that evening, the last night of camp, Cindy received her second and final card from me during mail call. I wrote, "Cindy, your smile not only brightened up this camp, but it brightened our hearts. It is obvious that you are a creation of God. He made you extra special. God loves you. Everyone at this camp loves you. When you are sad or afraid, please remember God is there to help you. Just like Joseph, the man we talked about in the Breakfast and Adventure Clubs, you can trust God too. Thank you for the banana sticker and the beautiful card you sent to me. Darren. P.S. Yes, I am Dr. Bogus."

Her counselor started to read it to Cindy, but she couldn't get through it without crying, so she asked another counselor to finish reading it to Cindy. The next morning, I was greeted with a big squeeze around my neck as she excitedly said, "I knew you were Dr. Bogus."

"I have one more thing to tell you," I said.

Cindy's face became serious as she replied, "You can trust me."

"Okay," I said. "I was the clown."

Her eyes lit up as she shouted in surprise, "You were the clown at *my* birthday party!"

A Little Gift

The bus was now at the end of the field, where it had arrived on Monday. This time, it was pointing in the opposite direction, prepared to transport kids away from camp. After packing my things, I walked out of the lodge to the field. Cindy sat in the middle of the field with two counselors. She called to me, waved, and ran over to me. This joyous little girl was somber for the first time. There was no smile—just tears.

She said, "We're leaving soon."

I choked back the tears with all my might as I said, "I know. We're going to miss you Cindy."

"Do you have kids?" she asked.

"Yes. I have three children, and my oldest is a girl who is also six years old."

Cindy then said something I wasn't expecting, "I bet you're a good daddy. I wish you were my daddy."

I stayed relatively composed even though I wanted to sob loudly. Then she made it more difficult. As from her own neck she removed a necklace she had made during the week and placed it around my neck.

"I hope you won't ever forget me," Cindy said.

My heart was broken as I assured her, "I will never forget you."

Cindy got on the bus with her counselor. As the bus pulled away, Cindy looked out the window at me, pointed to herself, crossed her arms over her chest, and pointed back at me. She had signed, "I love you."

My heart could not handle anymore. It was ironic that I cried next to the same bus, in the same location, on Monday. Those were tears of joy. I now had tears of sadness. I cried as I walked toward the van. I cried on the way home. I cried at the gas pump with my face in my sleeve. I had finally regained my composure before reading a billboard that said, "If you're not prepared to be a daddy, let someone who is." I wondered, *Where is her daddy?*

As when I first saw her, I asked myself a few questions: What reception will she receive when she arrives at home? Will anyone show her love as we have? Does anyone in her home love her as much as we do? Does she have a daddy who loves her as much as I love my daughter who is about the same age?

The unknown answers to these questions made my grief more difficult.

A BIG IMPACT

At the welcome-home dinner for the camp counselors and staff, I could barely speak. I had missed my family tremendously, but as I tried to tell my wife and children about the week, I couldn't get it out. I have been well acquainted with grief in my past, but I did not expect to feel such great loss at this time.

Later at the table, my wife politely said, "I feel like I lost part of you."

I responded, "Oh, Honey, I have gained so much."

Our camp director asked me to come to the front of the room to share a story or two with those at the banquet. I said two words, paused, and handed back the microphone. Tears ran down my face as I said, "I can't." I later thought I was ready for a second attempt, but the tears came again, and I didn't even approach the front of the room. Why does it hurt so much?

Many volunteers touched the life of Cindy that year, especially her counselor Joanna. I was just a small part of her camp story. In addition to Cindy, twenty-three other children were given the ability to "see" the love of God through the extravagant, unconditional acceptance of caring camp volunteers. God knows each of their individual stories, and we are so honored to have the privilege to be part of them. A number of those twenty-four campers returned to camp the following summer. The ones who stepped off the bus that first year, visibly hardened by their past, returned the second year with smiles on their faces.

Returning to Royal Family KIDS Camp for many children is like returning from a long, difficult tour of combat duty to a home where they are welcomed, loved, and celebrated. Before moving across the country, I was part of that Royal Family KIDS Camp for five years. Cindy was a camper for seven years in a row. I wasn't there for her last two years of camp, but my friends described how difficult it was to say good-bye to the twelve-year-old camper who grew up before our very eyes. Wherever she is, we pray that this now twenty-year-old woman is grounded in the love that was demonstrated for at least seven weeks of her life. We pray that the trajectory of her life was altered in a positive direction—even just a little—by the efforts of a team of people who still love her.

An Ongoing Legacy

I am the director of a Royal Family KIDS Camp, approximately one thousand miles from that first camp I attended. Just as a week of camp births a brand-new perspective in the lives of every camper, it birthed brand-new things in my life. That camp ignited in my wife and me a passion to help children who have been abused and neglected. It caused my wife and me and our three children to become a foster family to fourteen different children spanning ten years. It provided a ministry passion that we share today in our family, many years after that first camp. Without that first camp, at least three other camps would not exist, which means that the lives of hundreds of children in three other states would not have been positively impacted. Without that first camp, my oldest daughter would probably not be in a career in social work. Without that first camp, we wouldn't know Christina. Many events, children, and volunteers are tied to that first Royal Family KIDS Camp I attended, because without it, so much good would not have happened.

An Orphaned Camper

As our volunteer team was preparing for one of our most recent camps, our child placement team came to me with two special requests. They asked that two of our campers be one on one with counselors, forming a buddy group of two campers and two counselors. This was due to the history and needs of the two campers. Their second request was for two specific counselors to whom they wanted to assign these two girls. One of those counselors was my nineteen-year-old daughter, Daniela, who had served as an RFKC counselor during the previous summer. It was a good plan.

Daniela's camper was an eight-year-old girl who had been removed from her birth mother when she was two years old and adopted by a family who eventually abandoned her at the age of seven. That adoptive family adopted her only because they wanted her infant brothers, and she received that message loud and clear for five years. When Christina came to our camp, she had been with a foster family for seven months, and she was scheduled to move in with a new adoptive family after camp. Her negative behaviors at camp were indicative of her past, but she had a glimmer of hope about being adopted. Each time she made a craft, she informed Daniela that it was for her new mom or new dad. Christina visited this couple on numerous occasions before camp, and she was preparing for her forever family.

It was a challenging week with Christina, but it was also a good one. At times, Christina said that having Daniela as a counselor was like having a big sister—something she had never had. My son, David, was also a volunteer at the camp, and when Christina would walk by him, she'd say, "Hey, Big Bro." Throughout the week, our volunteers knew that Christina was challenging, but they were comforted by the fact that she was on her way to a new beginning through adoption.

At the end of the week, after the children had departed, our volunteers gathered for a time of debriefing. There were many stories shared and many tears shed. We cried together, prayed for the children, and thanked God for the great privilege to be part of something so amazing. As I stood at the front of the room, holding the microphone, one of our camp grandmas came in and asked if she could share some news she had just received. Christina's foster mom told this grandma that Christina's mom and dad-to-be had changed their minds and withdrawn from the adoption. The room was quiet except for sniffles and crying as the more than one hundred twenty volunteers were stunned by the unfairness of the situation. A girl who was failed by her birth mother and abandoned by her adoptive family now had to bear the news that her new adoptive parents—the ones for whom she had made many crafts— had changed their minds. Following the most amazing week of her life, she had to face another disappointment.

Three months after that disappointing news, Christina finally arrived home. She moved from her foster family to her forever family, where she gained a mom, dad, two older brothers, and an older sister. While at camp, Christina said that Daniela was like a big sister and David like a big brother, but there was no possibility of this being true. Three months after attending Royal Family KIDS Camp, it became true. Daniela and Christina went from camper–counselor to sister–sister, and our family was blessed with an opportunity to be part of a camper's new beginning and life story.

A Contagious Experience

Many have discovered Royal Family KIDS Camp as a contagious experience that affects their lives in wonderful and profound ways. We do it for the children, and we do it for God. In the process, we receive more than we ever expected. As I told our church congregation following that first camp, "Nothing I've done in ministry has been as meaningful as my week at Royal Family KIDS Camp."

After camp, volunteers often experience a sense of grief as they pray for each child and wonder where they are and what they are facing. Which ones are going back into homes in which they are abused, neglected, or ignored? A string of camp memories often brings back the tears. The "Royal Family Weep" is real for me and thousands of other volunteers. There is nothing like it. My wife was right—she did lose part of me at that first Royal Family KIDS Camp. I lost part of me. But God replaced it with so much more than I originally had.

I will not forget Cindy and many of the other kids, and I thank God that He forgets none of them. I am convinced that if Jesus was on earth in bodily form, a Royal Family KIDS Camp is where you would find Him.

22

KIM HOPPER
National Clubs and Mentors Coordinator

Being confident of this, that he who began a good work in you will carry it on to completion until the day of Christ Jesus. (Philippians 1:6, NIV)

Something that I am convinced of is that God desires to use his people to further His kingdom and glorify His name, and the question is not are we good enough, smart enough, wise enough, educated enough, or just enough for God to use us. But will we choose to be used by God whatever that looks like? I think most of us would like to believe that we would say yes to anything to which God calls us. But the truth is that when push comes to shove and the reality of what is expected of us is tough and outside our comfort zone, saying yes and living yes are two very different existences.

God has called me into various ministries throughout my adult life—MOPS, Teen MOPS, children's ministry, women's ministry, and others that I am sure I am forgetting at this moment. Each of those ministries were easy for me to say yes to. Each of them stretched me in various ways and allowed me to grow in my dependency on God, while at the same time giving me a clear look at my strengths and weaknesses. Through serving, I learned that I am a natural leader and I have great administrative skills. However, I also learned that I have exceptionally high expectations of myself and others. I like to control things so they turn out the way I expect.

Knowing my strengths and weaknesses has been a vital part of my growth as a leader and follower. I've always been a confident and strong-willed girl with an attitude of, "Where there's a will, there's a way." It's only when placed in positions where I could not rely on my "can-do attitude" that I was forced to look up and become dependent on a God who could. Looking back, I can honestly say that I was in no way aware that God was equipping or training me for what would be my "life calling" or "the thing God created me to do." But I can say that in those years I was realizing that God had given me specific gifts and He was indeed preparing me for more. I had no clue how much more, which was probably a good thing.

I grew up the youngest of three kids in a tight-knit family. My parents were not necessarily church goers, but they took us kids to church until about the time I was in fifth grade. Then we stopped. However, I accepted Jesus as my savior when I was nine years old during a church vacation Bible school. I can still picture the room I was in and the cold aluminum folding chair I was sitting on. I can remember the linoleum floor I was staring at when my eyes were supposed to be closed during prayer. I remember knowing deep down in my soul that Jesus was true. I knew I felt different that day, that something inside me had changed. I distinctly remember that defining moment of my life. I had some teen years where my life did not reflect it, but from the moment I asked Jesus to live in me I always had faith. I believed in God and I believed God. I carried in me a sense that God had something specific He wanted to do with my life; I just didn't know what yet. I often wondered, and sometimes asked others, if they too felt this strange calling on their life. I attribute much of where I am today to the power of prayer. My grandmother was a prayer warrior. She taught me about scripture and used memorization of scripture to punish me and my siblings when we would fight. I've never done that as a parent, but looking back I see it as her act of love for God and for us. She wanted us to know the Word of God and for us to hide it in our hearts. She talked to me about heaven and creation and warned me against things I would be taught in school that didn't line up with God's Word. Much would take place in my life before God revealed His purpose for me, and with everything in me I know the prayers of my grandmother were protecting me—hedging me in. She taught me the power of prayer; my life is a living example of it. I would later need to know that truth and believe it enough to live it. She also demonstrated to me the gift of time. She took time to teach me about the things that would shape my character, and I cherish every moment I had with her. All the while, my "calling" was out there, and I know now that God was leading me straight to it, preparing the way and preparing me. I just didn't see it coming.

My sophomore year of high school I met the guy who would five years later become my husband and the father of my three children. He was in a bit of a rebellious stage at that time and our relationship those first two years was not what I would call God honoring. However, something changed in both of us that third year and out of the blue he asked me to go to church with him. We started attending church regularly and in a short time I had rededicated my life to Christ. I was not perfect; far from it, still God pursued me, He still wanted me. I got married just shy of my twenty-first birthday and by the time I was twenty-seven had three kids under the age of five. At this point in time, I could not see past the changing of diapers, cooking, cleaning up after meals, and the constant work it took to keep a home running. I didn't have time to think about my life being anything more than a flurry of kid mayhem, let alone having some bigger and greater purpose!

Yet, in this, God was teaching me how to love even when it didn't feel reciprocated. During these years God showed me what unconditional love looks like, a small glimpse of the depth of his love for me even when I was a lot of work. I often told God that I couldn't grasp his love for me, and I wasn't sure I would ever really wrap my mind around the depth of it. Again, those questions, the love I had for my children and husband, that pondering, was preparing me for something bigger than myself. Had I not asked those questions, I don't believe I would have recognized what God showed me later—a depth of love I could not describe, a love so fierce and deep that it could only be the love of the Father. I am sure I would have missed it had I not been prepared beforehand.

When my oldest daughter was three I joined a group for moms called Mothers of Preschoolers (MOPS), and it was here that God grew my leadership and relational skills, brought me my "soul-mate" best friend (you will read later why she is so important to my RFK story), and introduced me to women who knew, loved, and followed Jesus so intimately I wanted to be like them. God drew me near to Him through MOPS, taught me about lifestyle evangelism, and it was through my leadership in this ministry that God deepened a sense in me that He had something very specific in mind for my life. He taught me that being a mom to my three kids was exactly where He wanted me and that was a worthy place to be. As a mom, God taught me to relinquish control and allow Him to work. He taught me that only He changes hearts and the most I could do for my family was to give them over to Him in prayer. I would later depend on that truth to get me through days when despair wanted to win out.

The MOPS ministry led me into another ministry called Teen MOPS, which was exactly what you would think it is: Teen Mothers of Preschoolers. I was a part of the committee of women who got the ministry off the ground at our church. We planned meetings, raised funds, secured speakers and childcare, and recruited teen moms in the community to attend. As a steering committee, we transported moms and their kids to and from our meetings and oftentimes to visit children they had lost custody of. The majority of our moms lived in government housing and the neighborhoods were sometimes scary to be in at night. We taught the girls about God and parenting. We told them they could have dreams and fulfill them. We told them they were valuable and loved. We just simply loved them. Even as I type these words, I have chills realizing just why God had me there. I would someday speak these same truths into the lives of children who often times came from similar backgrounds and neighborhoods.

I served as the coordinator for this group for two years and fell in love with the girls and their kids God brought to us. Often times the girls would call me with needs and situations I had *no* ability to meet or solve. I would be driven to my knees to ask God to help me help them. Here I learned that when God puts me in circumstances that I have no way to control, I allow Him to work in me and through me. God came through every time and in miraculous ways. Oh, how my faith grew in those years! Eventually I had to step down from leadership, but not before God instilled in me exactly what I needed for my future calling: dependence on Him to provide what I needed to serve those who needed Him.

A time came in 2006 when our family made the decision to go to another church in our area. We had been attending the same church, the church where we were married, for more than seventeen years. The transition was *hard*. No one knew me at this new church, and I went from being "known" to an unknown. I am a social girl and that was really difficult for me. My husband and I had prayed for three years before making the decision to leave our former church, and when we finally made the change, we believed it was God leading us. This, however, did not keep me from wanting to turn around and run back to where I was comfortable and known. I tried to volunteer for different ministries at this new church, but none seemed to fit. I felt like every door I opened closed. I came to an awareness of how much the security being known brings, that someone knows your name and knows you have something of value to offer. It's lonely when you feel invisible. It's scary and intimidating to make yourself known. Again, this was another lesson I would need to know intimately in order to serve God well in the very near future when He would begin to unveil my calling.

About a year into attending our new church I was sitting in the pew (well, a chair in our case), when a video was shown about a camp. The church was looking for volunteers. All I can say is that I knew that I knew that I knew that I knew I was supposed to volunteer at that camp. That camp, as you can probably guess based on the fact you are reading this book, was Royal Family KIDS Camp. Now I should stop here and say that I had *no* idea what I was getting myself into. I just knew I was supposed to volunteer and go.

I went through the application and interview process and then came the training. I knew nobody. I've always had the ability to come into a room full of strangers and make friends quickly. Here it didn't take long for me to come to the conclusion that most, if not all, of these people knew each other well and had history. At least that is what it felt like from my perspective. It felt lonely in my corner, and I learned something new about myself—when I am uncomfortable, my instinct is to get out as quickly as possible. I fought that feeling throughout the training process. I also learned something else about myself, which was that my heart desperately wanted to obey God and go where He led me, even if I was uncomfortable. So I stayed, and I went. I felt very close to God through that process and He was the one I talked to because in front of me I felt like I had no one else. What a gift. I learned that when I feel alone God is enough.

The training for Royal Family KIDS Camp is intense. I am ashamed to admit that up until that time in my life I had given little thought to foster children or foster care. I thought that once kids were taken from bad home environments and placed with new parents, things were good—problem solved. I never thought about what might have happened to them in that bad environment to get them removed. I didn't know or didn't want to know that children are abused in unspeakable ways, and just giving them a new and, hopefully, safe home does not heal them from the trauma and loss they feel. I didn't realize that children in foster care move *a lot* and they are constantly expected to adapt to new people, a new bed, new sets of rules, new adults who are supposed to love and care for them all without any control over any of it. They are expected to put the abuse and neglect behind them and just move on and trust that these new people, who someone else chose for them, are going to love them unconditionally. There is no time to grieve what is lost and heal from what has been done to them. That's a lot to ask of a child who maybe has never even known what love looks like, let alone what it feels like. I am ashamed I did not know these realities, yet I am so thankful God opened my eyes to them.

All that training educated me but, more than that, it scared me. Learning about abuse, abandonment, and neglect is hard, but knowing how those traumas show themselves in the children who experience them is scary. Night terrors, bed-wetting, angry outbursts, aggressiveness, and more were the next realities in effectively scaring me out of volunteering at the camp. Being unknown was beginning to look easy. Here is where some of those things God had taught me leading up to this point were going to sustain me and even keep me moving forward.

First and foremost, I was not in control and this was going to drive me to my knees. I had no control over the campers I would be paired with or their behavior. Would I respond appropriately? Would I have enough patience? Would I be able to love children I had just met, let alone children who may behave in ways that make them appear unlovable?

Those weeks leading up to camp had me in the Word daily ferociously looking for God to prepare me for what was to come. He reminded me that He had provided for me before in times when I felt helpless, and He would provide me with what I needed here too. That feeling I had when I watched the recruiting video at church—that I knew that I knew that I knew that I knew I was supposed to volunteer for Royal Family KIDS Camp—would be what kept me in the game. I wanted to obey God and to follow Him even here, even when I was scared to death! My can-do attitude was not enough in this situation. I needed God to show up big time!

God did show up that first year of camp. All that prayer leading up to camp and the prayer coverage by others while we were there was felt by me and every other volunteer. The kids that year were far less scary than I anticipated and I was paired with two great campers. I will never forget the girls I shared a cabin with that year, especially Angie. Angie was at camp for the first time and on top of that she was twelve years old and going to be graduating. Angie was sweet and obedient and an easy girl to spend time with. I had no idea those first two days of camp just how much she was hurting. In training, we are prepared as much as possible for the realities of our camper's lives and that they carry burdens within them that are deep and painful. It is one thing to hear this in training, and it's another to see it in the precious face and tears of a child.

Angie shared with me and another counselor that her mom was a drug addict and that she didn't know her dad. She was living with her grandma and her mom's boyfriend. Through sobs Angie asked us to pray for her mom because she just couldn't understand why she continued to choose drugs over her. She thought it was her fault. She believed she wasn't enough to get her mom to stop using so she could have her back. My heart broke as we prayed for Angie and then went on to tell her that she was perfect just the way she was and sometimes adults make poor choices. But that didn't mean her mom didn't love her. We told her she was worthy and loved by us and God and that we would always pray for her.

When the last day of camp came and it was time to say good-bye and put her on the bus back home, I was not prepared. I was actually a little excited that day because I missed my family. I was filthy dirty and needed a hot shower and a good night's sleep. I actually couldn't wait to get home.

I must stop and share at this point that up until Royal Family KIDS came into my life I was not a crier. I mean I literally almost never cried—not at the birth of my kids, not even at funerals. It's not that I didn't feel the emotion, it's just that tears never came. The bus scene I am about to describe changed that forever.

At Royal Family KIDS Camp, each counselor creates an album of pictures for their campers so each can remember their week at camp. One of RFK's values is "Make Moments Matter." The album represents the moments that mattered. I shared before how in detail I remember the day I accepted Jesus as my savior. That was a moment in time that forever changed me. I would never have believed had I not seen with my own eyes and experienced with my own breaking heart that the five days the campers spent with us were filled with moments that would forever change them. The first few minutes I spent going through the albums I had made with my campers, Angie could not stop crying the whole time. She clung to me and the other counselor from our cabin for dear life. She didn't want to leave. As I looked around me there were many, if not most, of the campers crying. As we loaded the bus there were literally children screaming and clinging to the legs of adults begging not be sent home. It struck me how different this was from my own children's experience with camp. They left for camp excited to get there and experience the week, and they loaded the bus excited to come home. Watching those campers it became very clear to me that much more had taken place that week than I could really comprehend. Moments matter and God orchestrates moments at camp that change lives. I am convinced.

I came home broken. I cried constantly and my husband had no idea what to do with this new wife who had returned home to him. I couldn't make anyone else understand what I was feeling. I felt helpless. I thought about Angie and the other campers constantly and I prayed for them.

I began to wrestle with the questions most RFK volunteers have to wrestle with. Does five days really make a difference? Are we doing more harm than good bringing them to camp and then sending them back? There must be more I can do, but what? Through this God began to shed light on some of those truths He had shown me earlier in my life. First, I came to the realization that I loved the kids I met at camp fiercely. Is that even possible in five days? I hurt for them like I did my own children.

Slowly I began to realize the love I was feeling was God's love for me and for his kids. No, I could not love that deeply on my own accord a child who was riddled with emotional baggage and pain; but God could. When I freely gave myself to be used by God, He freely poured his love into me and that allowed me to pour it into the campers. Once I understood, I began to see why God had allowed us those five days and He reminded me how powerful prayer was. Had I never met Angie and the other campers I would have never felt a burden to pray for them. I had to trust God with them and faithfully place them back in His care. I could not be there when they were alone and scared and felt invisible, but God could. Each camper is known by God and He loves them far more than I could. I know this because God had already made these truths evident in my own life, and He prepared me and others to demonstrate His love and tell them they are known and valuable.

I went on to serve another year as a counselor at camp. I had the best time this year. Some of my anxiety had lifted, and I just went expecting to enjoy the kids and the week. This is the year when I fully understood that moments matter. Sometimes it only takes a moment to have a conversation that will change your life. Year two God orchestrated just such a conversation. Our cabin of girls were the oldest, and they would be graduating from camp that year. On our last full day with them, we spent some time affirming each of them and encouraging them about their futures.

During our affirmation time, I told Kay that I saw kindness in her, and I appreciated how she treated other campers. When we finished, one of our campers approached me and told me that she was not kind at home. She was only kind at camp because everyone here was nice to her. It happened so quickly that I can honestly say, the only part of my response I remember was telling her that on my own, I am not kind either and that it was Jesus who lived in me that helped me to love. We hugged and started making our way down to the makeup area because we were going to get ready for the tea party.

When we reached the field, we saw a few motorcycles that a Bikers for Christ group had brought to show the kids. The motorcycle group had brought gifts for all of the kids. One of the things they gave the kids was a tract that told the story of Jesus and God's plan for our salvation through his son. Now, one thing we do not do at Royal Family KIDS Camp is proselytize. It's actually against the rules and I don't think our directors knew the group was handing them out. Just saying, because we follow the rules.

At this point I was not near Kay, but I could hear her reading something out loud. I quickly realized she was reading the tract and asking questions. Kay stayed behind with a camp staff person as the rest of our group headed to the makeup area. Probably five minutes had passed when she came running, I mean literally running, up to us yelling, "I'm saved! I'm saved!" She began asking the other girls if they wanted to be saved and told them about the prayer she had prayed. It was a very touching moment.

Once we were all ready for the tea party, we began walking towards the place where everything was set up and Kay and I were walking holding hands.

In one moment she looked at me and said, "Kim, I really do feel different."

I began to cry and responded, "That's because you are."

I believed Kay that day because I remembered how different I felt the day I invited Jesus into my life. What a precious moment for us both and I am so thankful I was there to be a part of it.

It was not easy saying good-bye to Kay that year. She was graduating and I knew I would probably never see her again. I struggled with just letting her go. God began to show me how those five days of camp and what we poured into the kids were so close to the lessons He had been teaching me. Foster children often feel out of control because they have no control over their lives. I had learned that in those very situations where we feel we have no control, God will be in control for us. He is trustworthy. I know the kids would struggle with this truth, but until they could know it for themselves, I would believe it for them. I would pray for them, and prayer is powerful. My grandmother had prayed and our family is where it is today because of those prayers. I believe that with everything in me. Feeling alone and unknown is scary.

Our campers leave the five days of camp knowing they are known by God and us. They know they can cry out to God and He is there. I believe God opened my eyes to a deeper understanding of how He loved me. I had asked for Him to help me understand His love and I began to understand when I realized how much I loved the campers. I understood that was God's love for them poured out through me. I felt helpless to help the kids past that week of camp, but God had equipped me with the truth that I can pray for them and trust Him. I am grateful for a God who prepares and equips His people—equips me. I could never have emotionally handled letting those kids go if God had not shown me in my own life that He was enough, especially when I am not. I was going to be an RFKC volunteer forever!

At this point in my life I had plans for my future. My plan was to take over as director of our local RFK camp as soon as the director stepped down. I was sure I was perfect for the job. I had good administrative skills, relational skills, I was a stay-at-home mom with kids in school, so I had free time. I had all that I needed to run our camp well. Pretty prideful, I know, but that's the truth. I would soon learn that was only my plan, not God's.

This was 2009 and the downturn in the economy was starting to hit my husband's business hard. It was becoming more and more obvious I would have to get a job to help out. So get a job, I did. There were more lessons to be learned by me, and the next two years were painful and productive growing years. I struggled with why God wanted me to work when I would joyfully volunteer all my time to ministry. My heart and soul were rooted in ministry, and working felt so unfulfilling. I wanted to be making a difference for the kingdom of God, not helping someone make more money. I wrestled with God a lot during this time, not understanding so many things and wanting so desperately for my life to go back to what it had been.

In my finite human brain, I couldn't begin to understand that this season of my life was also part of the training I needed to fulfill the call God would put on my life. So many times I wanted to take matters into my own hands and quit. I wanted to do it my way. On three separate occasions I woke up with the intention of going in to work to resign, and all three times when I had my quiet time I would hear God whisper to me, "You can quit today, Kim, but that's not what I am asking you to do." Again my heart's desire to obey God won out, and I am so glad it did. I resolved not to leave until God asked me to.

Sometime into my second year of this job and still volunteering, now as the assistant director of our local RFKC, I attended the RFK national leadership training with our camp leadership team. I knew nothing about RFK on a national level so everything was new to me. I expected nothing more from this day than to learn more about foster kids and how we could love and serve them. I definitely was not expecting God to speak to me that day.

I'm not sure how God speaks to others, but to me I clearly hear words, not audibly, just within me. I mostly hear His voice in the times when I am faithfully in the Word and prayer, times I am seeking Him like hidden treasure. This was such a time in my life. I was really still struggling with where God had me, and I was fighting hard not to follow my own desires but instead to remain in God's will. My heart and mind were very close to God in this season. On this day He chose to start me on the direct path to my calling.

It would be fun if I could share some amazing story of me seeing a vision or an angel appearing before me, but it was much simpler than that. There was a speaker on stage, I have no idea today what he was talking about, but I heard God say to me, "Kim, I want you to work for Royal Family."

Typically, when I think God is asking me to do something that I find kind of crazy, I will debate Him a bit, in my head, of course. This day, however, I immediately turned to my friend, our camp director, and said, "Charlie, I think I am supposed to go work for Royal Family."

His response to this day makes me giggle. He told me, "You don't want to do that; you have to raise your own support."

I think my first thought was, *You are right. I don't want to do that!* I didn't know it then, but my life was about to go in a direction I would have never dreamed, and I would need everything I knew to be true about God and those lessons God had taught me.

Everyone needs a friend who will tell you what you need to hear, not what you want to hear. I have a friend like that. She's the friend I mentioned earlier, my "soul-mate/best friend" I met while in MOPS. Sheri is her name and she gets me. She's not afraid to tell me when I am wrong or being weak or need an attitude adjustment. I love it. She can say things to me that my husband probably shouldn't.

When I came home that March from the RFK leadership training, I told my husband and Sheri what I heard God tell me. Both of them told me I shouldn't ignore it, but, of course, I don't like change, and I was afraid of raising support. As much as I wanted to serve God in ministry, I was going to be passive and let this go right by me because I was afraid. Sheri was the one who pushed me to contact Royal Family; she wasn't going to let me ignore God. Everyone needs a friend like that.

The day I decided to take the next step, I realized I had no idea how to contact the national office, and if I did figure it out would they laugh at my email. Lots of insecurities flourished at this moment, and it took everything in me to hit SEND. I wish I still had that first email, but I believe I basically wrote that I believed God was calling me to work for Royal Family and that I was taking a step of faith by emailing to see if I could meet with someone at the office. I received a response back from Wayne Tesch the same day, and he said he would love to meet with me. Now that got me even more scared.

What road was I walking down? So many unknowns and possibilities, and that is not a good combination for a control freak like myself. It's safe to say this is probably just where God wanted me and where I needed to be. The day I met with Wayne, I had two friends and my husband praying with me that through this meeting, I would know that I know that I know that I know that this was the path God was asking me to travel. I say it that way because there is something very distinct that happens within me when I am in God's will, and that is the only way I know to put it into words.

That day it happened and I left the office knowing I would continue to move forward with Royal Family as a possibility for my future. I was still scared to death, but I was confident this was what God was asking of me. I didn't fully understand it yet, but He had prepared me for the journey I was about to take.

The journey from my first meeting with Wayne until I sat at my new desk at Royal Family KIDS took about nine months. I met with Wayne in May, and in November I attended training on how to raise support. In those six months I did a lot of praying and a fair amount of negotiating with God.

I studied Scripture regarding raising support, and read everything I could from people who had been successful in raising funds. I was still working at my job and often questioned my ability to actually do this. *Missionary* and *Kim Hopper* had never crossed paths in my mind, ever. More specifically, Kim Hopper asking people for money was so far out of my reach, I never even considered it. My husband and I supported missionaries, but those were special people going to third-world countries and college campuses. I was not special and I was not going to a third-world country. The best way to sum up these six months is to say that I was in constant conversation with God about if He really knew what He was doing and if He really wanted me to do this. I would often tell Him that I would follow Him anywhere and that I would follow Him to Royal Family KIDS, but I desperately needed Him to confirm that calling in ways I couldn't deny. One particular morning I was driving home from my early morning workout and I was telling God how scared I was. I needed to know that He was going to help me do this and that I needed Him to be clear with me that I wasn't alone in this journey.

When I opened my Bible a short time later to spend some time in the Word, I read this passage in 2 Timothy 1:12: "That is why I am suffering as I am. Yet I am not ashamed, because I know whom I have believed, and am convinced that he is able to guard what I have entrusted to him for that day" (NIV).

Paul was in prison and he was suffering, but he knew in whom he trusted and that He was trustworthy. This spoke to me that day and reminded me that God knew exactly what I was feeling and I could trust Him with the burdens I was laying before Him.

Every time I asked God for a confirmation, He provided it. I wish I could say it only took a couple of confirmations, but that would be lying. I asked for many confirmations and God was so gracious providing exactly what I needed to keep moving forward.

The training for raising support is pretty intense. It lasts two-and-a-half days and there is a lot of information on everything you need to do to be successful. The key word here is "do." On the second day of training, right about when the instructor was telling us how to schedule our out-of-state appointments, I literally began to freak out in my head. I began a conversation with God that sounded something like this: "God I can't travel to other states. I am a wife and a mom to three kids. I have a job. I am only one person and I have no idea why you think I can do all of this, but I can't."

I was panicking. God's response to me that day has carried me through the last three years of raising support and RFK ministry: "Kim, can you give me today? That's all I am asking."

I don't know if I can describe how much peace that simple truth brought me and still brings me today. I give each day to God and I don't worry (or try not to) about next week or six months. When you are responsible to raise a certain dollar amount each year, it's easy to worry about losing donors or gaining new ones. This simple truth helps me wake up, surrender my day, and trust that God has it covered. I am convinced that He in whom I believe is able to guard what I have entrusted to Him for that day.

I left that November training, went home, and quit my job in December. My husband and I were so convinced that God was calling me to Royal Family KIDS that we knew He would be faithful in helping me raise the funds. I took the remainder of December to prepare for this new adventure, enjoy my family over the holidays, and pray that God would indeed give me the courage to meet with people I knew—my friends—and ask them to partner with me in Royal Family KIDS. Easy, right? *Not!*

Fear was knocking at my heart at every corner. I wanted to spend my days serving the children I had fallen so in love with, the children God broke my heart for, but I didn't want to ask people for money. I wanted to trust God in this, but I also didn't want Him to ask me to do this. That's a lot of conflict rolling around in one body and mind. I was practicing my presentation in my sleep, literally. One night in bed my husband asked me what I was saying, and I realized I was actually talking out loud when I thought I was dreaming. It takes a well-thought-out message, courage, and a lot of passion and faith to do the job of raising funds well. Turns out my courage would come from my faith.

January rolled around and it was time to actually do the job of raising support. I couldn't start at Royal Family KIDS until I had raised 100 percent of the money required for my position. I had a few friends who had been walking this journey with me. They stepped up right away and committed to generous monthly donations. This was exciting for me, and I was so very grateful. Then the day came when I had to do my first "real" donor meeting. By "real" I mean, sit down and give my presentation, the one I had been practicing, and then actually ask them to make a financial commitment to support the ministry. To say I was scared to death would be an understatement. I was shaking and not feeling courageous at all. That morning I went into my closet and got on my knees, raised my hands in the air, and told God that there was nothing in me that wanted to ask people for money, but if that's what He was asking me to do, then I would do it. I also begged Him to give me courage and get me through the meeting without throwing up! He did get me through that meeting. I was still really nervous, but I made it. It took a few weeks, but those friends became faithful supporters of me and Royal Family KIDS. Time and again God gave me the courage to ask, and He gave the people the heart to give. It only took me seven weeks to raise 100 percent of the funds I needed to start. I've heard that is not typical and is actually pretty amazing. To God be all the glory.

Through this process God has shown me His faithfulness to prepare me and to equip me for the work to which He calls me. When I started at Royal Family KIDS, I was the national coordinator for the Club and Mentor Program. I have such a heart for the mentoring program because I know it's what every camp volunteer wants when they say good-bye to their campers, and it's what every camper needs the remainder of the year when they are not at camp. Our campers need to know that someone sees them and cares about what happens to them. They need someone who will stick by them even after five placements in a year. They need to feel as though they belong somewhere and that they are special. God does all of that through the Club and Mentor Program and through the *amazing* men and women who have said yes to mentoring and club. I now serve as the director of the RFK Club and Mentor program, and I am humbled to do so.

In this ministry, every bit of what God has taught me about Himself, myself, and truth collides. I must trust Him alone for the answers. If I just give Him today, He will accomplish all that is necessary for that day through me. When I don't have the answers, I can rest assured that He does. Prayer is more important than anything. I'm often overwhelmed with the truth of how much and how deeply God loves us. If God went to all this work to prepare me to love and serve his kids, how vast must His love for them be? I think more than I can comprehend. I love how deep God has driven these truths into me because I know how deep I want them rooted in the children we serve. That is what drives me every day—children who are learning about the God who has not forgotten them.

God calls the best of the best into Royal Family KIDS. The world measures success by money, big houses, fast cars, and education. I think God measures success by the ones who will hear and answer the call to go, those who will push forward even when they are filled with fear because they trust the God who calls them. I have tasted and seen that God is faithful to His Word and to me. I see every day that He can use me to do great things if I live a life surrendered to Him. I see God using thousands of His very own to love and care for the children who often seem forgotten.

Royal Family KIDS is a ministry to the abused, abandoned, and neglected in this world but it is also a ministry to the "called." How awesome is that? I am forever grateful that I didn't let fear stop me from following God all the way to the RFK National Office. My prayer is that I will humbly serve my God so that He gets all the glory all the days of my life.

23

ERICK ALVAREZ
Former Camper

My Royal Family, My Real Family

"Who would like to pray for the food?" someone asked.

I had never prayed for anything, but I was thrilled to raise my hand and make the silly monkey noises every kid makes to get attention. This was my fourth and final year at camp. After this there was no returning, so I wanted to do everything and be a part of everything. After being picked, just like all of my friends at camp, I asked everyone to bow their heads, close their eyes, and please stop talking. That day, I didn't pray very long, but I did pray for the first time, and for the first time, I believed God was listening to me.

Royal Family KIDS Camp was the safest place in the world to me. Every day, my foster parents made it clear to me that I didn't belong in their family. At RFKC I had an aunt, an uncle, a grandma, and a grandpa. I was hit in my foster home, and had my hair pulled. At camp, I was given endless amounts of high fives that built up my self-esteem. My mother was a recovering twelve-year alcoholic and drug addict. She had abandoned me until I was six. During "weekend visits" she would hit me with a belt, yell, scream in my face, and leave me gasping for air after knocking the wind out of me.

At camp, I was told that I had a charming smile, that I was smart and that God made me because He loved me. During my week at camp, I had everything that every child deserves: a family, a lot of smiles and laughter, enough food, and even toys!

Every other week, in foster care, I was a twelve-year-old boy who didn't have a family and felt unloved, hopeless, and unaccepted.

One day, during my final year at camp, I found myself singing a song that I had learned there. Part of the song is:

I will change your name,

You will no longer be called:
Wounded, Outcast, Lonely or Afraid
I will change your name,
Your new name shall be:
Confident, Joyfulness, Overcoming One,
Faithfulness, Friend of God, One Who Seeks My Face

Because of this song, I started following Jesus at twelve years of age. I wanted God to change my name, I wanted to be God's friend, I wanted a new name, I wanted to be God's child. I could have turned to alcohol and drugs like my birth mother, or I could abandon my responsibilities like my birth father, but instead, I opened a Bible that I received at camp and asked God into my life.

Today, Jesus has changed my life. I have been adopted by a family that loves me, I feel accepted and unconditionally loved. But I wouldn't have any of this if I had not met Jesus at Royal Family KIDS Camp. Because I met Jesus, every time I am asked to speak about foster care, I speak about the need of belonging to a family. I speak about inviting foster kids into the family of God, about unconditional hope and unlimited love found in God's family.

That is how I met my adopted family. I was speaking to the board of governors in Ventura County, and a couple with four kids, two of whom were biological and two who had been adopted, invited me to their home. And after endless invitations back to their home, I asked them if they wanted to be my forever Royal Family. After we prayed together, they said yes!

24

DJ BUTLER
Songwriter, "I Will Change Your Name"

How "I Will Change Your Name" Came to Be

Three years had passed since I tossed those words into that old cluttered drawer of mine. I had been unable to create a tune for "I Will Change Your Name," but I knew that the real problem went much deeper than just writer's block. I still carried a secret anger at God for allowing hurtful things to come into my life.

When I held that small piece of paper in my hand and read again those reassuring promises from Scripture, I knew I had to end my quarrel with God and surrender my *will*, as best I could, to whatever He had allowed. I needed to really *believe* what He was saying and make it mine. Only a fool reads a "Love Note" in the Bible and then walks away empty-handed like I had done.

Our loving Father knows we all have hurts and painful memories, but that is why He runs to us with such healing words. They are meant to go deep. They are meant to be medicine for our broken hearts.

Let us beg Him to heal us and make us powerful sons and daughters in this Royal Family He is creating. We don't want to miss any of it.

With love,

DJ Butler

25

BILL CLARKSON
Camp Director and Advisor, Midland, Michigan

My story is perhaps typical at the start, but "the rest of the story" is a bit unique. I was speaking at an International Network of Children's Ministry conference in 1995 and my topic was "How to Run Your Own Church Kids' Camp." I sat down at a lunch next to Wayne Tesch. I had just finished running my home church's third camp, and our children's pastor, Curt Zastrow, asked me to meet someone he knew. Wayne and I started a discussion, then Curt and I went to RFK directors' training, and now, eighteen years later, I sit here reflecting on the changes that have happened.

One of the more difficult things for me was the predictable "crisis" during training—either a crisis around the clientele, crisis around the church and volunteers, or crisis around the money. For me, I could not fathom how the money was going to work. Our senior pastor had told us before going to training that although we could start the camp, we would not have any money from the church budget, and could not make a direct appeal to the congregation from the pulpit to support our efforts. We (I) had to think very differently about how to approach the issue.

Long story short, we were able to raise hundreds of thousands of dollars in a small community of forty thousand people "for the kids" by talking to individuals, churches, businesses, and local foundations. The money miracle was that it was always an easy sell, and always an opportunity to vision cast for the children!

At one point, Wayne invited me to come to Southern California as part of a long-range planning group (the future of Royal Family KIDS). Through that process, I became friends with Mitch McConnell, Randy Martin, Tim Howell, and Glenn Garvin. "You are the future of this movement/ministry. How do we proceed? What thoughts do you have?" This was the start of a process during which Wayne allowed me to "speak into the organization."

Along the way, we were constantly dealing with the numbers of abused and neglected children, and lack of space at camp. The solution? Start more camps! We started Midland #2, planted Bay County, and assisted Bill and Jan Kreuger with their start-up in the Chicago area. I also was proud to serve on the director's cabinet for several years, including chairing the mentor and club group.

I was "in the room" when Wayne and Joanne Feldmeth worked through the initial vision of the mentoring program, taking notes, writing on a flip chart, asking critical questions.

MY STORIES FROM CAMP

The very first meal that I sat down to as director my first year was at a table opposite a seven-year-old girl named Ike. I noticed that she had only taken two carrots and a piece of celery and set them in front of her. There was a massive amount of food on the table, so I asked her if she was okay, if she was hungry. She said yes, and after the prayer, she started nibbling. I asked her two or three times during the meal if she wanted anything else, and she shook her head no. I finally gave her something and her eyes panicked. Later that day, I found out that in her house, if a child takes more than three of anything, they are punished and beaten if they grab for something to eat.

The one year when I was a counselor I had two eight-year-old boys. One boy knew more about the Bible than me (a children's pastor) and the other was continuously frustrated with any kind of structure, threw his hat on the ground, and swore like a sailor. At one point, I had a massive migraine and needed some respite. I asked the dean of men to relieve me, but before handing the two boys off, I asked them to pray for me. They were both less than enthusiastic, but the headache went away. I continually testified to them for the rest of the camp that "God healed me and took away my headache."

The next year, I was a carpenter helping a camper with a treasure box, and the camper had a headache. One of my campers from the previous year was behind him and immediately said, "We should pray for him, because God can take away headaches. Right, Carpenter Bill?" My past camper prayed for the boy and winked at me when he was done. (By the way, this was the kid with the hat and sailor-esque vocabulary the year before.)

One of our years, we had a nine-year-old girl who did not show up for registration. She had been moved from foster care back to her biological parents. We finally tracked down where she was. Our registration people asked if the family was still interested in having the girl attend and if they could come and pick her up. "Meet us at a rest stop" was the arrangement. When the registration staff and Grandma came to camp with the girl, she had on a T-shirt and shorts, no underwear, and was not in good shape. The "body check" that was conducted by our nurse and social worker revealed about 60 recent cigarette burns on the girl's body. We jumped into action several ways, including getting her a complete set of clothes and bedding for the week, contacting social services, and so on. The girl did *not* go back to her bio parents. After camp, she was immediately placed into a strong, healthy foster home. This camper came back for two years afterward and this past year was on our teen staff at camp.

How Has RFK Transformed My View of Children

There are several elements of RFK that we immediately brought back to our church and other camp programs that improved our ministry to all children:

Two deep rules for all interactions:

1. Always be observable and observed.
2. The child's current behavior is a result of something that may not be seen or experienced recently. It could be a reaction to some circumstance that has happened in the past. Give the kid a break!

The Rest of the Story

Perhaps the largest, lasting thing that happened to me with RFK was initiated in a phone call with Wayne several years ago.

"What do you know about succession planning?" I was in the process of working on my doctorate, and was at a point in my program of trying to find a dissertation topic. I was able to change a course paper topic to start developing the initial research information and "poke around the edges" of the literature.

The title of my dissertation, *The Effect of Founder Succession on Key Loyalty Factors in Faith Based Nonprofits—The Case of Royal Family KIDS Camps*, was published in 2009, after many trips to national headquarters and lots of interviews with employees, board members, and key donors. All that to say, this was the start of documenting the impending changes in the organization as Wayne and Diane moved on with their lives, and the organization adjusted to life beyond the founders.

One of the more telling parts of all of this is that now, I am a professor at the University of Valley Forge in Phoenixville, Pennsylvania. For the past four years, I have had the opportunity to teach nonprofit start-up and fundraising during the fall semester. My course lectures are rich with examples of RFK and the life that I have lived over the past eighteen years.

26

TIM AND SERENA HOWELL

Camp Directors; Co-Founders of Teen Reach
Adventure Camps, Sherwood, Oregon

The Beginning

Everyone would ask me, "What is your favorite thing about camp?" All I ever had to say was that I don't have a favorite. It has been my first time being here, and the first day, I knew I wouldn't want to leave. Everyone has been helpful, kind, peaceful, and hopeful. Their faces are all imprinted in my heart, soul, and mind. I will never forget these three days at camp. I love camp.

Can three days impact a life? Ask the teenager who penned the words above. This girl, like others in foster care whose stories fill these pages, experienced three fun-filled days at one of the many gender-specific Teen Reach Adventure Camps (TRAC), now across the country.

Tim and I founded TRAC to provide hope and a future to at-risk teens ages twelve to fifteen. For many wards of the state, life is a series of changes from one temporary home to another. Leaving behind siblings, special pets, and favorite belongings manifests itself in behavioral and medical issues that make attending other summer camps difficult. Multiple medications for depression, mood swings, anxiety, hyperactivity, and insomnia are common among TRAC campers. Life is a minefield where survival trumps fun.

* * *

The dream of serving abused children awakened in Tim on a spring Sunday morning in 1996. Sitting in a pew at Horizon Community Church in Tualatin, Oregon, Tim listened to Wayne Tesch, co-founder of Royal Family KIDS, talk about ministering to foster kids through a summer camp.

"Maybe someone here today will respond to God's call," Wayne's deep voice boomed across the audience. "Perhaps God is asking you to help a child find hope for the future."

Time stood still for Tim.

"Experiencing God's love in the cathedral of the outdoors changes lives," Wayne's voice trailed off.

Tim's heart thumped in the silence, as he heard God whisper. *You need to help.*

After the service, Tim spoke to Wayne. As a licensed counselor, he would start by volunteering as a therapist for the Tualatin camp. Deep down, Tim knew Royal Family KIDS would change the course of his life.

As Tim expected, the week at camp touched him deeply. He wanted to do more, but doubt set in, so he waited to share the stirring inside him until my birthday. "If Serena wavers at all," Tim bargained with God, "I'll know the call I heard a year ago wasn't your voice."

After dinner at Timberline Lodge, Tim tried to mask his nervousness as he casually brought up the topic. "I feel God calling us to help Wayne Tesch expand Royal Family KIDS Camps on a national level. What do you think?"

I didn't hesitate. "Sounds like we need to be obedient."

Tim exhaled. God had answered his prayer. It was time to invite Wayne to dinner.

***

Tim and I continued to volunteer at the Tualatin camp for many years while developing Royal Family KIDS Camps in Oregon, Washington, and Alaska. Two years later, we headed to directors' training in Houghton, New York. For a week, we studied a Royal Family KIDS Camp in action with other directors-in-training observing foster kids reclaiming their childhoods as they romped around the campground, splashed in the pool, and spent time with camp grandparents and loving camp counselors.

After watching graduation for the eleven- and twelve-year-olds the last night, we returned to our dorm room after the ceremony, broken and emotionally spent. We collapsed on our bunk beds, both staring at the ceiling with tears streaming. Neither of us said a word.

Tim finally spoke. "Watching those kids graduate tore me up."

My eyes still stung. I pictured the teary eleven-year-olds on stage, trying to keep a stiff upper lip as they realized they wouldn't return to "their family." Many had come for five years. "There needs to be another camp for the graduates." My voice caught. "But it seems so impossible." We had two young daughters and a fast-growing counseling business.

"That's how I've been feeling," Tim confessed. "But I'm so confused. Why would God call us to develop more Royal Family KIDS Camps then break our hearts for the graduates?"

Once again, we prayed for the next step.

***

Four years earlier, we began looking at land outside of Portland, Oregon. When a deal fell through, a friend mentioned property in Sherwood needing a quick sale. Incredibly, the home on the five-acre plot matched the dream home I had sketched. Our house sold in two weeks, and we purchased the place in Sherwood on contract and finished six months of work in two.

We took a step of faith and began to develop two separate gender camps for abused teenagers. A training model provided by Wayne and Diane Tesch served as a stepping-off point, and Hope Unlimited, Inc., a public nonprofit, was born.

One Indian summer day, we shared our dream with a good friend who had a compassionate heart for hurting teens.

"What's the budget?" he asked after listening intently.

We exchanged a look of surprise. I shared the printout of the budget we'd estimated a week earlier.

Our friend pulled out his checkbook and wrote a check for $10,000. "I will give you this on one condition: these camps need to serve abused teens next summer. Is that going to be a problem?"

We didn't waste time. We started work on our property the following weekend. Friends too numerous to list gave up weekends to help clear vine maple and wild blackberry bushes. Volunteers also leveled areas that would later house tents and Cross Talk, a time of worship and teaching about biblical characters who overcame difficulties with God's help.

God's hand of protection was clearly evident. One afternoon, Tim and two friends piled debris on a fire when the wind shifted. No sooner had the track hoe operator put down the safety protector, when a shot rang out, instantly shattering the glass on the machine. An old bullet had been left in the forest and ignited in the heat.

Tim and the men blinked in disbelief, realizing how narrowly they'd missed a fatal blow.

***

God was growing the dream in others too, like friends and volunteers Don and Gayle Brown. Tim did not know Don's own background mirrored the lives Hope Unlimited would later serve. The youngest of seven kids, Don watched his mother fight with various boyfriends over rent or grocery money wasted on booze. By age twelve, Don was regularly picking up his mother from the local bar.

Summer camp changed the course of Don's life. When the YMCA offered him a scholarship, he met other teens like himself who struggled with fear and lack of confidence. For the first time in his life, Don experienced unconditional love from his counselor and other staff. He shot his first bullseye, caught his first crawdad, rode horses, hiked, and heard about the love of Jesus. At camp at age sixteen, he asked Jesus into his heart. This decision grounded him when his mother abandoned him the following year. He credits camp for setting him on the right path—finishing school, working hard, and a thirty-two-year marriage—so working with TRAC was a perfect fit. Don and Tim were still digging tent railings when the first bus of campers rolled into Sherwood in the summer of 2002.

***

After the first year of TRAC, we felt something was missing from the overall program. Three days didn't leave much time for trust to develop. We thought a challenge course would help connect campers as a team and build self-value, but weren't sure how to begin.

Enter Dennis Roach from Spokane, Washington, whom we had met when we were developing Royal Family KIDS Camps.

Dennis made an unplanned stop at our home one evening that fall. After friendly conversation in front of the fire, Dennis confided feeling a prompting to visit.

"I don't really know why I'm here. I could've driven home a much shorter way." He looked from Tim to me. "Is there something I can do for you?"

Tim shared our desire to add a challenge course at TRAC.

"Isn't that interesting?" A glimmer shined in Dennis's eye. "I happen to be a certified builder and trainer of challenge courses."

Dennis soon designed the TRAC challenge course program, which has proven successful in breaking down walls of distrust through team-building activities. Facilitators frame challenges in scenarios that stretch campers to work together. The challenges increase in difficulty over the three days from the "teepee shuffle" and "minefield" to the "spider web" and "trust fall." Debriefing helps campers process their thoughts and feelings, a skill many lack.

* * *

Seeing the impact three days made in the lives of foster teens, two friends and volunteers, Lloyd and Colleen West, saw a larger vision.

"You should do this on a national level," Lloyd told Tim over coffee on their deck. He and his wife had adopted two kids, so they knew firsthand how much these children needed hope and stable adults to speak encouragement into their lives.

"No," Tim shook his head. Running camp had been a huge undertaking. He and I couldn't imagine running a large-scale ministry.

Lloyd kept pressing, and others encouraged us to develop a model that could operate both nationally and internationally. With a great deal of guidance from the Teschs and Lloyd West, we agreed, and TRAC held its first national directors' training in 2005.

God had a dream to share, and it was bigger than we could ever imagine.

* * *

At the time of this writing, TRAC, a program of Hope Unlimited, has served thousands of youth ages 12–16 in 14 different states, 56 separate gender camps in 28 locations. In 2009, Hope Unlimited launched TRAC *life*, a mentoring program that pairs TRAC campers with TRAC staff for a yearlong mentoring relationship.

We and the board of Hope Unlimited continue to dream. We envision other ministries for foster teens, including forever homes, self-sustaining ranch and camp facilities that would house aged-out foster teens year-round.

An endowment fund and succession plan are being established to ensure the long-term stability of the organization.

Two verses underscore the mission of Hope Unlimited. Jeremiah 29:11 says, "'For I know the plans I have for you,' declares the Lord, 'plans to prosper you and not to harm you, plans to give you hope and a future.'" Not only does God have a hope and a future for the fatherless in the foster care system, He will renew their strength as stated in Isaiah 40:30–31: "Even youths grow tired and weary, and young men stumble and fall; but those who hope in the Lord will renew their strength."

Can three days impact a life?

Thirteen years of Teen Reach Adventure Camp is proving three days does make a difference, turning heartbreak to hope.

27

MIKE AND ALICE LALLY
Directors, Arlington, Texas

During a Sunday morning Bible study class in 1998, an announcement was made by two friends who were Child Protection Services caseworkers.

"We need help with a summer camp for abused children."

We later found out that Wayne Tesch, co-founder of Royal Family KIDS, referred to them as "Texas-T." So our journey began in 1998. Alice, a camp counselor, and Mike, a Jack-of-all-trades staff member.

Our real journey began in 1996 when our youngest daughter started having night terrors and could not sleep through the night. Every night was filled with one of us holding her for hours while she screamed and we cried. Day after day, night after night, therapist after therapist, our tempers were short and our frustrations grew. Fortunately, we were able to recognize when one of us needed a break. The night terrors eventually subsided, but other trials bore similar challenges.

The final diagnosis came in 2001, when a behavioral pediatrician pronounced our daughter had obsessive compulsive disorder. Knowing what it was and getting the right counseling didn't make dealing with it any less exasperating. Without each other and the prayers of many friends, our two children might have been campers at a Royal Family KIDS camp. As we look back, we believe God was preparing us for the work we are now doing.

The first camp looked completely different for both of us. If you had talked to us about our experience, you might not have even thought we had been to the same camp at all. That week was an extremely emotional week for Alice and a trying week for Mike. One of Alice's campers, Angel, had one of the worst cases of lice ever seen by our caseworker friends from CPS. Angel required much attention from Alice, the camp nurse and the dean of women on Monday afternoon and all day Tuesday. During this time, Angel talked excitedly about the fact that she and her brother, who was also at camp, were going to be moving from their mother's house to their father's house as soon as camp was over.

Wednesday morning came with tragic news: we received a call from Angel's caseworker telling us that Angel's father had accidentally drowned the day before and that she would be coming to get them. Their bags were quickly packed with everything they had received at camp that week, as well as the birthday boxes from the party that had not even happened yet. The ride into town to meet the caseworker was long and quiet but full of reassuring hugs.

Angel and her brother were sent off with hugs, prayers, and words of encouragement letting them know that we would never forget their time with us at camp. Needless to say, Alice was emotionally drained. Alice never would have thought that the worst case of lice ever would actually be a blessing in disguise for a sweet little girl who got some much needed undivided attention. The biggest takeaway for Alice after that first camp was that we are never promised another week or even another day with these kids, so work to make every moment matter. Alice shares this statement with every volunteer that comes to camp. Anyone who has ever worked with abused and neglected children knows that every moment is unpredictable. Mike, on the other hand, spent the whole week working behind the scenes and never interacted with the campers.

People who have volunteered at camp know that the support staff works tirelessly to make camp look like it is running smoothly all the time. Between Mike's servant heart and his engineering mind, he is the kind of guy who sees a problem and immediately jumps in to fix it. A first-year camp has lots of those situations, and Mike was busy working behind the scenes non-stop. After camp, when Alice asked Mike what he thought about camp, he declared, "I'm never doing that again!" But he did and we haven't missed a year yet. Mike was eventually dubbed "Make-it-happen-Mike" for his ability to get, make, or fix anything, even when it was a hairweave on a panicked camper's head who was afraid her foster mother was going to be mad that it had come out.

By our third camp, we were making memories as the activities directors. After that third camp, "Texas-T" stepped down as directors and we were asked to step in. This change occurred in December 2000. A few short weeks later, we were on our way to California for a three-day Passing the Scepter training session with a huge director's manual and feelings of overwhelming inadequacy. During this same time, our church (Fielder Road Baptist Church) began studying "The Prayer of Jabez." As we flew to California, Mike read this short book. The Bible verse this book centers on is 1 Chronicles 4:10: "Jabez cried out to the God of Israel, 'Oh that you would bless me and enlarge my territory! Let your hand be with me, and keep me from harm so that I will be free from pain.'" And God granted his request. Mike perceived this as the first indication God was confirming that becoming the camp's directors was His plan for us.

After we returned from training, we had five months to pull together what seemed almost impossible. With a small group of returning volunteers determined to help make camp happen and the prayers of many, we began to broaden our territory, together. We soon identified the two concerns of any camp director: finances and volunteers. God again was working in the details when he sent someone to Mike with a $20,000 check on a Sunday morning at church. Mike, an engineer by profession and an introvert by nature, doesn't show a lot of emotion, but he was floored. He practically fainted and began to weep. This whole adventure has softened Mike's heart, and he weeps at a lot of things now. God has worked on Mike since the first camp. He jokes about God's sense of humor but also acknowledges how he has seen God orchestrate every detail of this journey.

Alice, on the other hand, was sold out from day one. Even though Alice was raising two daughters and teaching preschool, she loved helping young girls learn about the Lord and she loved creating positive memories. She loved being a camp counselor, but now sees how much more of an impact she is making in the lives of hundreds of children as director.

By the end of 2001, with one year as camp director under our belts, we realized that God had a bigger plan than just one week of camp. Not only are there more abused, neglected, and abandoned children in North Central Texas, but there are also many teenagers in need of the same positive memories and safe adult role models. Mike sensed a call to take the next step, so he met with the church leadership and talked to Wayne about creating a stand-alone, nonprofit organization. In February 2002, Trinity Kids, Inc. was created, taking on the financial and legal responsibility for Royal Family KIDS Camp #47.

The name Trinity Kids recognizes the fact that the Trinity River, which links North Central Texas communities together, cuts through neighborhoods of kids who fall victim to abuse, neglect, and abandonment every day. The name also recognizes the biblical reference to the Trinity: Father, Son and Holy Spirit. God provided a name that allows us to reach businesses and church members throughout the Dallas and Fort Worth Metroplex. Trinity Kids now sponsors an annual Christmas party for any child who has ever been to camp and a ConnecTeen program to continue the relationship building with the teens who have graduated from Royal Family KIDS camp.

Through the partnership between Trinity Kids and Royal Family KIDS, we have been able to create positive memories for nearly 1,100 children. Most of the time these opportunities are planned by camp staff, but sometimes they are divinely planned. Mike recalls a birthday box situation from a few years ago.

I work painstakingly to make sure that each birthday box in a cabin is very similar and this particular year was no different. But sometimes our eyes are blinded. During the afternoon before our birthday party, Elijah got upset at the swimming pool and refused to put his shoes on because his socks were wet. His counselor, Barry, assured him it would be fine to go without his socks and he would get him some clean and dry ones back at the cabin. Once there, Barry discovered that Elijah had worn all the socks he had, and he gave him an old pair to wear. Elijah was not happy, but agreed to put them on and headed to the next activity: the surprise birthday party. When Elijah opened his very own birthday box he discovered a brand new pair of white socks sitting right on top. None of the other birthday boxes had socks in them. We were all amazed, but blessed. God has continued to show us that He sees and knows our every need.

After seventeen years of camp, the stories are many, but the favorite ones seem to be the ones where God's hand is plainly evident, like, for example, the time we found out at registration that one of our campers, Maria, spoke only Spanish. The foster mother assumed she and her sister would be staying together and her sister would be able to translate for her. In a panic, we tried to solve the problem ourselves. Do we move some campers so that both sisters will be in the same cabin? No, it is really too late for that. Can we find someone who might speak a little Spanish that could possibly help? We even thought, we have a longtime volunteer that does sign language in her cabin, but then that doesn't really help. Then we paused, took a deep breath, called back to the camp, and found out that Maria's counselor spoke fluent Spanish.

Our only one! Only God can orchestrate miracles like that. When Maria got off the bus, her counselor welcomed her to camp in Spanish, and the anxiety on her face disappeared. There was so much that Maria did not understand at camp because of the language differences, but by the end of the week she was singing the songs and had heard through her counselor that God loved her and had a plan for her.

Time at camp is spent creating new positive memories and putting the traumatic negative ones behind. Few people at camp really know what the kids have been through, but everyone does know that something horrific has happened to them or they would not be at a Royal Family KIDS Camp. Mike remembers a camp where he spent a lot of activity time helping a camper named Kayla. When camp was over and Kayla was leaving with her foster mom, she ran over to Mike and gave him a huge hug. Kayla's foster mom asked Alice who Mike was and what had happened at camp. Alice explained that Mike was the camp director and that he had spent a lot of time with Kayla during the activities centers. Kayla's foster mom then shared Kayla's background of severe sexual abuse and her extreme fear of men. She was amazed at Kayla's response to Mike and felt this was a breakthrough in the healing process for Kayla. Once again, God began the healing in a child and Mike was privileged to play a small part in the healing.

To say Royal Family KIDS camps and Trinity Kids activities have affected the Lally family would be an understatement. Both of their daughters are fully involved and have been since we were activities directors. They have helped with cutting, coloring, and creating supplies plus they have been teen volunteers and have now been camp counselors. The training they have received has had other useful benefits too. Our oldest daughter became an elementary school teacher in 2012 in a central Texas community. When she saw signs of abuse, which she had learned to recognize as a result of camp training, she was able to engage her school's principal and counselor. Camp has given her the experience to recognize abuse and share that knowledge with other teachers at her school. This awareness has also given her the passion to realize that some children come to school to be loved first and taught second. She pours love into each child she encounters, whether it is through a hug, kind words, or a snack because they didn't have breakfast. She thinks nothing about taking home a student's jacket to wash every week because no one else cares enough to do it.

In 2014, our youngest daughter was sought out at camp by a camper she had not seen in four years. When she was a teen helper she seemed to be the only one to connect with this teeny tiny camper named Julie, who spent more time hiding under the chairs than she did being a part of camp. Our youngest daughter worked to build a relationship with Julie when she seemed to be connecting with no one else and then as soon as the week was over, she was gone. Julie moved to another state. She was told that she would never return to Texas or camp. But only by God's providence, Julie moved back to Texas and back to her original foster family four years later. Everyone was so excited to have Julie back at camp after four years of having to place her in God's hands to watch over and protect. The first thing Julie wanted to know was if our youngest daughter was going to be at camp. We all learned from this experience that whether we remember each child's name or if they remember ours, they do remember the acceptance and the love. Julie even laughed when she talked about hiding under the chairs and how silly she must have seemed.

God has blessed our entire family through this ministry and has shown us that He doesn't need *capable* servants, just *available* servants. We have all learned to get outside our comfort zones and stretch our territories. When we get comfortable, God gives us another challenge or two or three. One year it was losing our camp facility one week before camp. Only to get it back and then having the petting zoo eaten by a mountain lion and experiencing a stampede of horses running right through the middle of the camp. Obviously, Texas-style challenges!

Another year the challenge was the news our camp pastor was moving to Thailand. We found out later that he was willing to take his vacation and fly back to Texas because he believes in the ministry to these kids.

One more challenge came when we were told that our new insurance underwriters would not approve several fundraisers we had in place in the same year. (We were planning to add a second week of camp.) God had a plan and provided us enough money for two camps without those fundraisers, leaving money in the bank at the end of both camps.

Despite the challenges, God has met every need every step of the way. In 2013, Trinity Kids was approved to start camp #293, two camps back-to-back. We determined the best way to do two weeks was to schedule the camps back-to-back. But that meant Mike had to negotiate with the new camp facility and convince the board of directors this was the best option. There were logistical opportunities to work out, but we were not packing and unpacking twice. After all was said and done, we finished two weeks of camp with more energy than we had had in the past just doing one week of camp. So, we did it again in 2014.

We must recognize that all of the challenges have resulted in blessings we could never imagine and friendships we never sought and spiritual growth we never believed could happen. Most camps have prayer partners but we have a prayer mentor, Clyde Hodson (www.PrayerMentor.org). Clyde joined our team to remind and help us focus on the power of prayer. He organizes prayer partners, leads precamp prayer times, sends out daily prayer updates to our prayer partners, and spends eight hours each day at camp prayer walking and praying for the specific needs at camp. We have seen the answers to Clyde's prayers appear right before our eyes.

During Clyde's first year of camp, on Thursday evening we were doing the memory balloon release. The good and bad memories were written and the balloons were filled with helium. We were about forty-five minutes from releasing the balloons when a huge rainstorm began. We took a balloon outside to test it and see if it would rise in the rain; the answer was no. Someone asked if we had a plan B. We did not. Clyde had already sent an email to our prayer partners the day before asking for prayer that the children would be able to release their bad memories to God through the tangible balloon release. When the camp pastor had finished his prerelease share time, everyone stood up wondering how this balloon release would go in the rain. I am pretty sure we were all sending up "arrow" prayers at that point. We headed outside to see that the rain had stopped and a beautiful rainbow was filling the sky where dark clouds had been only a few minutes earlier. Needless, to say we were all praising God for His miracle and reminding ourselves that Clyde's prayer for the release had gone out before the rain ever started. Our appreciation for prayer has been eternally influenced by having Clyde as a prayer mentor, and we all recognize that God is the master of answered prayers.

We look forward to seeing God open more doors, challenge us to grow and break the cycle of child abuse through Trinity Kids events.

28

KEN AND SANDY HAMLIN
Directors, St. Joseph, Missouri

My story with Royal Family began on a weekday in 1992 as I was teaching my high school accounting class. I received a note to see my church minister, Charles Bayer, as soon as school was out. This was quite unusual, so I hurried the twelve miles to discover my husband, Ken, had been in to talk with Charles earlier in the day.

Our church had decided on a new ministry a year earlier, brought to us by a new member from California. She showed our Outreach Committee a story in the *Guidepost* magazine about a new camp starting nationwide for abused, neglected, and abandoned children sponsored via Christian churches. Our church newcomer was selected to attend training (which she did) and began organizing for the following summer. However, she decided she was not the right person for the job and had told Charles. Word reached the church membership. I thought, *What a shame, but I am sure someone will step up.*

Ken knew that I had spent many summers leading a language and culture camp for foreign exchange students, and proceeded to meet with Charles telling him I was the right choice. Unaware of this conversation, I had no idea the note I had just received at school would turn into a twenty-three-year commitment to direct a camp for abused and neglected children! As I thought and prayed about this journey, I kept hearing God tell me, "You have dedicated your life to teaching and helping children. This is just one more step toward that dedication in My name."

CAMP STORIES
Our first year of camp included twin boys who were ten years old and their sister who was twelve. They had been locked in a small house, windows boarded up, on the outskirts of town along the Missouri River. Mom and

boyfriend had decided to take a vacation from the children. They were discovered a week later and turned over to the state authorities. Unfortunately, there was little food and the children developed an eating disorder because of this lack of available food.

Each child was grossly overweight and couldn't be satisfied with any amount of food. At the beginning of the week, they were told they could have as much as they wanted. Not believing us, they gorged themselves at every meal. However, as the week progressed, instead of four or five plates of food, the children only took seconds or thirds. By our last day, they were eating the same amounts as the other children. Our daily staff prayers for them were working. The children's social worker told our camp child placement coordinator that the foster family was amazed at the difference. They wanted to know if the children could return the following year!

* * *

Dale was an older camp counselor with grandchildren. He was paired with nine-year-old Mikey, who simply would not participate. He never sang the camp songs and just wanted to run around. Dale was very patient and wanted to say a special prayer for Mikey at each staff meeting. Then, on Thursday night, the night before camp ended, Dale lay awake listening to the tiny voice above him sing "Jesus Loves Me." Dale thought to himself, *Yes, he does.*

REWARDS/AWARDS GIVEN

Because of Royal Family KIDS, numerous awards and recognition have been bestowed on us and the organization. One of the most significant items came from the Missouri Department of Social Services' Division of Family Services in March 1994. This date was three months prior to our second year of camp. I believe Royal Family received a copy of the letter, which read, in part:

> The camp activities such as horseback riding, swimming, crafts, and music exposed the children to experiences they might not otherwise have had in their own environment . . . It was obvious on the day the children returned from the camp that they had had a wonderful time! The children were sad to leave the new friends, but happy to have made new friendships with both the other

children and the adult staff. Some of the children would never have had a camping experience had it not been for this endeavor. We view the camp experience as very successful and are hopeful that this year other children will be awarded the opportunity to attend this camp.

Boy, did this letter come at the right time! We learned many things from hosting our first camp but still had apprehension about the second year.

In January 2002, I received the Service to Mankind award from the East Hills Sertoma Club for significant and meritorious service to mankind. Wayne Tesch sent greetings on behalf of the Royal Family national organization to the Sertoma Club president. Diane Tesch sent a bouquet of flowers to me. The award was a complete surprise until I reached the club thinking, I was to give a presentation about Royal Family KIDS.

In April 2006, Ken and I received the Dr. Larry A. Jones Humanitarian Award from St. Joseph Rotary East Club in recognition of the advocacy of the importance of human welfare, our leadership, and personal work in providing goodwill and improving the quality of life of those with the greatest need.

Ken and I also received recognition at our church, First Christian, for our work with this children's mission in our community. Our names are on a plaque located in our church. In 1995, our church and I received a proclamation from the city in appreciation for our work with abused children through Royal Family KIDS. In 1995 and 2011, we received proclamations from the Missouri House of Representatives for our work with abused children through Royal Family. Of course, Royal Family has given us recognition each five years. This means I have five-year, ten-year, fifteen-year, and twenty-year trophies, as well as a Royal Bear and a Royal Jacket.

I say this not for personal credit, but to give gratitude for how the answer yes to the request by my pastor broadened the awareness of the community, city, and state to focus on abused, abandoned, and neglected children.

ME AND MY FAMILY

Since starting this mission to work with abused and neglected children, I find myself more aware of the children around me and my family and their circumstances. Stories in the newspaper and television about abuse and foster children grab my attention. The growing statistics make me very angry. I find myself saying yes to requests to join advisory groups and various not-for-profit boards that deal in children's issues. On my own, I attend workshops and lectures on child abuse and neglect, which I would not have done before Royal Family KIDS came into my life. The number of presentations I have given on Royal Family and on abuse and neglect in our community have increased greatly. Requests for presentations to church groups, service organizations, social work classes at our university, high schools, and ladies groups have quadrupled since 1993. There have been numerous radio talk shows and television appearances promoting benefits and fundraisers for our camp.

Royal Family KIDS has become the center of my life and my family's life. My husband, Ken, is the assistant director, and I joke during presentations that camp is the only time I get to boss him around! However, over the years the camps could not have happened without his help, encouragement, and guidance. He honestly should have been named co-director long ago.

Our youngest daughter, Heather, was a camp counselor for several years. She tells me her experience has helped her in her job as a school counselor in California. She is passionate about children's needs and is very popular with the staff and, especially the students. Our oldest daughter, Melissa, has worn several hats at camp. She has been a camp counselor and director of the camp play. She helped buy needed camp items during camp, and used her social work degree when needed. She is the executive director locally for Habitat for Humanity and has guided several qualifying children to our camp. Our two oldest granddaughters have been involved as camp counselors and referred several friends as well. One still lives here and continues to be a camp counselor. These granddaughters are twenty-two and nineteen years old. We are preparing for our twenty-third camp, so they know nothing else for one week each summer. These girls have helped with every aspect of the camps from counting and unpacking supplies, running camp errands, making signs, helping with fundraisers, as well as being camp counselors. They associate Royal Family with us as grandparents and as a family. This is a wonderful legacy for our family. We have also recruited Ken's sister and a brother-in-law to become counselors over the years. God has blessed our family with knowing Royal Family and the Tesch family. I thank God every day for leading us to Royal Family and all the wonderful people involved in any way.

The year 2015 will be my last camp as director and Ken's as assistant director. After twenty-three years associated with Royal Family KIDS and staff, we are sad to leave these positions. We know God will lead us to the right people to continue this journey and give HIM the glory.

29

DAN AND BECKY BUHR
Directors, Hastings, Nebraska

Royal Family KIDS Camp will change your life. Ever heard that famous statement from Wayne Tesch before? When Dan and Becky Buhr of Hastings Nebraska heard this statement in 1993, they had no idea how incredibly true it would be over the next twenty years.

One Sunday morning at Keystone Baptist church, we attended a morning service for the second time. Searching for a new church home, an invitation came from some friends who attended there. That morning Pastor Dale Phillips just happened to be preaching on "divine visions."

Dan was in Pastor Dale's office the following morning. He said, "I think I had one of those recently, Pastor Dale."

After describing the vision from a few weeks earlier, the outdoor setting, children laughing and playing, but having a look of hurt on their faces, Pastor Dale encouraged Dan to share this story with others in the church so they could pray for understanding of the vision. Three whole years passed without any understanding or direction, yet the vision was as fresh in Dan's mind as if it were yesterday.

There was, however, much preparation that happened within our hearts, including a close family member's experience of abuse. God was preparing our hearts for what they would face as Royal Family KIDS directors. One day, after three years of waiting, the youth pastor at the church handed Dan a *Summer Camp Youth Activities* magazine with an article about Royal Family KIDS Camp. There seemed to be no doubt in Dan's mind that this was where God was leading. We phoned Diane Tesch, co-founder of Royal Family KIDS, and were invited to attend training at a church of less than one hundred members. It was a step of faith leaving seven children at home with grandparents, along with a certainty of a calling, that set us off on an adventure that neither of us expected. During the training in Bellingham, Washington, both our hearts were broken many times throughout the week.

It was as if all of a sudden our eyes were opened to a need that was so overwhelming. Watching the volunteers with the kids during the week immediately convinced us that we could make a difference in the lives of foster children in our own community. As we saw faces with that look of fear at first, then later transformed into continuous smiles and small steps toward trust, we knew we were experiencing something very special.

Returning home, reality set in and doubts began to surface. How can we raise the funds and find the volunteers in such a small church? Are there really enough children in those situations living in our town of under twenty thousand? What had we really committed to, with seven children of our own and a business to run as well? So many questions.

Our first step was to invite every child protection worker, judge, and Health and Human Services provider to a luncheon where we told them about Royal Family KIDS Camp and that we planned to offer it the next summer. We asked the director of DHHS if they could give us an idea of just how many children in our three-county area would qualify. A few days later we got that answer. We were shocked to learn that there were 238 children in the system who could come to camp. Whoa! Over the next twenty years, we never asked that question again.

Finding a camp facility was the second step we needed to take. Covenant Cedars Bible Camp was one of the places to check out to see if it was a facility that met all the criteria for a Royal Family KIDS Camp. We made the appointment with the director, Kathy. We were prepared to share our heart and about the training we had received. To our surprise, after we were finished sharing about this special camp for foster children, Kathy shared with us how her board of directors had just met and had prayed and asked God if Covenant Cedars Bible Camp could be a safe place for children with special needs. As we were saying our good-byes to Kathy, she said to us, "I think I have caught the vision for this Royal Family KIDS Camp!" Whoa! That was exactly one of the final things Wayne Tesch had told us in training: "Find a Camp facility that catches the vision of Royal Family KIDS." We knew Covenant Cedars Bible Camp was the place to have our first Royal Family KIDS Camp!

To sum it up: God gave us assurance and provided all that was needed in the way of funds, volunteers, and campers matched in amazing ways to counselors. He provided the energy and perseverance needed by all. The Hastings camp was #21 in the country, the first in Nebraska, and is now one of eleven serving that state. After five years, our camp therapist, Sandy Kroeker, felt called to start another Nebraska camp. In the seventh year, a young man who had been a counselor for two years launched another camp in the state's capital, Lincoln. A few years later, a friend of his started another camp out of Omaha. A female counselor from our first year of camp started another in Columbus, Nebraska. On and on we saw God continuing to plant that seed in the hearts of other directors. And if that were the end of the story, that would be enough, but God had bigger plans.

After about five years of renting the camp facility of Covenant Cedars Bible Camp, the director asked if we could come and share some training on abuse with their own camp staff. Of course, we were delighted to do so. A few years later, we were asked to apply for management roles after several of the camp staff had left for various reasons. After being offered a couple of key positions, we sold our home, sold our business, and moved our family.

We have now served as executive director and guest services director for fourteen years, where many of the Royal Family KIDS methods have been implemented in the "regular camping weeks." Five RFKC weeks are held at this facility, along with six TRAC weekends where we see many of the RFKC graduates. And yes, the statistics are true even among the so called "normal kids" in our regular camping weeks, and because of Royal Family KIDS training, we are able to help hundreds of youth recognize abuse and help them toward a solution. Royal Family KIDS Camp has simply carried out and done so many things "right" in the camping world from the very beginning, it continues to amaze us. So you see, Royal Family KIDS has the potential to "change your life" in unbelievable ways. We Praise God for RFKC!

There are far too many stories to tell from the last twenty years of RFKC, both relating to personal growth and amazing, miraculous things that we have witnessed. But please, let us just tell you a few of our favorites.

DAN'S MOST IMPACTFUL STORY

A young boy that we had as a camper our very first year simply broke my heart! He was nine and had been in at least fourteen different foster homes. He was the angriest little boy I had ever known. He continued to come back to Royal Family KIDS Camp for six years. His dream was always to someday live with his biological mother, who had become pregnant with him in high school and couldn't care for him. Later, she had two daughters (which she kept), each child from a different father. The boy knew where his mom lived, and vowed to one day live with her. I had kept in contact with him over the years as he continued to move around. I helped him get enrolled in a community school after high school where he was doing fairly well. On his eighteenth birthday, he disappeared from his independent living program and his school. After giving some thought, I figured out where he had likely gone. His mom had allowed him to come with the following conditions: He could have a small room to sleep in for $350 per month, (not big enough for a bed) and could eat meals with them, but would be charged for food according to how much he ate. So he slept on the floor, worked two or three jobs to meet his mom's financial requirements, and his dream had finally come true. This went on for a year and a half, when he summed up his feelings with this question: "My mom is never going to change, is she Dan?"

After he moved out, he went from one relative to another, living in carports, garages, and wherever he could find a place to sleep. One particular night, he made a phone call to Dan with an alarming message.

"I'm in a bad part of town, I'm hungry, it's midnight, and I don't know where to go. I'm really scared."

Two hours away is not a good place to be when receiving that kind of phone call. So I called the Omaha RFKC director, who was close by. He helped him find safety for the night. After returning to his last foster home at nearly twenty years of age, just because they considered him one of their own, he is living a somewhat peaceful life. He is still going from job to job, sabotaging relationships along the way, but he has hope through faith in Jesus Christ and has discovered the source of his anger, which the Lord showed him was fear. It has been an adventure to say the least. I am so thankful that he has had a family called Royal Family to lean on!

Becky's Favorite Story

So many stories but one of my favorites is about a camper who got to change his name!

As I was traveling one day to Lincoln, Nebraska, to help with my grandchildren, I was praying and telling Jesus that I was discouraged and felt really down about how the plans for that year's Royal Family KIDS Camp were not coming together. I had just received another call from a counselor who had to back out; funds were not totally in the bank; we had two staff positions that needed to be filled; camp was coming up; and I was crying, whining, and wondering if this was really worth all the time, effort, and ups and down in the planning process. I was crying out to the Lord with all my concerns when my cell phone rang and I answered it.

I recognized the number and knew it was a social worker that needed to talk to me. She said, "Becky, I have something to tell you about Johnny, the camper you have had for three years at Royal Family. He has been adopted and, guess what. He got to change his name. During the court proceeding, the judge asked him if he would like to change his first name and Johnny said 'Yes, I would like the name of my Royal Family KIDS Camp counselor. His name is Shane!'"

Oh my, the tears were streaming down my face, as Shane had been Johnny's counselor for those years, and Shane never felt like he had made an impact in his life, but he trusted and had faith that God would work in Johnny's life in some way. We called Shane and told him what had happened, and through that social worker and the adoptive parents, Shane got to visit Shane (Johnny) and got to witness what God had done through his dedication of volunteering one week for three years in a little boy who loved his counselor Shane and wanted his name forever!

Our God is good, as this was just the thing I needed to hear. My prayer had been answered, that yes, this is worth every ounce of energy, tears, time, money, and volunteers God provides to help the abused, abandoned, and neglected in our community.

Royal Family KIDS Camp changes lives, not only in the campers but also for everyone who is available to be the hands and feet of Jesus to His children! One week does make a difference!

APPENDIX

THE ORIGINAL VOLUNTEERS OF ROYAL FAMILY KIDS, 1985

Listed below are the names of the first volunteers of Royal Family KIDS Camps. They are the pioneers who "risked the week" and made the first year work. RFK is built on their shoulders of distinction and compassion.

1.	Mike Anderson	Counselor
2.	Lynell Brooks	Nurse
3.	Michelle Brown	Counselor
4.	Dave Childers	Recreation Leader
5.	Kim Choi	Counselor
6.	Melinda DeVito	Counselor
7.	Jeff Hann	Counselor
8.	June Hunt	Crafts
9.	Gary Huntley	Counselor
10.	Dan Irwin	Counselor
11.	Ken Low	Counselor
12.	Marlene Marx	Assistant Director
13.	Alisa McAfee	Counselor
14.	Valerie Norris	Counselor
15.	Cecilia Potter	Counselor
16.	Karen Reistad	Counselor
17.	Wayne Tesch	Director
18.	Johanna Townsend	Spiritual Life Leader
19.	Debbie Tracy	Music

20.   Diana Wahlstedt   Counselor
21.   Lisa Walsh   Counselor
22.   Dave Watkins   Dean of Men
23.   Sue Watkins   Dean of Women

WHAT ABOUT *YOUR STORY?*

You have just read some of the incredible stories that come from Royal Family KIDS. Each story is personal and powerful, just like yours. If you have been moved by these stories, consider how others may be moved by *Your Story*.

We invite you to share your own memories of how Royal Family KIDS impacted your life. It takes a little time and effort, but putting your thoughts onto paper may be helpful and healing for you. Your story may open doors that have yet to be opened. Writing it out allows family and friends to get a more complete picture of your experiences, and you may be surprised how many people will enjoy learning the details of your story.

Teresa Mummert said, "Things spoken can be forgotten and forgiven, but the written word has the power to change the course of history, to alter our lives."

Your story about how Royal Family KIDS has impacted your life has the power to help, to heal, and to alter lives—perhaps even change the course of history!

You'll never know unless you write it down.

We invite you to submit your story on our website, so we can share it with others to encourage, to help, and to heal.

Visit **RoyalFamilyKIDS.org/YourStoryMatters** to share your
story today.*

*By posting your story at: RoyalFamilyKIDS.org/YourStoryMat-
ters you agree to allow Royal Family KIDS to use your story, or
parts of it, in our marketing and promotional materials.